Excursions In The Mountains Of Ronda And Granada, With Characteristic Sketches Of The Inhabitants Of Southern Spain
Vol. II

by

C. Rochfort Scott

Double 9
BOOKS

Excursions In The Mountains Of Ronda And Granada, With Characteristic Sketches Of The Inhabitants Of Southern Spain
Vol. II
by C. Rochfort Scott

ISBN: 978-93-61424-10-6

Published by

DOUBLE 9 BOOKS

2/13-B, Ansari Road
Daryaganj, New Delhi – 110002
info@double9books.com
www.double9books.com
Tel. 011-40042856

ABOUT THE AUTHOR

Major-General Charles Rochfort Scott was a British Army officer who served as Lieutenant Governor of Guernsey. Rochfort Scott was commissioned into the Royal Staff Corps and served until 1834, when he changed to the 81st Regiment of Foot. near same year, he visited the Messara Labyrinth near Gortyn, Crete, and reported his impressions. He spent the majority of 1840 and 1841 surveying areas of Syria; in January 1842, he was relocated to Gibraltar, and in 1845, to Wales, but he continued to work on his Syrian maps throughout. He was appointed Assistant Quartermaster-General in Dublin in 1849, but by 1854 he was Assistant Quartermaster-General for the Northern District, and in 1857 he was named Lieutenant Governor of the Royal Military College, Sandhurst. He was appointed Lieutenant Governor of Guernsey in 1864. He was also the Colonel of the 100th Regiment of Foot.

CONTENTS

CHAPTER I

ON leaving Cordoba, we turned our horses' heads homewards, taking the *arrecife*, or high road, to Seville and Cadiz. This appears to follow the *direct* Roman military way given in detail in the Itinerary of Antoninus; the distances from station to station, on the modern road, agreeing perfectly with those specified in the Itinerary, which, as it runs very straight as far as Ecija, would not be the case if the Roman road had diverged either to the right or left, as some are disposed to make it, placing *Adaras* (one of the intermediate stations) on the margin of the Guadalquivír.

Several monuments, bearing inscriptions alluding to this military way, are preserved at Cordoba. They all describe it as being from the temple of Janus *to* the Bœtis, (meaning, it must be presumed, the *mouth* of the river) and to the ocean.

The road is no longer paved, as it is described to have been in those days; but, nevertheless, it is good enough to enable a lumbering diligence to pulverize the gravel daily on its tedious way between Madrid and Seville. It is also furnished with relays of post horses, [1] but the posting establishments being, as in most other countries of Europe, under the direction of the government, is a satire upon the term *post haste*.

From Cordoba to Ecija is ten leagues. [2] The road, on reaching the river *Badajocillo*, or Guadajoz, which is crossed by a lofty stone bridge, commanding a fine view of Cordoba, leaves the rich alluvial valley of the Guadalquivír, and enters upon an undulated tract of country, that extends nearly all the way to Ecija. At three leagues is the scattered village and post-house of Mango-negro, and three leagues beyond that again, the settlement of Carlota. The ride is most uninteresting; as, besides being tamely outlined and thinly peopled, the country is nearly destitute of wood, and, in the summer season, of water; though, judging from the extraordinary number of bridges, especially on drawing near Carlota, there must be a superabundance in winter. Carlota is one of the numerous villages which Charles the Third colonized from the Tyrol. It consists principally of isolated cottages, standing some hundred yards apart, and the same distance from the road; but there is a small congregation of houses round the chapel, post-house, and *Casa del Ayuntamiento*, [3] and a *Gasthof*, which I can say, from personal experience, would do no discredit to Innsbruck itself.

The parish contains 250 houses, and a population of 1500 souls. The fields round Carlota certainly appear to be better tilled than those in other parts of the country, and there is a German tidiness about its white cottages, as well as a platterfacedness about the little white-headed urchins assembled round the doors, that are quite anti-Spanish.

We obtained an excellent dinner at the *Tyroler Adler*, and, in the afternoon, taking a by-road that struck off from the post route to the right, cantered through plantations of olives nearly all the way to Ecija,—four leagues. In the whole of the distance we did not see a drop of running water, until we arrived on the brow of the hill overlooking the river Genil. From this spot there is a fine view of the city of Ecija, situated on the opposite bank.

The volume of the Genil increases but little between Granada and Ecija; for its principal feeders, though falling into it below Granada, are expended in irrigating the *vega*; and the *salados*, on the western side of the *Serranía de Ronda*, are mostly dry during the summer. In winter, however, the Genil is so increased, that the bridge at Ecija (a solid stone structure of eleven arches,) is carried quite across the valley, although the bed of the river is not above 100 yards wide.

Ecija is the Astigi of the Romans. It stands on a gentle acclivity, some little distance from the Genil, and bears evident marks of antiquity. Almost all traces of its walls have disappeared, however; and what little remains of its tapia-built castle shows it to have been a work of the Moors. The principal streets are wide, and contain many good houses; and the *plaza* is particularly well worth a visit from the lovers of the picturesque.

The city contains sixteen convents, and two hospitals, with churches in proportion. None of them offers much to interest the protestant traveller; but, I believe, several boast of possessing valuable relics. The Royal stud-house is fast going to decay.

The population of Ecija is estimated at 30,000 souls; a number that appears totally disproportioned to the size of the city; particularly, as it contains but a few tanneries, and trifling manufactories of shoes, saddlery, &c. But, from the extreme fertility of the soil in its neighbourhood—considered the most productive and best cultivated in Andalusia—it is very possible this amount may not be exaggerated; for in Spain the agriculturalists do not scatter themselves about in small villages and hamlets over its surface, as in other countries, but assemble together in large towns; so that those places which are situated in fertile districts are as densely populated as our manufacturing towns.

The distance that a Spanish peasant sometimes travels daily, to and from his work, is truly surprising, in a people that, generally speaking, like to save themselves trouble. Whilst getting in the harvest, however, they erect *ranchas*, or rush huts, to shelter them from the midday sun and night dews, and dwell in these temporary habitations until their work is completed.

The crops of corn in the neighbourhood of Ecija are remarkably fine, yielding forty to one, and though not so tall, perhaps, as those of the *vega* of Granada, the grains are larger and better ripened.

I must not omit to say a good word for the *Posada*,—the Post-house,—which I do the more willingly from being so seldom called upon to speak in terms of commendation of Spanish "houses of entertainment." Suffice it to observe, that, provided the traveller be very hungry, and moderately fatigued, he may reckon on getting a supper that he will be able to eat, and a bed whereon—albeit hard—he may obtain some hours' unmolested repose.

The remainder of the post road to Seville is so perfectly uninteresting, that, reserving the Andalusian capital for a future tour, I shall take a more direct route back to Gibraltar, through the *Serranía* de Ronda; merely offering a few remarks on the town of Carmona, which is situated about two thirds of the way between Ecija and Seville, and referring my readers to the Itinerary in the Appendix for any further details as to the distances from place to place along the road.

Carmona is one of the few Roman towns of Bœtica of whose identity there is scarcely a doubt; its name having undergone little or no change. It is mentioned by most of the ancient writers, and called by them, indifferently, Carmo and Carmona, and by Julius Cæsar was esteemed one of the strongest posts in the whole country. Its position, considered relatively with the adjacent ground, is, indeed, most commanding; being on the edge of a vast plateau of very elevated land, which, stretching many miles to the south, falls abruptly along the course of the river Corbones.

The Roman name for this river is, I think, doubtful. Florez, and most antiquaries, suppose it to be the *Silicensis*. Some, and, as it appears to me, with better reason, give that name to the Badajocillo. Be that as it may, the Corbones is but an inconsiderable stream, and is now crossed by a stone bridge of three arches.

The ascent to Carmona is very steep and tedious. The city is entered through a triumphal Roman arch, which was repaired and spoilt by order of Charles III. Another Roman gateway stands at the southern extremity of the town, by which the road to Seville leaves it; and various parts of the walls which yet encompass the place are the work of the same people. The castle, however, is a relique of the Moors, and in a very ruinous condition.

This stronghold was wrested from the Moors by San Fernando, after a six months' investment. It was a favourite place of residence of Peter, surnamed the Cruel, who, looking upon it as impregnable, left his children there in fancied security when he took the field for the last time against his brother. Soon after Peter's death, however, it fell into the hands of his rival, who, according to some accounts, caused the children (his nephews) to be put to death in cold blood.

The streets of Carmona are wide, clean, and well-paved; and the alameda is enchanting, commanding a superb view of the ruined fortress, and over the rich vales of the Corbones, and more distant Guadalquivír, and embracing, at the same time, the whole chain of the Ronda mountains to the eastward.

The population of the place is about 10,000 souls. The inn is execrable.

The post road to Cadiz is directed from Carmona on Alcalà de Guadiara, where a branch to Seville strikes off, nearly at a right angle, to the east, thereby making a considerable détour. But in summer, carriages even may proceed to Seville by a cross road, which not only lessens the dust, but reduces the distance from six *long* to the same number of *short* leagues; or, in other words, effects a saving of about three miles.

I now return to Ecija, and take the road from that city to Osuna; which is tolerably good, and practicable for carriages during the greater part of the year. The distance is five (very long) leagues. The country presents a slightly undulated surface, and, excepting round the edges of some basins wherein extensive lakes have been formed, is altogether under the plough. At a little distance from the road, on the left hand, a stream, called *El Salado*, flows towards the Genil. It does not communicate with these lakes, nor has the name it bears been given from its being impregnated with salt.

During our ride, we observed a number of men advancing in skirmishing order across the country, and thrashing the ground most savagely with long flails. Curious to know what could be the motive for this Xerxes-like treatment of the earth, we turned out of the road to inspect their operations, and found they were driving a swarm of locusts into a wide piece of linen spread on the ground at some distance before them, wherein they were made prisoners. These animals are about three times the size of an English grasshopper. They migrate from Africa, and their spring visits are very destructive; for in a single night they will entirely eat up a field of young corn.

The *Caza de Langostas* [4] is a very profitable business to the peasantry; as, besides a reward obtained from the proprietor of the soil in consideration for service done, they sell the produce of their *chasse* for manure at so much a sack.

Osuna is generally admitted to be the Urso, [5] Ursao, and Ursaon, of the Roman historians; though it agrees in no one particular with the description given of that place by Hirtius; for it is not by any means "strong by nature;" it is in the vicinity of extensive forests—rendering it perfectly absurd to suppose that Cæsar's troops "had to bring wood thither all the way from Munda;"—and, so far from "there being no rivulet within eight miles of the place," [6] a fine stream meanders under its very walls.

The town is situated at the foot of a hill that screens it effectually to the eastward, and the summit of which is occupied by an old castle of considerable strength and size, but now fast crumbling to decay. The streets are wide and well paved, the houses particularly good;—indeed, some of the palaces of the provincial nobility (with whom it was formerly a favourite place of residence) are strikingly handsome; in particular, that of the Duke who takes his title from the city; and notwithstanding that the streets are overgrown with grass, and the houses covered with mildew, I am, nevertheless, disposed to call Osuna the best built and handsomest city in Andalusia, it contains a university, fourteen convents, for both sexes, and a population of 16,000 souls; but has little or no trade—in fact, though on the crossing of two high roads, (viz., from Gibraltar to Madrid, and from Granada to Seville) it has all the dullness of a secluded country village.

The vicinity is very fruitful in olives and corn; the soil is a whitish clay. To the S.E. the country is tolerably level all the way to Antequera, and to the west is nearly flat to Seville; but at about a mile southward from the city, shoot up the entangled roots of the mountains of Ronda, presenting on that side a belt of very intricate country. There are two roads to that place, the distance by the better, which, I think, is also rather the shorter, of the two, is nine leagues. It leaves Osuna by the gate of Granada, and, crossing the before-mentioned stream (which is one of the sources of the Corbones), advances some distance along a wide olive-planted valley. It then quits the great road to Granada (which continues along the valley), and ascends a steep and very long hill, from the crest of which, distant about three miles from Osuna, there is a splendid view of the city, and of the spacious plains extending to and bordering the distant Guadalquivír, studded with the towns of Marchena, Fuentes, Palmar, and Carmona.

The road continues along the summit of the elevated range of hills which it has now attained, for about five miles, winding amongst some singularly mammillated hummocks, that have very much the appearance of the tumuli left in an exhausted mining country. A succession of strongly marked and peculiarly rugged ravines present themselves along the eastern side of the ridge, and the ground falls also very abruptly in the opposite direction; but to the south, whither the road is directed, the descent is much more gradual; and from the foot of the hill, which is bathed by a rivulet wending its way to the Genil, the country is tolerably level, and the road extremely good the remaining distance to Saucejo.

In former days, this route was practicable for carriages throughout, and with very little labour it might again be made so; but, though the high road from the capital to Algeciras and Gibraltar, it is but little travelled. The other road from Osuna to Ronda joins in here on the right.

The village of Saucejo is a post station three leagues from Osuna, and six from Ronda. It contains some eight hundred inhabitants, great abundance of stabling, but not one decent house. The posada is a peculiarly unpromising establishment, and the landlady's face such as to shut out all hope of any sound wine being found within its influence. We had left Osuna so late in the day, however, that it would have been vain to attempt reaching Ronda ere nightfall.

We, therefore, reluctantly took possession of the *sala*, and, presenting our sour-faced hostess with a rabbit and some partridges that we had purchased on the road, asked if she could furnish the other requisites for the concorporation of an *olla*, and whether it would be possible to let us have our meal ere midnight; to both of which questions, with sundry consequential nods of the head, she replied severally, *en casa llena, presto se guisa la cena.* [7] Notwithstanding this assurance, our supper was long in making its appearance, for the operations of an *olla* cannot be hurried. But, when it did come, it bespoke our landlady to be a *cordon bleu* of the first class; the *pimento* [8] had been administered with judgment; the *berza* [9] had duly extracted the flavour from the rabbit and partridges; the *chorizo* [10] had imparted but the desirable smack of garlic to the other ingredients; and the nutty savour of the *tocino* [11] was beyond all praise. Nor was her wine such as we had expected; though somewhat too light to have much influence on the digestion of the unctuous mess placed before us.

From Saucejo the road again branches into two, one route proceeding by way of Almargen, the other by the Venta del Granadal. Both are *reckoned* six leagues; but the last mentioned is better than the other, as well as shorter by several miles. It crosses a considerable stream (here called the Algamitas, but which is, in fact, the main source of the Corbones) by a ford, about three miles from Saucejo. The descent to the stream is very bad, and, after keeping along its bank for another mile, the road mounts to some elevated table land, from which the view to the westward is obstructed by the rocky peaks of two detached mountains about a mile off. These may be considered the outposts of the Serranía in that direction; and, on the rough side of the more considerable of the two, is the *Hermita de Caños Santos*.

The country becomes very wild as the road advances, and rugged tors, partially covered with wood, rise on all sides. At nine miles from Saucejo is the lone venta of Grañadal, and beyond it the mountains rise to a yet greater height, but their slopes are less abrupt, and are covered with forests of oak and cork. At twelve miles a track branches off to the right, proceeding to the little town of Alcalà del Valle, which, though distant only about half a mile, is not visible from the road. Soon after, a wide valley opens to the view, at the bottom of which, encased by steep rocky banks, flows the river *Guadalete*. This river is by some considered the *Lethe* of the ancients; but, if it be so, our long-cherished notions of the beauty of the Elysian fields have been wofully faulty, for the country is rather tame, and the soil stony and ungrateful. Thus far, however, it answers the description of Virgil, that you

"Breathe in ample fields the soft Elysian air."

The town of Setenil is perched on a crag overhanging the left bank of the Guadalete, and distant about three miles from the road, which keeps under the broad summit of the hills forming the northern boundary of Elysium. The sides of these are partially cultivated, and, from time to time, a low cottage is met with as the road proceeds; but it soon enters a cork-forest, and, threading its dark mazes for about four miles, gradually gains the crest of the chain of hills overlooking the vale of Ronda to the north, whence a splendid view is obtained of the fertile basin, its rock-built fortress, and jagged sierras.

The descent on the southern side of the hills is rather rapid, and, after proceeding downwards about a mile, the road is joined on the left by the other route from Saucejo. From hence to Ronda is two short leagues. The road still continues descending for another mile; and, in the course of the two following, it crosses three deep ravines, watered by copious streams, and planted with all sorts of fruit-trees.

In the bottom of one of these dells is ensconced the village of Arriate. The last is a deep and very singular rent that extends, east and west, quite across the basin of Ronda. Immediately after crossing this fissure, the road begins to ascend the range of hills whereon Ronda is situated, and, after winding for three miles amongst vineyards, olive grounds, and corn-fields, enters the city on its north side.

We were seven hours performing the journey, although the distance is but six *leguas regulares*.

I have already given so full a description of Ronda, that I will pass on without further remark.

To vary the scenery, and moved by curiosity to visit some of the scenes of our acquaintance Blas's exploits, we determined to take a somewhat circuitous route homewards, by way of Grazalema and Ubrique.

The distance to the first named town is three long leagues. The road descends gradually to the south-western extremity of the basin of Ronda, where the Guadiaro, forming its junction with the Rio Verde, enters a rocky defile, and is lost sight of amidst the roots of the rugged sierras that spread themselves in all directions towards the Mediterranean.

Crossing the last named stream just before its confluence with the Guadiaro, the road at once begins ascending towards a deeply marked gap, that breaks the ridge of the mountains which rise along the right bank of the stream.

The pass is about four miles from Ronda, and commands a splendid view of the fruitful valley, which lies, like an outspread *cornucopia*, at its foot. On the other side, too, the scenery is not less fine, though of a totally different nature. There a singular double-peaked crag rises up boldly and darkly on the left hand, casting its shadow on the bright foliage of an oak forest, which, deep sunk below the rest of the country, spreads its verdant covering as far to the eastward as where the huge Sierra Endrinal raises its cloud-enveloped head above all the other mountains of the range. High seated on the side of this, a white speck is seen which, in the course of time, proves to be the town of Grazalema, whither we are bending our steps.

Proceeding onwards, from the pass about a mile, the little village of Montejaque shows itself, peeping from between the two peaks of the mountain on the left, and, seemingly, quite inaccessible, even to a goat.

It is inhabited by a horde of half-tamed Saracens, who pride themselves greatly on having foiled all the attempts of the French to make themselves masters of the place; [12] and, as this elevated little village is but three quarters of a mile from the high road, (which is the principal communication between Malaga and Cadiz) it must have possessed the means of annoying the enemy considerably.

For the next two miles our way lay along the spine of a somewhat elevated ridge; whence we looked down upon the before-mentioned wooded country on one side, and on the other into a well cultivated valley. From the bed of this, but at several leagues' distance, the rock-built town of Zahara rears its embattled head.

This little fortress is very noted in Moorish history; its capture by Muley Aben Hassan, during a period of truce, having provoked the renewal of the war which led to the loss of the crown, not only to himself first, but to his race afterwards.

One of the sources of the Guadalete flows in this valley, bathing the walls of Zahara, which stands on the site of the Roman town of Lastigi. [13] The present name, I should imagine, (considering the locality) is derived rather from the Arabic word *Zaharat* (mountain top) than *Záhara*, (flowery) as supposed by Mr. Carter; for the streets are cut out of the live rock on which the place is built.

The road to Grazalema, now mounting another step, enters a dark forest, and, continuing for five miles along the top of a narrow ridge, descends into a vine-clad valley, that spreads out at the foot of the rough sierra on the side of which Grazalema is seated.

The ascent to the town is very bad, and is rendered worse than it otherwise would be by being paved—for a paved road in Spain is sure to be neglected. We scrambled up with much difficulty, and alighting at the posada, remained for an hour or two, to procure some breakfast, and examine the place.

It is a singularly built town, the streets being heaped one above another, like steps; and in several instances they are even worked out of the native rock. There is, nevertheless, a fine open market-place, which we found well supplied with fruit, vegetables, and game, including venison and wild boar; and the town possesses several manufactories of coarse cloths and serges.

From its situation, immediately over the mouth of a deep ravine, by which alone access can be obtained to one of the principal passes in the Serranía, Grazalema occupies a very important military position, and may considered almost inassailable; for, whilst at its back a perfectly impracticable mountain covers it from attack, it is protected to the north and east by the precipitous ravine it overlooks; up the side of which, even the narrow road from Ronda has not been practised without much labour. The only side, therefore, on which it has to apprehend danger, is that fronting the pass above it—i.e. to the westward. But it has the means of offering an obstinate resistance, even in that direction.

Commanding, as it thus does, so important a passage over the mountains, there can be but little doubt that Grazalema stands upon, or near, the site of some Roman fortress; and, for reasons which I shall hereafter mention, I feel inclined to place here the town of Ilipa. [14]

The inhabitants amount to about 6,000, and are a savage, ruffianly-looking race. During the "War of Independence," assisted by their brethren of the neighbouring mountain fastnesses, they frequently rose against their invaders, driving them out of the place; and on one occasion they repulsed a French column of several thousand men, which was sent to dispossess them of their stronghold.

On leaving Grazalema, the road enters the narrow, rock-bound ravine leading up to the pass, down which a noisy torrent rushes, leaping from precipice to precipice, and lashing the base of the crag-built town, whence we had just issued. A newly-built bridge, whose high-crowned arch places it beyond the anger of the foaming stream, gives a passage to the road to Zahara, which winds along the eastern face of the Sierra del Pinar. Our route, however, continues ascending yet a mile and a half along the right bank of the torrent, ere it reaches the long descried gap in the mountain chain, the name of which is *El Puerto Bozal*.

This is considered one of the most elevated passes in the whole Serranía de Ronda, and must be at least 4,000 feet above the level of the sea. The mountains on either side rise to a far greater elevation; that on the right, distinguished by the name of *El Pico de San Cristoval*, is said (as has already been stated) to have been the first land made by Columbus on his return from the discovery of the "New World."

The views from this pass are truly grand. At our backs lay the beautifully wooded country we had travelled over in the morning—Ronda and its vale, and the distant sierras of El Burgo and Casarabonela. Before us, a wild mountain country extended for several miles; and beyond, spreading as far as the eye could reach, were the vast plains of Arcos, through which the gladdening Guadalete, winding its way past Xeres, turns to seek the bay of Cadiz, whose glassy surface the white walls of its proud mistress, and the deep blue ocean, could be seen distinctly on the left, though at a distance of more than fifty miles.

From the Puerto Bozal, a *trocha*, directed straight upon Ubrique, strikes off to the left; but the saving in point of distance which this road offers, is counterbalanced by its extreme ruggedness. We, therefore, took the more circuitous route to that place by El Broque, which, for the first five miles, is itself sufficiently bad to satisfy most people. The views along it, looking to the south, are very fine; but the lofty barren range of San Cristoval, on the side of which it is conducted, shuts out the prospect in the opposite direction.

At length, crossing over a narrow tongue that protrudes from the side of the rugged mountain, we entered a dark, wooded ravine, and began to descend very rapidly, and, to our astonishment, by a very good road. After proceeding in this way about a mile, the valley gradually expanding, we emerged from the wood, and found ourselves in a sequestered glen of surpassing loveliness. A neat white chapel, with a picturesque belfry, stood on a sloping green bank on our right hand, and, scattered in all directions about it, were the trim, vine-clad cottages of its frequenters, each screened partially from the sun in a grove of almond, cherry, and orange trees. A crystal stream gurgled through the fruitful dell, which was bounded at some little distance by high wooded hills and rocky cliffs.

This secluded retreat is called *La Huerta* [15] *de Benamajáma*,—the peculiarly guttural name proving it to have been a little earthly paradise of the Moors.

The road, which had thus far been nearly west, here, continuing along the course of the little river Posadas, turns to the south; and, keeping under a range of wooded hills on the left hand, in about an hour reaches El Broque. This portion of the road is very good, and from it, looking over the great plain bordering the Guadalete, may be seen the lofty tower of *Pajarete*, perched on a conical mound, at about a league's distance. The justly celebrated sweet wine called by this name was originally produced from the vineyards in its vicinity, but it is now made principally at Xeres.

El Broque is a small clean town, abounding in wood and water, and containing from 1500 to 2000 inhabitants. To the east it is overshadowed by a range of lofty, wooded hills, which may be considered the last buttresses of the Serranía; for the road to Cadiz, which here branches off to the right, crossing the Posadas, traverses an uninterrupted plain all the way to Arcos.

The route to Ubrique, on the other hand, again strikes into the mountains; though, for yet two miles further, it follows the course of the little river and its impending sierra. Arrived, however, at the mouth of a ravine, which brings down another mountain-torrent to the plain, it turns to the north, keeping along the margin of the stream, until the bridge of Tavira offers the means of passage; when, crossing to the opposite bank, it once more enters the intricate belt of mountains.

The name of the stream which is here crossed is the Majaceite; and on its right bank, close to the bridge, is a solitary venta. The scenery is extremely beautiful. The mountains of Grazalema, which we had traversed in the morning, form the background; the ruined tower of Alamada, perched on an isolated knoll, stands boldly forward in middle distance; and close at hand are the rough, coppiced banks and crystal current of the winding Majaceite.

From hence to Ubrique the country is very wild and rugged. The town is first seen (when about a league off) from the summit of a round-topped hill, six miles from El Broque. It is nestled in the bottom of a deep valley, hemmed in by singularly rugged mountains. The first part of the descent is gradual, but a steep neck of land must be crossed ere reaching the town; and, as if to render the approach as difficult as possible, the road over this mound has been paved.

Amongst the rude masses of sierra that encompass Ubrique, numerous rivulets pierce their way to the lowly valley, where, collected in two streams, they are conducted to the town, and, fertilizing the ground in its neighbourhood, cause it to be encircled by a belt of most luxuriant vegetation. The mountains in the vicinity abound also in lead-mines, but they are no longer worked. "Where are we to find money? Where are we to look for security?" were the answers given to *my* question, "Why not?"

The streets of Ubrique are wide, clean, and well paved; the houses lofty and good; but the inn, alas! affords the wearied traveller little more than bare walls and a wooden floor. The population of the place may be estimated at 8000 souls. It contains some tanneries, water-mills, and manufactories of hats and coarse cloths. It does not strike me as being a likely site for a Roman city.

We were on horseback by daybreak, having before us a long ride, and, for the first five leagues (to Ximena), a very difficult country to traverse. For about a mile the road is paved, and confined to the vale in which Ubrique stands by a precipitous mountain. But, the westernmost point of this ridge turned, the route to Ximena (leaving a road to Alcalà de los Gazules on the right) takes a more southerly direction than heretofore, and, entering a hilly country, soon dwindles into a mere mule-track. Ere proceeding far in this direction, another road branches off to Cortes, winding up towards some cragged eminences that serrate the mountain-chain on the left. The path to Ximena, however, continues yet two miles further across the comparatively undulated country below, which thus far is under cultivation; but, on gaining the summit of a hill, distant about four miles from Ubrique, a complete change takes place in the face of the country; the view opening upon a wide expanse of forest, furrowed by numerous deep ravines, and studded with rugged tors.

The road through this overshadowed labyrinth is continually mounting and descending the slippery banks of the countless torrents that intersect it, twisting and winding in every direction; and, on gaining the heart of the forest, the path is crossed and cut up by such numbers of timber-tracks, and is screened from the sun's cheering rays by so impervious a covering, that the difficulty of choosing a path amongst the many which presented themselves was yet further increased by that of determining the point of the compass towards which they were respectively directed.

The guide we had brought with us, though pretending to be thoroughly acquainted with every pathway in the forest, was evidently as much at a *nonplus* as we ourselves were; and his muttered *malditos* and *carajos*, like the rolling of distant thunder, announced the coming of a storm. At length it burst forth: the track he had selected, after various windings, led only to the stump of a venerable oak. Never was mortal in a more towering passion; he snatched his hat from his head, threw it on the ground, and stamped upon it, swearing by, or at—for we could hardly distinguish which—all the saints in the calendar. After enjoying this scene for some time, we spread ourselves in different directions in search of the beaten track; and, at last, a swineherd, attracted by our calls to each other, came to our deliverance; and our guide, after bestowing sundry *malditos* upon the wood, the torrents, the timber-tracks, and those who made them, resumed his wonted state of composure, assuring us, that there was some accursed hobgoblin in this *hi-de-puta* forest, who took delight in leading good Catholics astray; that during the war an entire regiment, misled by some such *malhechor*, [16] had been obliged to bivouac there for the night, to the great detriment of his very Catholic Majesty's service.

Soon after this little adventure we reached a solitary house, called the *Venta de Montera*, which is something more than half way between Ubrique and Ximena; *i.e.* eleven miles from the former, and nine from the latter. A little way beyond this the road reaches an elevated chain of hills, that separates the rivers Sogarganta and Guadiaro; the summit of which being rather a succession of peaks than a continuous ridge, occasions the track to be conducted sometimes along the edge of one valley, sometimes of the other. The mountain falls very ruggedly to the first-named river, but in one magnificent sweep to the Guadiaro.

The views on both sides are extremely fine; that on the left hand embraces Gibraltar's cloud-wrapped peaks, the mirror-like Mediterranean, Spain's prison-fortress of Ceuta, and the blue mountains of Mauritanía; the other looks over the silvery current of the Sogarganta, winding amidst the roots of a peculiarly wild and wooded country, and towards the rock-built little fortress of Castellar.

The road continues winding along this elevated heather-clad ridge for four miles, and then descends by rapid zig-zags towards Ximena.

The town lies crouching under the shelter of a rocky ledge, that, detached from the rest of the sierra, and crowned with the ruined towers of an ancient castle, forms a bold and very picturesque feature in the view, looking southward. The town is nearly a mile in length, and consists principally of two long narrow streets, one extending from north to south quite through it, the other leading up to the castle. The rest of the *callejones* [17] are disposed in steps up the steep side of the impending hill, and can be reached only on foot.

The old castle—in great part Roman, but the superstructure Moorish—is accessible only on the side of the town (east), and in former days must have been almost impregnable. The narrow-ridged ledge whereon it stands has been levelled, as far as was practicable, to give capacity to this citadel, which is 400 yards in length, and varies in breadth from 50 to 80. It rises gently, so as to form two hummocks at its extremities; and the narrowest part of the inclosure being towards the centre, it has very much the form of a calabash.

A strongly built circular tower, mounting artillery, and enclosed by an irregular loop-holed work of some strength, occupies the southern peak of the ridge; and a fort of more modern structure, but feeble profile, covers that in which it terminates to the north. An irregularly indented wall, or in some places scarped rock, connects these two retrenched works along the eastern side of the ridge; but, in the opposite direction, the cliff falls precipitously to the river Sogarganta; rendering any artificial defences, beyond a slight parapet wall, quite superfluous.

Numerous vaulted tanks and magazines afforded security to the ammunition and provisions of the isolated little citadel; but they are now in a wretched state, as well as the outworks generally; for the fortress was partially blown up by Ballasteros, (A.D. 1811) upon his abandoning it, on the approach of the French, to seek a surer protection under the guns of Gibraltar.

In exploring the ruined tanks of this old Moorish fortress, chance directed our footsteps to an unfrequented spot where some smugglers were in treaty with a revenue *guarda*, touching the amount of bribe to be given for his connivance at the entry of sundry mule loads of contraband goods into the town on the following night.

We did not pry so curiously into the proceedings of the contracting parties, as to ascertain the precise sum demanded by this faithful servant of the crown for the purchase of his acquiescence to the proposed arrangement, but, from the elevated shoulders, outstretched arms, and down-stretched mouth, of one of the negociators, it was evident that the demand was considered unconscionable; and the roguish countenance of the custom-house shark as clearly expressed in reply, "But do you count for nothing the sacrifice of principle I make?"

From the ruined ramparts of Fort Ballasteros (the name by which the northern retrenched work of the fortress is distinguished) the view looking south is remarkably fine. The keep of the ancient castle, enclosed by its comparatively modern outworks, and occupying the extreme point of the narrow rocky ledge whereon we were perched, stands boldly out from the adjacent mountains; whilst, deep sunk below, the tortuous Sogarganta may be traced for miles, wending its way towards the Almoraima forest. Above this rise the two remarkable headlands of Gibraltar and Ceuta; the glassy waterline between them marking the separation of Europe and Africa.

That Ximena was once a place of importance there can be no doubt, since it gave the title of King to Abou Melic, son of the Emperor of Fez; and that it was a Roman station (though the name is lost,) is likewise sufficiently proved, as well by the walls of the castle, as by various inscriptions which have been discovered in the vicinity. At the present day, it is a poor and inconsiderable town, whose inhabitants, amounting to about 8000, are chiefly employed in smuggling and agriculture.

On issuing from the town, the road to Gibraltar crosses the Sogarganta, having on its left bank, and directly under the precipitous southern cliff of the castle rock, the ruins of an immense building, erected some sixty years back, for the purpose of casting shot for the siege of Gibraltar!

The distance from Ximena to the English fortress is 25 miles. The road was, in times past, practicable for carriages throughout; and even now is tolerably good, though the bridges are not in a state to drive over. It is conducted along the right bank of the Sogarganta; at six miles, is joined by a road that winds down from the little town of Castellar on the right; and, at eight, enters the Almoraima forest by the "Lion's Mouth," of which mention has already been made. The river, repelled by the steep brakes of the forest, winds away to the eastward to seek the Guadiaro and Genil.

Here I will take a temporary leave of my readers, to seek a night's lodging at a cottage in the neighbourhood, which, being frequented by some friends and myself in the shooting season, we knew could furnish us with clean beds and a *gazpacho*.

CHAPTER II

HOPING that the taste of my readers, like my own, leads them to prefer the motion of a horse to that of a ship, the chance of being robbed to that of being sea-sick, and the savoury smell of an *olla* to the greasy odour of a steam engine, I purpose in my next excursion to conduct them to Cadiz by the rude pathway practised along the rocky shore of the Straits of Gibraltar, and thence, "*inter æstuaria Bætis*," to Seville, instead of proceeding to those places by the more rapid and now generally adopted means of fire and water. From the last named "fair city" we will return homewards by another passage through the mountains of Ronda.

To authorise *me*—a mere scribbler of notes and journals—to assume the plural *we*, that gives a Delphic importance to one's opinions (but under whose shelter I gladly seek to avoid the charge of egotism), I must state that a friend bore me company on this occasion; our two servants, with well stuffed saddle-bags and *alforjas*, "bringing up the rear."

Proceeding along the margin of the bay of Gibraltar, leaving successively behind us the ruins of Fort St. Philip, which a few years since gave security to the right flank of the lines drawn across the Isthmus in front of the British fortress; the crumbling tower of *Cartagena*, or *Recadillo*, which, during the seven centuries of Moslem sway, served as an *atalaya*, or beacon, to convey intelligence along the coast between Algeciras and Malaga; and, lastly, the scattered fragments of the yet more ancient city of Carteia, we arrive at the river Guadaranque.

The stream is so deep as to render a ferry-boat necessary. That in use is of a most uncouth kind, and so low waisted that "Almanzor," who was ever prone to gad amongst the Spanish lady Rosinantes, could not be deterred from showing his gallantry to some that were collected on the opposite side of the river, by leaping "clean out" of the boat before it was half way over. Fortunately, we had passed the deepest part of the stream, so that I escaped with a foot-bath only.

The road keeps close to the shore for about a mile and a half, when it reaches the river Palmones, which is crossed by a similarly ill-contrived ferry. From hence to Algeciras is three miles, the first along the sea-beach, the remainder by a carriage-road, conducted some little distance inland to avoid the various rugged promontories which now begin to indent the coast, and to dash back in angry foam the hitherto gently received caresses of the flowing tide.

The total distance from Gibraltar to Algeciras, following the sea-shore, is nine English miles; but straight across the bay it is barely five.

Algeciras, supposed to be the Tingentera of the ancients, and by some the Julia Traducta of the Romans, received its present name from the Moors—*Al chazira*, the island. In the days of the Moslem domination, it became a place of great strength and importance; and when the power of the Moors of Spain began to wane, was one of the towns ceded to the Emperor of Fez, to form a kingdom for his son, Abou Melic, in the hope of presenting a barrier that would check the alarming progress of the Christian arms. From that time it became a constant object of contention, and endured many sieges. The most memorable was in 1342-4, during which cannon were first brought into use by its defenders. It, nevertheless, fell to the irresistible Alfonso XI., after a siege of twenty months.

At that period, the town stood on the right bank of the little river Miel (instead of on the left, as at present), where traces of its walls are yet to be seen; but its fortifications having shortly afterwards been razed to the ground by the Moors, the place fell to decay, and the present town was built so late as in 1760. It is unprotected by walls, but is sheltered from attack on the sea-side by a rocky little island, distant 800 yards from the shore. This island is crowned with batteries of heavy ordnance, and has, on more occasions than one, been found an "ugly customer" to deal with. The anchorage is to the north of the island, and directly in front of the town.

The streets of Algeciras are wide and regularly built, remarkably well paved, and lined with good houses; but it is a sun-burnt place, without a tree to shelter, or a drain to purify it. Being the port of communication between Spain and her *presidario*, Ceuta, as well as the military seat of government of the *Campo de Gibraltar*, it is a place of some bustle, and carries on a thriving trade, by means of *felucas* and other small craft, with the British fortress. The population may be reckoned at 8,000 souls, exclusive of a garrison of from twelve to fifteen hundred men.

The Spaniards call the rock of Gibraltar *el cuerpo muerto*, [18] from its resemblance to a corpse; and, viewed from Algeciras, it certainly does look something like a human figure laid upon its back, the northernmost pinnacle forming the head, the swelling ridge between that and the signal tower, the chest and belly, and the point occupied by O'Hara's tower the bend of the knees.

The direct road from Algeciras to Cadiz crosses the most elevated pass in the wooded mountains that rise at the back of the town, and, from its excessive asperity, is called "*The Trocha*," the word itself signifying a *bad* mountain road. The distance by this route is sixty-two miles; by Tarifa it is about a league more, and this latter road is not much better than the other, though over a far lower tract of country.

On quitting the town, the road, having crossed the river Miel, and passed over the site of "Old Algeciras," situated on its right bank, edges away from the coast, and, in about a mile, reaches a hill, whence an old tower is seen standing on a rocky promontory; which, jutting some considerable distance into the sea, forms the northern boundary of a deep and well sheltered bay. The Spanish name for this bight is *La Ensenada de Getares*; but by us, on account of the high beach of white sand that edges it, it is called "Sandy bay." It strikes me this must be the *Portus albus* of Antoninus's Itinerary, since its distance from Carteia corresponds exactly with that therein specified, and renders the rest of the route to Gades *intelligible*, which, otherwise, it certainly is not. But more of this hereafter.

Within two miles of Algeciras the road crosses two mountain torrents, the latter of which, called *El Rio Picaro* [19] (I presume from its occasional *treacherous* rise), discharges itself into the bay of Getares. Thenceforth, the track becomes more rugged, and ascends towards a pass, (*El puerto del Cabrito*) which connects the *Sierra Santa Ana* on the right with a range of hills that, rising to the south, and closing the view in that direction, shoots its gnarled roots into the Straits of Gibraltar.

The views from the pass are very fine—that to the eastward, looking over the lake-like Mediterranean and towards the snowy sierras of Granada; the other, down upon the rough features of the Spanish shore, and towards the yet more rugged mountains of Africa; the still distant Atlantic stretching away to the left. The former view is shut out immediately on crossing the ridge: but the other, undergoing pleasing varieties as one proceeds, continues very fine all the way to Tarifa.

The road is now very bad, being conducted across the numerous rough ramifications of the mountains on the right hand, midway between their summits and the sea. At about seven miles from Algeciras it reaches the secluded valley of Gualmesi, or Guadalmesi, celebrated for the crystaline clearness of its springs, and the high flavour of its oranges; and, crossing the stream, whence the romantic dell takes its name, directs itself towards the sea-shore, continuing along it the rest of the way to Tarifa; which place is distant twelve miles from Algeciras.

The stratification of the rocks along this coast is very remarkable: the flat shelving ledges that border it running so regularly in parallel lines, nearly east and west, as to have all the appearance of artificial moles for sheltering vessels. It is on the contrary, however, an extremely dangerous shore to approach.

The old Moorish battlements of Tarifa abut against the rocky cliff that bounds the coast; stretching thence to the westward, along, but about 50 yards from, the sea. It is not necessary, therefore, to enter the fortress; indeed, one makes a considerable détour in doing so; but curiosity will naturally lead all Englishmen—who have the opportunity—to visit the walls so gallantly defended by a handful of their countrymen during the late war; and those who cannot do so may not object to read a somewhat minute description of them.

The town closes the mouth of a valley, bound by two long but slightly marked moles, protruded from a mountain range some miles distant to the north; the easternmost of which terminates abruptly along the sea-shore. The walls extend partly up both these hills; but not far enough to save the town from being looked into, and completely commanded, within a very short distance. Their general lines form a quadrangular figure, about 600 yards square; but a kind of horn work projects from the N.E. angle, furnishing the only good flanking fire that the fortress can boast of along its north front. Every where else the walls, which are only four feet and a half thick, are flanked by square towers, themselves hardly solid enough to bear the *weight* of artillery, much less its blows.

At the S.W. angle, but within the enceinte of the fortress, and looking seawards, there is a small castle, or citadel, the *alcazar* of its Moorish governors; and immediately under its machicoulated battlements is one of the three gateways of the town. The two others are towards the centre of its western and northern fronts.

In the attack of 1811, the French made their approaches against the north front of the town, and effected a breach towards its centre, in the very lowest part of the bed of the valley; thus most completely "taking the bull by the horns;" (and Tarifa bulls are not to be trifled with—as every Spanish *picador* knows,) since the approach to it was swept by the fire of the projecting *horn*-work I have before mentioned.

When the breach was repaired, a marble tablet was inserted in the wall, bearing a modest inscription in Latin, which states that "this part of the wall, destroyed by the besieging French, was re-built by the British defenders in November, 1813."

When the French again attacked the fortress, in 1823, profiting by past experience, they established their breaching batteries in a large convent, distant about 200 yards from the walls on the west front of the town; and, favouring their assault by a feigned attack on the gate in its south wall, they carried the place with scarcely any loss.

The streets of Tarifa are narrow, dark, and crooked; and, excepting that they are clean, are in every respect Moorish. The inhabitants are rude in speech and manners, and amount to about 8000.

From the S.E. salient angle of the town, a sandy isthmus juts about a thousand yards into the sea, and is connected by a narrow artificial causeway with a rocky peninsula, or island, as it is more generally termed, that stretches yet 700 or 800 yards further into the Straits of Gibraltar. This is the most southerly point of Europe, being in latitude 30° 0' 56", which is nearly six miles to the south of Europa Point.

The island is of a circular form, and towards the sea is merely defended by three open batteries, armed *en barbette*; but to the land side, it presents a bastioned front, that sweeps the causeway with a most formidable fire. A lighthouse stands at the extreme point of the island, which also contains a casemated barrack for troops, and some remarkable old tanks, perhaps of a date much prior to the arrival of the Saracens.

The foundation of the town of Tarifa is usually ascribed to Tarik Aben Zaide, the first Mohammedan invader of Spain; who probably, previous to crossing the Straits, had marked the island as offering a favourable landing-place, as well as a secure depôt for his stores, and a safe refuge in the event of a repulse. Mariana, however, imagined, that Tartessus, or Carteia—which he considered the same place—stood upon this spot; and, under this persuasion, he speaks of the admiral of the Pompeian faction retiring there, after his action with Cæsar's fleet, and drawing a chain across the mouth of the port to protect his vessels; a circumstance which alone proves that Carteia was not Tarifa; since it must be evident to any one who has examined the coast attentively, that no port could possibly have existed there, which could have afforded shelter to a large fleet, and been closed by drawing a chain across its mouth.

Others, again, suppose Tarifa to occupy the site of Mellaria. But I rather incline to the opinion of those who consider it doubtful whether *any* Roman town stood upon the spot; an opinion for which I think I shall hereafter be able to assign sufficient reason.

As Tarifa was the field wherein the Mohammedan invaders of Spain obtained their first success, so, six centuries after, did it become the scene of one of their most humiliating defeats; the battle of the *Salado*, gained

A.D. 1340, by Alphonso XI., of Castile, having inflicted a blow upon them, from the effects of which they never recovered. Four crowned heads were engaged in that sanguinary conflict—the King of Portugal, as the ally of the Castillian hero; Jusuf, King of Granada; and Abu Jacoob, Emperor of Morocco. The last-named, according to the Spanish historians, had crossed over from Africa, with an army of nearly half a million of men, to avenge the death of his son, Abou Melic; killed the preceding year at the battle of Arcos.

The little river, which gave its name to that important battle gained by the Christian army on its banks, winds through a plain to the westward of Tarifa, crossing the road to Cadiz, at about two miles from the town. [20] The valley is about three miles across, and extends a considerable distance inland. It is watered by several mountain streams that fall into the Salado. That rivulet is the last which is met with, and is crossed by a long wooden bridge on five stone piers.

The term *Salado* is of very common occurrence amongst the names of the rivers of the south of Spain; though in most cases it is used rather as a term signifying a *water-course*, than as the name of the rivulet: thus *El Salado de Moron* is a stream issuing from the mountains in the vicinity of the town of Moron; *El Salado de Porcuna* is a torrent that washes the walls of Porcuna; and so with the rest. As, however, the word in Spanish signifies salt, (used adjectively) it has led to many mistakes, and occasioned much perplexity in determining the course of the river *Salsus*, mentioned so frequently by Hirtius; but to which, in point of fact, the word *Salado* has no reference whatever, being applied to numerous streams that are perfectly free from salt.

On the other hand, it might naturally be supposed that the word *Salido* (the past participle of the verb *Salir*, to issue) would have been used if intended to signify a source or stream issuing from the mountains.

It seems to me, therefore, that the word *Salado* must be a derivation from the Arabic *Sāl*, a water-course in a valley; which, differing so little in sound from *Salido*, continued to be used after the expulsion of the Moors; until at length, its derivation being lost, it came to be considered as signifying what the word actually means in Spanish, viz. impregnated with salt.

At the western extremity of the plain, watered by the *Salado de Tarifa*, a barren Sierra terminates precipitously along the coast, leaving but a narrow space between its foot and the sea, for the passage of the road to Cadiz. Under shelter of the eastern side of this Sierra, standing in the plain, but closing the little Thermopylæ, I think we may place the Roman town of

Mellaría, [21] eighteen miles from Carteia, and six from Belone Claudia, according to the Itinerary of Antoninus; and mentioned by Strabo as a place famous for curing fish.

Tarifa, which, as I have said before, is supposed by some authors to be on the site of Mellaría, is in the first place rather too near Calpe Carteia to accord with that supposition; and in the next, it is far too distant from Belon; the site of which is well established by numerous ruins visible to this day, at a *despoblado*, [22] called Bolonia.

It may be objected, on the other hand, that the position which I suppose Mellaría to have occupied, is as much too far removed from Carteia, as Tarifa is too near it: and following the present road, it certainly is so. But there is no reason to take for granted that the ancient military way followed this line; on the contrary, as the Romans rather preferred straight to circuitous roads, we may suppose that, as soon as the nature of the country admitted of it, they carried their road away from the coast, to avoid the promontory running into the sea at Tarifa. Now, an opportunity for them to do this presented itself on arriving at the valley of Gualmesi, from whence a road might very well have been carried direct to the spot that I assign for the position of Mellaría; which road, by saving two miles of the circuitous route by Tarifa, would fix Mellaría at the prescribed distance from Carteia, and also bring it (very nearly) within the number of miles from Belon, specified in the Roman Itinerary, viz. six; whereas, if Mellaría stood where Tarifa now does, the distance would be nearly *ten*.

The city of Belon appears to have slipped bodily from the side of the mountain on which it was built (probably the result of an earthquake), as its ruins may be distinctly seen when the tide is out and the water calm, stretching some distance into the Atlantic. Vestiges of an aqueduct may also be traced for nearly a league along the coast, by means of which the town was supplied with water from a spring that rises near Cape Palomo, the southernmost point of the same Sierra under which Belon was situated.

In following out the Itinerary of Antoninus—according to which the total distance from Calpe to Gades is made seventy-six miles [23] —the next place mentioned after Belon Claudia is Besippone, distant twelve miles. This place, it appears to me, must have stood on the coast a little way beyond the river Barbate; and not at Vejer, (which is several miles inland) as some have supposed; for the distance from the ruins of Bolonia to that town far exceeds that specified in the Itinerary.

Vejer (or Beger, as it is indifferently written) may probably be where a Roman town called Besaro stood, of which Besippo was the port; the latter only having been noticed in the Itinerary from it being situated on the direct military route from Carteia to Gades; the former by Pliny, [24] as being a place of importance within the *Conventus Gaditani.*

From Besippone to Mergablo—the next station of the Itinerary—is six miles; and at that distance from the spot where I suppose the first of those places to have stood, there is a very ancient tower on the sea side, (to the westward of Cape Trafalgar) from which an old, apparently Roman, paved road, now serving no purpose whatever, leads for several miles into the country. From this tower to Cadiz—crossing the Santi Petri river *at its mouth*—the distance exceeds but little twenty-four miles; the number given in the Itinerary.

The distances I have thus laid down agree pretty well throughout with those marked on the Roman military way; which, it may be supposed, were not *very exactly* measured, since the fractions of miles have in every case been omitted. The only objection which can be urged to my measurements is, that they make the Roman miles too long. Having, however, taken the Olympic stadium (in this instance) as my standard, of which there are but 600 to a degree of the Meridian, or seventy-five Roman miles; and as my measurements, even with it, are still rather *short*, the reply is very simple, viz. that the adoption of any *smaller* scale would but *increase the error.*

From the spot where I suppose Mellaría to have stood—which is marked by a little chapel standing on a detached pinnacle of the *Sierra de Enmedio,* overhanging the sea—the distance to the Rio Baqueros is two miles; the road keeping along a flat and narrow strip of land, between the foot of the mountain and the sea.

The coast now trends to the south west, a high wooded mountain, distinguished by the name of the Sierra de *San Mateo,* stretching some way into the sea, and forming the steep sandy cape of *Paloma,* a league on the western side of which are the ruins of Belon.

The road to Cadiz, however, leaves the sea-shore to seek a more level country, and, inclining slightly to the north, keeping up the *Val de Baqueros* for five miles, reaches a pass between the mountains of San Mateo and Enmedio.

The valley is very wild and beautiful. Laurustinus, arbutus, oleander, and rhododendron are scattered profusely over the bed of the torrent that rushes down it; and the bounding mountains are richly clothed with forest trees.

From the pass an extensive view is obtained of the wide plain of Vejer, and *laguna de la Janda* in its centre. Descending for two miles and a half,— the double-peaked Sierra *de la Plata* being now on the left hand, and that of *Fachenas*, studded with water-mills, on the right—the road reaches the eastern extremity of the above-named plain, where the direct road from Algeciras to Cadiz falls in, and that of Medina Sidonia branches off to the right. The Cadiz route here inclines again to the westward, and, in three miles, reaches the *Venta de Tavilla*.

From hence two roads present themselves for continuing the journey; one proceeding along the edge of the plain; the other keeping to the left, and making a slight détour by the *Sierra de Retin*; and when the plain is flooded, it is necessary to take this latter route. Let those who find themselves in this predicament avoid making the solitary hovel, called the *Venta de Retin*, their resting-place for the night, as I was once obliged to do; for, unless they are partial to a guard bed, and to go to it supperless, they will not meet with accommodation and entertainment to their liking.

We will return, however, to the *Venta de Tabilla*, which is a fraction of a degree better than that of Retin. From thence the distance to Vejer is fourteen miles. The first two pass over a gently swelling country, planted with corn; the next six along the low wooded hills bordering the *laguna de la Janda*; the remainder over a hilly, and partially wooded tract, whence the sea is again visible at some miles distance on the left.

In winter the greater part of the plain of Vejer is covered with water, there being no outlet for the *Laguna*; which, besides being the reservoir for all the rain that falls on the surrounding hills, is fed by several considerable streams.

A project to drain the lake was entertained some years ago; but, like all other Spanish projects, it failed, after an abortive trial. In its present state, therefore, the whole surface of the plain is available only for pasture; and numerous herds are subsisted on it. The gentle slopes bounding it, being secure from inundation, are planted with corn.

Vejer is situated on the northern extremity of a bare mountain ridge, that stretches inland from the coast about five miles, and terminates in a stupendous precipice along the right bank of the river Barbate. Towards the sea, however, it slopes more gradually, forming the forked headland, for ever celebrated in history, called Cape Trafalgar.

When arrived within half a mile of the lofty cliff whereon the town stands, the road enters a narrow gorge, by which the Barbate escapes to the ocean; this part of its course offering a remarkable contrast to the rest, which is through an extensive flat.

A stone bridge of three curiously constructed arches, said to be Roman, gives a passage over the stream; and a venta is situated on the right bank, immediately under the town; the houses of which may be seen edging the precipice, at a height of five or six hundred feet above the river.

The road to Cadiz, and consequently all others,—it being the most southerly,—avoids the ascent to Vejer, which is very steep, and so circuitous as to occupy fully half an hour. But the place is well worth a visit, if only for the sake of the view from the church steeple, which is very extensive and beautiful; and taken altogether, it is a much better town than could be expected, considering its truly out-of-the-way situation. That it was a Roman station, its position alone sufficiently proves; but whether it be the Besaro, or Belippo, or even Besippo of Pliny, seems doubtful.

It occupies a tolerably level space; though bounded on three sides by precipices, and is consequently still a very defensible post, notwithstanding its walls are all destroyed. The streets are narrow, but clean and well paved; and the place contains many good houses, and several large convents. The inns, however, are such wretched places, that on one occasion, when I passed a night there, I had to seek a resting-place in a private house.

The Barbate is navigable for large barges up to the bridge; but the difficulty of access to the town prevents its carrying on much trade. The population amounts to about 6,000 souls.

There is a delightful walk down a wooded ravine on the western side of the town, by which the road to Cadiz and the valley of the Barbate may be regained quicker than by retracing our footsteps to the Venta. Of this latter I feel bound to say—after much experience—that there is not a better halting-place between Cadiz and Gibraltar; albeit, many stories are told of robberies committed even within its very walls. Let the traveller take care, therefore, to show his pistols to mine host, and to lock his bedroom door.

We resumed our journey with the dawn. The road keeps for nearly a mile along the narrow, flat strip between the bank of the river, and the high cliff whereon the town is perched. The gorge then terminates, and an open country permits the roads to the different neighbouring places to branch off in their respective directions. From hence to Medina Sidonia is thirteen miles; to Alcalá de los Gazules, twenty; and to Chiclana—whither we were bound—fifteen;—but, leaving these three roads on the right, we proceeded by a rather more circuitous route to the last mentioned place, by Conil and Barrosa.

The distance from Vejer to Conil is nine miles; the country undulated and uninteresting. Conil is a large fishing town, containing a swarming population of 8,000 souls. The smell of the houses where the tunny fish (here taken in great abundance) are cut up and cured, extends inland for several miles; but the inhabitants consider it very wholesome; and to my animadversive remarks on the filth and effluvium of the place itself, answer was made, "*no hay epidemia aqui;*" [25] — quite a sufficient excuse, according to their ideas, for submitting to live the life of hogs.

We arrived just as the fishermen had enclosed a shoal of Tunny with their nets; so, putting up our horses, we waited to see the result of their labours. The whole process is very interesting. The Tunny can be discovered when at a very considerable distance from the land; as they arrive in immense shoals, and cause a ripple on the surface of the water, like that occasioned by a light puff of wind on a calm day. Men are, therefore, stationed in the different watch towers along the coast, to look out for them, and, immediately on perceiving a shoal, they make signals to the fishermen, indicating the direction, distance, &c. Boats are forthwith put to sea, and the fish are surrounded with a net of immense size, but very fine texture, which is gradually hauled towards the shore.

The tunny, coming in contact with this net, become alarmed, and make off from it in the only direction left open to them. The boats follow, and draw the net in, until the space in which the fish are confined is sufficiently small to allow a second net, of great strength, to circumscribe the first; which is then withdrawn. The tunny, although very powerful, (being nearly the size and very much the shape of a porpoise) have thus far been very quiet, seeking only to escape under the net; and have hardly been perceptible to the spectators on the beach. But, on drawing in the new net, and getting into shallow water, their danger gives them the courage of despair, and furious are their struggles to escape from their hempen prison.

The scene now becomes very animated. When the draught is heavy — as it was in this instance — and there is a possibility of the net being injured, and of the fish escaping if it be drawn at once to land, the fishermen arm themselves with harpoons, or stakes, having iron hooks at the end, and rush into the sea whilst the net is yet a considerable distance from the shore, surrounding it, and shouting with all their might to frighten the fish into shallow water, when they become comparatively powerless.

In completing the investment of their prey, some of the fishermen are obliged even to swim to the outer extremity of the net, where, holding on by the floats with one hand, they strike, with singular dexterity, such fish as approach the edge, in the hope of effecting their escape, with a short harpoon held in the other. The men in the boats, at the same time, keep up a continual splashing with their oars, to deter the tunny from attempting to leap over the hempen enclosure; which, nevertheless, many succeed in doing, amidst volleys of "*Carajos!*"

The fish are thus killed in the water, and then drawn in triumph on shore. They are allowed to bleed very freely; and the entrails, roes, livers, and eyes, are immediately cut out, being perquisites of different authorities.

The flesh is salted, and exported in great quantities to Catalonia, Valencia, and the northern provinces of the kingdom. A small quantity of oil is extracted from the bones.

Some years since, the Duke of Medina Sidonia enjoyed the monopoly of the tunny fishery on this part of the coast, which was calculated to have given him a yearly profit of £4000 sterling. But, at the time of my visit, he had been deprived of this privilege, much to the regret of the inhabitants of Conil; for the nets and salting-houses, being the property of the duke, had to be hired, and as there were no capitalists in the place able to embark in so expensive a speculation as the purchase of others, the "company" that engaged in the fishery was, necessarily, composed of strangers to Conil, whose only object was to obtain the greatest possible profit during the short period for which they held the duke's property on lease. They, consequently, drove the hardest bargain they could with the poor inhabitants, who, accustomed all their lives to this employment, could not turn their hands to any other, and were forced to submit.

I do not mean to defend monopolies in general, but what I have stated shows, that in the present state of Spain they are almost unavoidable evils. The inhabitants of Conil, at all events, complained most bitterly of the change.

The fishery lasts from March to July, and the season of which I write (then drawing to a close,) was considered a very successful one, 1300 tunny having been taken at Conil, and 1600 at Barrosa. Each fish is worth ten dollars, or two pounds sterling. The falling off has, however, been most extraordinary, as in former days we read of 70,000 fish having been taken annually.

From Conil the road keeps along the coast for twelve miles, to Barrosa, a spot occupying a distinguished place in the pages of history, but marked only by an old tower on the coast, and a small building, called a *vigia*, or watch-house, situated on a knoll that rises slightly above the general level of the country. This was the great object of contention on the celebrated 5th March, 1811.

Never, perhaps, were British soldiers placed under greater disadvantages than on this glorious day, through the incapacity or pusillanimity, or both, of the Spanish general who commanded in chief. And though far more important victories have been gained by them, yet the cool bearing and determined courage that shone forth so conspicuously on this occasion, by completely removing the erroneous impression under which their opponents laboured, as to the fitness of Englishmen for soldiers, produced, perhaps, better effects than might have attended a victory gained on a larger scale, under *more favourable* circumstances.

I have met with Spaniards who absolutely shed tears when speaking of this battle, in which they considered our troops had been so shamefully abandoned by their countrymen, or rather by the general who led them. Nor is it surprising that the English character should stand so high as it does in this part of the Peninsula, when, within the short space of a day's ride, three such names as Tarifa, Trafalgar, and Barrosa, are successively brought to recollection.

The walls of the watch-house of Barrosa still bear the marks of mortal strife, and the hill on which it stands is even yet strewed with the bleached bones of the horses which fell there; but so slight is the command the knoll possesses—indeed in so unimportant, pinched-up a corner of the coast is it situated—that those who are not aware of the unaccountable events which led to the battle, may well be surprised at its having been chosen as a military position.

Striking into the pine-forest, which bounds the field of battle to the west, we arrived in about half an hour at the bridge and mill of Almanza, and proceeding onwards, in four miles reached Chiclana; first winding round the base of a conical knoll, surmounted by a chapel dedicated to *Santa Ana.*

Chiclana is the Highgate of the good citizens of Cadiz, and contains many "genteel family residences," adapted for summer visiters; but the place is disgracefully dirty, so that little benefit can be expected from *change of air.* The gardens in its vicinage offer agreeable promenades, however; and there is a fine view from the chapel of *Santa Ana,* whence may be seen

"Fair Cadiz, rising o'er the dark blue sea."

Chiclana contains a population of about 6000 souls, and boasts of possessing a tolerably good *posada,* whereat *calesas,* and other vehicles, may be hired to proceed to the neighbouring towns; the roads to all, even the direct one to Vejer, being open to wheel carriages.

A rivulet bathes the north side of the town, dividing it from a large suburb, and flowing on to the Santi Petri river. The Cadiz road, crossing this stream by a long wooden bridge, proceeds for three miles and a half (in company with the routes to *Puerto Santa Maria, Puerto Real,* and *Xeres,*) [26] along a raised causeway, which keeps it above the saltpans and marshes that render the *Isla de Leon* so difficult of approach. Arrived at a wide stream, a ferry-boat affords the means of passage; and, on gaining the southern bank, the great road from Cadiz to Madrid (passing through the towns above mentioned) presents itself.

Taking the direction of Cadiz, our passports were immediately demanded at the entrance of a fortified post, called the *Portazgo*, [27] the first advanced redoubt of the multiplied defences of the *Isla de Leon*. From thence the road is conducted, for nearly a mile, through bogs and saltpans, as before, to the *Puente Zuazo*, a bridge over the river *Santi Petri*, or *San Pedro*. This, by the way, is rather an arm of the sea than a river, since it communicates between the bay of Cadiz and the ocean, and forms the *Isla* (island) *de Leon*, which otherwise would be an isthmus. The channel is very wide, deep, and muddy; the bridge has five arches, and was built by a Doctor *Juan Sanchez de Zuazo* (whence its name), on the foundation of one that existed in the days of the Romans, and is supposed to have served as an aqueduct to supply Cadiz with water from the *Sierra de Xeres*. It is protected by a double tête de pont; and has one arch cut, and its parapets pierced with embrasures, to enable artillery to fire down the stream.

Soon after reaching the right bank of the San Pedro, the long straggling town of the Isla, or, more properly, *San Fernando*, commences. The main street is upwards of a mile in length, wide, and rather handsome. The population of this place is estimated at 30,000 souls; but it varies considerably, according to the date of the last visitation of yellow fever.

At the southern extremity of the city a low range of hills begins, which stretches for a mile and a half towards the sea. The causeway to Cadiz, however, is directed straight upon the *Torre Gorda*, standing upon the shore more to the westward, and three miles distant from the town of *San Fernando*.

Here commences the narrow sandy isthmus that connects the point of land on which Cadiz is built with the *Isla*. It is five miles long, and in some places so narrow, that the waves of the Atlantic on one side, and those of the bay of Cadiz on the other, reach the walls of the causeway. About half way between the *Torre Gorda* and Cadiz, the isthmus is cut across by a fort called the *Cortadura*, beyond which it becomes much wider.

At five miles to the eastward of the *Torre Gorda*, or Tower of Hercules, as it is also called, is the mouth of the Santi Petri river, and four miles only beyond it is the *Vigia de Barrosa*; so that the distance from thence to Cadiz is almost doubled by making the détour by Chiclana. It is more than probable, therefore, that the Romans had a military post, commanding a *flying bridge*, at the mouth of the river; for, in the Itinerary of Antoninus, the coast-road from *Calpe* to *Gades* was not directed from *Mergablo* "*ad pontem,*" as in the route laid down from *Gades* to *Hispalis* (Seville), but "*ad Herculem;*"—that is, it may be presumed, to the temple of Hercules, [28] situated, according to common tradition, on a part of the coast near the mouth of the Santi Petri river, over which the waves of the Atlantic now roll unobstructed; and the supposed site of which temple is the same distance from Cadiz as the bridge of Zuazo, thereby agreeing with the Roman Itineraries.

At the distance of 1200 yards from the river's mouth a rocky islet rises from the sea, bearing on its scarped sides the inapproachable little castle of *Santi Petri*, the bleached walls of which are said to have been built from the ruins of the famed temple of Hercules.

Contemptible as this isolated fortress appears to be, as well from its size as from any thing that art has done for it, the fate of Cadiz, nevertheless, depends in a great measure upon its preservation; since, from the command the castle possesses of the entrance of the river, an enemy, who may gain possession of it, is enabled to force the passage of the stream under its protecting fire, and take in reverse all the defenses of the *Isla de Leon*. Cadiz would thereby be reduced to its own resources; and strong as Cadiz is, yet, like all fortresses defended only by art, it must eventually fall.

The surrender of the castle of *Santi Petri* to the French, in the siege of 1823, occasioned the immediate fall of Cadiz, its defenders seeing that further resistance would be unavailing; whereas, the capture of the *Trocadero*, about which so much was thought, did little towards the reduction of the place. Indeed, the *Trocadero* was in possession of the enemy during the whole period of the former siege, 1810-12.

CHAPTER III

THE date of the foundation of Cadiz is lost in the impenetrable chaos of heathen mythology. One of the numerous conquerors, distinguished by the general name of Hercules, who, in early ages, carried their victorious arms to the remotest extremities of Europe, appears to have erected a temple at the westernmost point of the rocky ledge on which Cadiz now stands; and round this temple, doubtless, a town gradually sprung up. But the place came only to be known and distinguished by the name *Gadira*, when the commercial enterprise of the Phœnicians led them to make a settlement on this defensible island; and the foundation of the temple dedicated to Hercules, which Strabo describes as situated at the eastern extremity of the same island, "where it is separated from the continent by a strait only about a stadium in width," is ascribed to Pygmalion, nearly nine centuries before the Christian era.

Gadira, or Gades, to which the name now became corrupted, was the first town of Spain forcibly occupied by the Carthagenians, who, throwing off the mask of friendship, took possession of it about the year B.C. 240. It was the last place that afforded them a refuge in the war which shortly followed with the Romans, into whose hands it fell, B.C. 203. From the Romans it afterwards received the name of Augusta Julia, probably from its adherence to the cause of Cæsar, who restored to the temple of Hercules the treasures of which it had been plundered during the civil wars that had previously distracted the country. But its old name, altered apparently to its present orthography by the Moors, seems always to have prevailed.

Under the Moslems, Cadiz does not appear to have enjoyed any very great consideration; and it was wrested from them without difficulty by San Fernando, soon after the capture of Seville.

On the discovery of America, Cadiz became, next to Seville (which was endowed with peculiar privileges), the richest city of Spain. Its imports at that time amounted annually to eleven millions sterling. But since the loss of the American colonies, its prosperity has been rapidly declining; and some years back, when the intestine troubles of Spain rendered it impossible for her to afford protection to her commerce, the trade of Cadiz may be said to have ceased.

A *fillip* was, however, given to its commerce, for it would be absurd to call it an attempt to restore it—about nine years since, by making it a free port. But this apparently liberal act, not having been accompanied by any reduction of the duties imposed on foreign produce introduced for consumption into the country, was merely a disgraceful contrivance on the part of the king and his ministers to obtain money.

On the promulgation of the edict constituting Cadiz a free port, it became at once an entrepôt for the produce of all nations; the goods brought to it being subjected only to a trifling charge for landing, &c. The proceeds of this pitiful tax went to the coffers of the municipality, which had paid the king handsomely for the "act of grace" bestowed upon the city; and no source of revenue was opened to the public treasury by the grant of this special privilege, since the goods landed at Cadiz could only be carried into the interior of the country on payment of duties that amounted to an absolute prohibition of them, and they were, consequently, introduced surreptitiously by bribing the city authorities and custom-house officers; who, in their turn, paid large sums for their respective situations to the ministers of the crown!

Such is the way in which the commercial concerns of Spain are conducted. The whole affair was, in fact, a temporary expedient to raise money by selling Cadiz permission to smuggle. At the same time, the Spanish government—by offering foreign merchants a mart which, at first sight, seemed more conveniently situated for disposing of their goods than Gibraltar—hoped to give a death-blow to the commerce of the British fortress, which it had found to thrive, in spite of all the iniquitous restrictions imposed upon it; such, for instance, as the exaction of duties on goods shipped from thence, double in amount to those levied on the *same articles*, if brought from the ports of France and Italy; the depriving even Spanish vessels, if coming from, or touching at, Gibraltar, of all advantages in regard to the rate of duty otherwise granted to the national flag; [29] and various other abuses, to which it is astonishing the British government has so long quietly submitted.

The scheme, however, though successful for a time against Gibraltar, did no permanent good to Cadiz; and the trade of the place has relapsed into its former sickly state.

"Cadiz! sweet Cadiz," has been so extolled by modern authors, that I am almost afraid to say what I think of it. It strikes me, that the very favourable impression it usually makes on my countrymen is owing to its being, in most cases, the first place they see after leaving England; or, perchance, the first place they have seen out of England; to whose gloomy brick-built towns its bright houses and battlements offer as agreeable a contrast, as the picturesque costume of its inhabitants does to the ill-cut garments of the natives of our island.

Under any circumstances, however, the first impression made by Cadiz is favourable, unless you enter by the fish-market. The streets are straight, tolerably well lighted, and remarkably well paved, many of them having even the convenience of a *trottoir*. There is one handsome square, and the houses, generally, are lofty, and those which are inhabited are clean. But many are falling rapidly to decay, from the diminished population and prosperity of the place.

On the other hand, the city does not contain one handsome public building; and, if one leaves the principal thoroughfares, its boasted cleanliness and "sweetness" turn out to be mere poetical delusions. In fact, the vaunted *agrémens* of the city to me were undiscoverable. There is but one road to ride upon, one promenade to walk upon, one sheet of water to boat upon. The Alameda, on which much hyperbolical praise has been bestowed, is a dusty gravel walk, extending about half a mile along the ramparts. It is lined—not shaded—with stunted trees, and commands a fine view of the marsh-environed bay when the tide is in, and a disagreeable effluvium from it when the tide is out; and, I must say, that I never could perceive any more "harmony and fascination" in the movements of the pavonizing *gaditanas* who frequent it, than in those of the fair promenaders of other Spanish towns. The *Plaza de San Antonio* is a square, situated in the heart of the city, which, paved with large flag-stones, and lighted with lamps, may be considered a kind of treadmill, that fashion has condemned her votaries to take an hour's exercise in after the fatigues of the day.

The society of Cadiz is now but second rate; for it is no longer inhabited as in bygone days, when the nobility from all parts of the kingdom sought shelter behind its walls. At the Tertulias of the first circle, gaming is the principal pastime, and I have been given to understand that the play is very high. The public amusements are few. There is a tolerable theatre, where Italian Operas are sometimes performed; but, for the great national diversion, the bull-fight, the inhabitants have to cross the bay to Puerto Santa Maria.

In fine, for one whose time is not fully occupied by business, I know of few *less* agreeable places of residence than Cadiz. The transient visiter, who prolongs his stay beyond two days, will find time hang very heavy on his hands; for having, in that short space, seen all the place contains, he will be driven to wile away the tedious hours after the usual manner of its inhabitants, viz., by devoting the morning to the *cafés* and billiard-rooms, the afternoon to the *siesta*, evening to the Alameda, dusk to the Plaza San Antonio and its *Neverias*, [30] and night to the Tertulias—for such is the life of a Spanish *man of pleasure*!

The hospitable mansion of the British Consul General affords those who have the good fortune to possess his acquaintance a happy relief from this monotonous and wearisome life; and, besides meeting there the best society the place affords, the lovers of the fine arts will derive much gratification from the inspection of Mr. Brackenbury's picture gallery, which contains many choice paintings of Murillo, and the best Spanish Masters.

What few other good paintings Cadiz possesses are scattered amongst private houses. The churches contain none of any merit. In one of the Franciscan convents, however, is to be seen a painting that excites much interest, as being the last which occupied the pencil of Murillo, though it was not finished by him. Our conductor told me that a most distinguished English nobleman had offered 500 guineas for it, but the pious monks refused to sell it to a heretic!—Perhaps, His Grace did not know before on what *conscientious* grounds his liberal offer had been declined.

The old Cathedral is not worth visiting. The new one, as it is called, was commenced in the days of the city's prosperity; but the source from whence the funds for building it were raised, failed ere it was half finished; and there it stands, a perfect emblem of Spain herself!—a pile of the most valuable materials, planned on a scale of excessive magnificence, but put together without the slightest taste, and falling to decay for want of revenue! [31]

The walls of the city—excepting those of its land front, which are remarkably well constructed, and kept in tolerable order—are in a deplorable state of dilapidation, and in some places the sea has undermined, and made such breaches in them, as even to threaten the very existence of the city, should it be exposed to a tempest similar to that which did so much mischief to it some seventy years since. This decay is particularly observable, too, on the south side of the fortress, where the sea-wall is exposed to the full sweep of the Atlantic; and here the mischief has resulted chiefly from the want of timely attention to its repairs, for the wall itself is a perfect masterpiece of the building art. Regarding it as such, I venture to devote a small space to its description, conceiving that a hint may be advantageously taken therefrom in the future construction of piers, wharfs, &c. in our own country; and I am the more induced to do so, since so small a portion of the work remains in its pristine state, that it already must be spoken of rather as a thing that *has been*, than one which *is*.

The great object of the builder was to secure the foundation of his wall from the assaults of the ocean, which, at times, breaks with excessive violence upon this coast. For this purpose, he formed an artificial beach, by clearing away the loose rocks which lay strewed about, and inserting in the space thus prepared and levelled, a strong wooden frame-work formed of cases dovetailed into and well fastened to each other. These cases were filled with stones, and secured by numerous piles. The surface was composed of beams of wood, placed close together, carefully caulked, and laid so as to form an inclined plane, at an angle of eight degrees and a half with the horizon.

This beach extended twenty-seven yards from the sea-wall; and its foot, by resting against a kind of breakwater formed of large stones, was saved from being exposed, vertically, to the action of the sea. The waves, thus broke upon the artificial beach, and running up its smooth surface without meeting the slightest resistance, expended, in a great measure, their strength ere reaching the foot of the wall.

To avoid, however, the shock which would still have been felt by the waves breaking against the ramparts, (especially when the sea was unusually agitated) had the planes of the beach and wall met at an angle, the upper portion of the surface of the artificial beach—for about fifteen feet—was laid with large blocks of stone, and united in a curve, or inverted arch, with the casing of the walls of the rampart; and the waves being, by this means, conducted upwards, without experiencing a check, spent their remaining strength in the air, and fell back upon the wooden beach in a harmless shower of spray.

So well was the work executed, that many portions of the arch which connected the beach with the scarped masonry of the rampart are yet perfect, and may be seen projecting from the face of the wall, about twenty feet above its foundation; although the beach upon which it rested has been entirely swept away.

Another cause, besides neglect, has contributed greatly to the destruction of this work; namely, the injudicious removal of the stones and ledges of rock which formed the breakwater of the beach, for erecting houses and repairing the walls of the city.

The ride round the ramparts would be an agreeable variety to the *eternal paseo* on the *Camino de Ercoles*, [32] but for the insufferable odours that arise from the vast heaps of filth deposited on one part of it. To such an extent has this nuisance reached, that, without another river Alpheus, even the hard-working son of Jupiter (the city's reputed founder) would find its removal no easy task.

The arsenal of the *Carracas* is situated on the northern bank of the Santi Petri river, about half a mile within the mouth by which that channel communicates with the bay of Cadiz, and at a distance of two leagues from the city, to which it has no access by land. Its plan is laid on a magnificent scale, and it may boast of having equipped some of the most formidable armaments that ever put to sea; but it is now one vast ruin, hardly possessing the means of fitting out a cockboat. A fire, that reduced the greater part of it to ashes some five and thirty years since, furnishes the national vanity with an agreeable excuse for its present condition.

The road from Cadiz to Port St. Mary's is very circuitous, and offers little to interest any persons but military men and salt-refiners. I will, therefore, pass rapidly over it—which its condition enables me to do—merely observing that, from the branching off of the Chaussée to Chiclana at the *Portazgo*, it makes a wide sweep round the salt marshes at the head of the bay of Cadiz, to gain *Puerto Real* (eighteen miles from Cadiz); and then leaving the peninsula of the *Trocadero* on the left, in four miles reaches a long wooden bridge over the Guadalete—here called the river San Pedro. Two miles further on it crosses another stream by a similar means; and this second river, which is connected with the Guadalete by a canal, has become the principal channel of communication between Xeres and the bay of Cadiz.

A road now turns off to the right to Xeres; another, on the left, to Puerto Santa Maria; and that which continues straight on proceeds to San Lucar, on the Guadalquivír.

Puerto Real is a large but decayed town, possessing but little trade, [33] and no manufactories. Its environs, however, are fertile—enabling it to contend with Port St. Mary's in supplying the Cadiz market with fruit and vegetables;—and a good crop of hay might even be taken from its streets after the autumnal rains!—The population is estimated at 12,000 souls.

Puerto Santa Maria is a yet larger town than Puerto Real, and is computed to contain 18,000 inhabitants. It is situated within the mouth and extending along the right bank of the river, into which the Guadalete has been partly turned. The entrance to the harbour is obstructed by a sand bank, which is impassable at low tide; and at times, when the wind is strong from the S. W., this bar interrupts altogether the water communication with Cadiz. [34]

The distance between the two places, across the bay, is but five miles; by the causeway, twenty-four.

The main street of Puerto Santa Maria is of great length, wide, and rather handsome; and the place has, altogether, a very thriving look; for which it is indebted, as well to the great share it enjoys of the Xeres wine trade, [35] as to the fruitfulness of its fields and orchards. The country, to some considerable extent round the town, is perfectly flat; and the soil (a dark alluvial deposit,) is rich, and highly cultivated; it is, in fact, the market-garden of Cadiz, the inhabitants of which place would die of scurvy, if cut off for six months from the lemon-groves of Port St. Mary.

The position of Puerto Santa Maria seems to correspond pretty well with that of the Portus Gaditanus of Antoninus, viz., 14 miles from the Puente Zuazo, (*Pons;*) the difference being only that between English and Roman miles. But, besides that there is every appearance of the Guadalete having altered its course, and consequently swept away all traces of the Roman port, (or yet more ancient one of *Menesthes*, according to Strabo,) a fertile soil is, of all things, the most inimical to the *preservation* of *ruins*; for gardeners will have no respect for old stones when they stand in the way of cabbage-plants. It would, therefore, be vain to look for any vestiges of the ancient town, in the vicinity of the modern one.

To proceed to Xeres, we must retrace our steps, along the chaussée to Cadiz, for about a mile; when, leaving the two roads branching off to Puerto Real and San Lucar on the right and left, our way continues straight on, traverses a cultivated plain for another mile, and then ascends a rather steep ridge, distinguished in this flat country by the name of *Sierra de Xeres*, though scarcely 500 feet high.

The view from the summit of this ridge is, nevertheless, remarkably fine. It embraces the whole extent of the bay of Cadiz; the bright towns which stand upon its margin; the curiously intersected country that cuts them off from each other; and the winding courses of the Guadalete and Santi Petri.

The slope of the hill is very gradual on the side facing Xeres, and the view is tame in comparison with that in the opposite direction. The road, which traverses a country covered with corn and olives, is *carriageable* throughout; but there is a better route, which turns the Sierra to the eastward, keeping nearer the marshes of the Guadalete. The distance from Puerto Santa Maria to Xeres, by the direct road, is nine miles; by the post route, ten.

Xeres is situated in the lap of two rounded hillocks, which shelter it to the east and west; and it covers a considerable extent of ground. The city, properly so called, is embraced by an old crenated Moorish wall, which, though enclosing a labyrinth of narrow, ill-built, and worse drained streets, is of no great circuit, and is so intermixed with the houses of the suburbs, as to be visible only here and there. The limits of the ancient town are well defined, however, by the numerous gateways still standing, and which, from the augmented size of the place, appear to be scattered about it without any object. Some of the old buildings and narrow streets are very sketchy, and the number of gables and chimneys cannot fail to strike one who has been long accustomed to the flat-roofed cities of Andalusia.

The principal merchants of the place reside mostly in the suburbs; where, besides having greater space for their necessarily extensive premises, their wine stores are better situated for ventilation; a very important auxiliary in bringing the juice of the grape to a due state of perfection. The numerous clean and lofty stores, interspersed with commodious and well-built houses, gardens, greenhouses, &c., give the suburbs an agreeable, refreshing appearance. But it is needful to walk the streets with nose in air, and eyes fixed on things above; for, though much wider, and consequently more freely exposed to the action of the sun and air, than those of the circumvallated city, they are yet more filthy, and quite as nauseating. Now and then, indeed, a generous brown sherry odour salutes the third sense, counteracting, in some degree, the unwholesome effects of the noxious cloacal miasms. But the bad scents prevail in the proportion of ten to one; and, like the far-famed distilling city of Cologne, Xeres seems to have bottled up, and hermetically sealed, all its sweets for exportation.

The population of the place is enormous—being estimated at no less than 50,000 souls. But the amount is subject to great variations, dependant on the recentness of the last endemic fever, generated in its pestiferous gutters. The inhabitants are all, more or less, connected with the wine trade—which is the only thing thought of or talked of in the place.

The store-houses are all above ground. They are immense buildings, having lofty roofs supported on arches, springing from rows of slender columns; and their walls are pierced with numerous windows, to admit of a thorough circulation of air. Some are so large as to be capable of containing 4000 butts, and are cool, even in the most sultry weather. The exhalations are, nevertheless, rather *overcoming*, even unaided by the numerous *samples*, of which one is tempted to make trial. The number of butts annually made, or, more correctly speaking, *collected*, at Xeres, amounts to 30,000. Of this number, one half is exported to England, and includes the produce of nearly all the choicest vineyards of Xeres; for, in selecting their wines for shipment, the Xeres houses carefully avoid mixing their first-growth wines with those of lighter quality, collected from the vineyards of Moguer, San Lucar, and Puerto Real; or even with such as are produced on their own inferior grounds.

The remaining 15,000 butts are in part consumed in the country; where a light wine, having what is called a *Manzanilla* [36] flavour, is preferred—or sold to the shippers from other places, where they are generally mixed with inferior wines.

The total number of butts shipped, annually, from the different ports round the bay of Cadiz, may be taken at the following average—

From	Xeres	15,000	almost all to England.
"	Puerto Santa Maria	12,000	chiefly to England and the United States.
"	Chiclana	3,000	principally to the Habana,
"	Puerto Real	500	the Ports of Mexico, and Buenos Ayres.
	Total	30,500	

But, besides the above, a prodigious quantity of wine finds its way to England from Moguer and San Lucar, which one never hears of but under the common denomination of Sherry.

Most of the principal merchants are growers, as well as venders of wine; which, with foreign houses, renders it necessary that one partner of the firm, at least, should be a Roman Catholic; for "heretics" cannot hold lands in Spain. Those who are growers have a decided advantage over such as merely make up wines; for the latter are liable to have the produce of the inferior vineyards of San Lucar, Moguer, and other places, mixed up by the grower of whom they purchase. All Sherries, however, are *manufactured*; for, it would be almost as difficult to get an unmixed butt of wine from a Xeres merchant, as a direct answer from a quaker. But there is no concealment in this mixing process; and it is even quite necessary, in order to keep up the stock of old wines, which, otherwise, would soon be consumed.

These are kept in huge casks—not much inferior in size to the great ton of Heidelberg—called *"Madre"* [37] butts; and some of these old ladies contain wine that is 120 years of age. It must, however, be confessed, that the plan adopted in keeping them up, partakes somewhat of the nature of *"une imposture delicate;"* since, whenever a gallon of wine is taken from the 120 year old butt, it is replaced by a like quantity from the next in seniority, and so on with the rest; so that even the very oldest wines in the store are daily undergoing a mixing process.

It is thus perfectly idle, when a customer writes for a "ten-year old" butt of sherry, to expect to receive a wine which was grown that number of years previously. He will get a most excellent wine, however, which will, probably, be prepared for him in the following manner:—Three-fourths of the butt will consist of a three or four year old wine, to which a few gallons of *Pajarete*, or *Amontillado*, [38] will be added, to give the particular flavour or colour required; and the remainder will be made up of various proportions of old wines, of different vintages: a dash of brandy being added, to preserve it from sea-sickness during the voyage.

To calculate the age of this mixture appears, at first sight, to involve a laborious arithmetical operation. But it is very simply done, by striking an average in the following manner:—The *fond*, we will suppose, is a four-years' old wine, with which figure we must, therefore, commence our calculations. To flavour and give age to this foundation, the hundred and twenty years' old "*madre*" is made to contribute a gallon, which, being about the hundreth part of the proposed butt, diffuses a year's maturity into the composition. The centiginarian stock-butt next furnishes a quantity, which in the same way adds another year to its age. The next in seniority supplies a proportion equivalent to a space of two years; and a fourth adds a similar period to its existence. So that, without going further, we have $4 + 1 + 1 + 2 + 2 = 10$, as clear as the sun at noon-day, or a demonstration in Euclid.

This may appear very like "*bishoping*," or putting marks in a horse's mouth to conceal his real age. But the intention, *in the case of the wine*, is by no means fraudulent, but simply to distribute more equally the good things of this life, by furnishing the public with an excellent composition, which is within the reach of many; for, if this were not done, the consequence would be, that the Xeres merchant would have a small quantity of wine in his stores, which, from its extreme age, would be so valuable, that few persons would be found to purchase it, and a large stock of inferior wines, which would be driven out of the market by the produce of other countries.

The quality of the wine depends, therefore, upon the quantity and age of the various *madre* butts from which it has been flavoured; and the taste is varied from dry to sweet, and the colour from pale to brown, by the greater or less admixture of *Pajarete*, *Amontillado*, and *boiled* sherry. I do not think that the custom of adding boiled wine obtains generally, for it is a very expensive method of giving age. It is, however, a very effectual mode, and one that is considered equivalent to a voyage across the Atlantic, at the very least.

I have heard of an extensive manufacturer (not of wine) in our own country, who had rather improved on this plan of giving premature old age to his wines. He called one of the steam-engines of his factory *Bencoolen*, and another *Mobile*; and, slinging his butts of Sherry and Madeira to the great levers of the machinery, gave them the benefit of a ship's motion, as well as a tropical temperature, without their quitting his premises; and, after a certain number of weeks' oscillation, he passed them off as "East and West India *particular*."

The sweet wines of Xeres are, perhaps, the finest in the world. That known as *Pajarete* is the most abundantly made, but the *Pedro Ximenes* is of superior flavour. There is also a sweet wine flavoured with cherries, which is very delicious.

The light dry Sherries are also very pleasant in their pure state, but they require to be mixed with brandy and other wines, to keep long, or to ship for the foreign market. Those, therefore, who purchase *cheap Sherry* in England may be assured that it has become a *light* wine since its departure from Spain.

The number of *winehouses* at Xeres is quite extraordinary. Of these, as many, I think, as five-and-twenty export almost exclusively to England. The merchants are extremely hospitable; they live in very good style, and are particularly choice of the wines that appear at their tables.

The Spanish antiquaries have by no means settled to their satisfaction what Roman city stood on the site of modern Xeres. The common opinion seems to be, that it occupies the place of *Asta Regia*, mentioned by Pliny as one of the towns within the marshes of the Guadalquivír. Florez, however, labours to prove that it agrees better with *Asido*. But I do not think his arguments get over the difficulty arising from the expression "*in mediterraneo*," applied to that city; which agrees better with *Medina Sidonia* than Xeres, the latter being close upon the flats of the Guadalquivír, whereas the other is decidedly *inland* with reference to them.

The medals of Asido, Florez describes as having sometimes a bull, and at others a "fish of the *tunny* kind," upon them. Now this latter emblem is, most certainly, more applicable to Medina Sidonia than Xeres, since no fish of the "tunny kind" ever could have frequented the shallow muddy stream of the Guadalete. And though the city of Medina Sidonia is situated on the summit of a high hill, sixteen miles from the sea, yet we may take it for granted that its jurisdiction extended as far as the coast, to the eastward of the Isla de Leon; since it does not appear that any town of note intervened between Cadiz and Besaro, or Besippone.

The same author derives the name Xeres from the Persian *Zeiraz* (Schiras); supposing it may have been so called from that having been the country of the Moslem chief who captured Regia.

The word assimilates with our mode of pronouncing the name of the existing town; and the wine of Schiraz was not less esteemed of old amongst the easterns, than Sherry is now by us, and appears ever to have been by the ancients; for tradition ascribes to Bacchus the foundation of Nebrissa, in the vicinity of Xeres. May not, therefore, the celebrity of its vineyards have led the Arabs to call the town Schiraz, or Xeres, rather than the country of the chief who conquered it?

Xeres was captured from the Moors by San Fernando, and, becoming thenceforth one of the bulwarks of the Christian frontier, changed its name from *Xeres Sidonia* to *Xeres de la Frontera*, by which it continues to be distinguished from others.

The Guadalete does not approach within a mile and a half of Xeres. This river is the Chryssus of the Romans; and the Spaniards, ever prone to boast of the ancient celebrity of their country, maintain it to be the mythological Lethe of yet more remote times. On its right bank (about three miles on the road to Medina Sidonia) stands a Carthusian convent of some note. The pious founders of this edifice—as indeed was their wont—located themselves in a most enviable situation. The *"elisios xerexanos prados"* were spread out before them, covered with fat beeves, and herds of high caste horses, belonging to the order. The perfume of the surrounding orange-groves penetrated to the innermost recesses of this house of prayer and penance. The juice of the luscious grape, and the oil of the purple olives that grew upon the sunny bank whereon it stands, found their way, with as little obstruction, into its cells and cellars. But still, with this Canaan in their possession, these austere disciples of St. Bruno affected to despise the things of this world, and held not communion with their fellow-creatures!

The edifice is fast falling to decay; the brotherhood is reduced to a score of decrepit old men; and—what alone is to be regretted—the celebrated breed of horses has become extinct.

The Guadalete winds through the valley overlooked by the *Cartuja*, [39] and is crossed by a stone bridge of five arches. On gaining the southern bank of the river, roads branch off in all directions. That to the left—keeping up the valley—proceeds to Paterna (sixteen miles from Xeres), and *Alcalà de los Gazules* (twenty-five miles). Another, continuing straight on, goes to Medina Sidonia (eighteen miles); and a third, that presents itself to the right, is directed across the country to Chiclana, reducing the distance to that place from twenty-six miles (by the post-road) to sixteen.

About four miles below the bridge are some store-houses, a wharf, and ferry, called *El Portal*, from whence the river is navigable to Port St. Mary's. *El Portal* may be considered the port of Xeres, to which place (distant about three miles) there is a good wheel-road.

The fatal battle which gave Spain up to the dominion of the Saracens (A.D. 714) was fought on the southern bank of the Guadalete, about five miles from Xeres, on the road to Paterna. The robes and "horned helmet" of Roderick, which he is supposed to have thrown off to facilitate his escape, were found on the bank of the river, where a small chapel, dedicated to

Our Lady of *Leyna*, now stands. The sanguinary fight is stated—with the customary Spanish exaggeration—to have lasted eight days! and then only to have been decided in favour of the Mohammedans by treason.

But however much we may admire the valour displayed by the Gothic monarch, in thus obstinately defending his crown, yet the rashness he was guilty of, in drawing up his forces on such a field (in a country abounding in strong positions, where the enemy's superiority of numbers would not have availed them), proves him to have been as little fitted to command an army as to govern a kingdom.

CHAPTER IV

THE traveller who journeys on horseback has the choice of several roads between Xeres and Seville. The shortest is by the marshes of the Guadalquivír, visiting only one town, Lebrija, in the whole distance of eleven leagues. The longest is the post route, or *arrecife*, which makes a very wide circuit by Utrera and Alcalá de Guadaira, to avoid the swampy country bordering the river. From this latter road several others diverge to the left, cutting off various segments of the arc it describes; and in summer these routes are even better than the highway itself, though heavy and much intersected by torrents in winter.

On the first-named or shortest road, the town of Lebrija alone calls for observation. It is about fifteen miles from Xeres, and stands on the side of a slightly-marked mound, that stretches some little way into the wide-spreading plain of the Guadalquivír. The knoll is covered with the extensive ruins of a castle—a joint work of Romans and Moors—which during the late war was put into a defensible state by the French. Most writers agree in placing here the Roman city of Nebrissa; [40] in which name that of the modern town may readily be distinguished. It is distant about five miles from the Guadalquivír, and contains three convents, and a population of 4,000 souls. The Posada is excellent.

The country from Xeres to Lebrija presents an undulated surface, which is clothed with vines and olives; but thenceforth the banks of the "*olivifero Bœtis*" are devoted entirely to pasture, and the road is most uninterestingly flat: so flat, indeed, that there is scarcely a rise in the whole twenty-eight miles from Lebrija to Seville. It is not passable in winter, and but one wretched hovel, called the *Venta del Peleon*, offers itself as a resting-place. The river winds occasionally close up to the side of the road, and from time to time a barge or passage boat, gliding along its smooth surface, breaks the wearisome monotony of the scene; but in general the tortuous stream wanders to a distance of several miles from the road, and is altogether lost to the sight in an apparently interminable plain, that stretches to the westward.

The misty vapour, or *mirage*, which rises from and hangs over the low land bordering the river, produces singular deceptions; at times giving the whole face of the country in advance the semblance of a vast lake; at others, magnifying distant objects in a most extraordinary manner. On one occasion, we were surprised to see what had every appearance of being a large town rise up suddenly before us; and it was only when arrived within a few hundred yards of the objects we had taken for churches and houses, that we became convinced they were but a drove of oxen. These imaginary oxen proved in the end, however, to be only a flock of sheep. The *Marisma*, [41] for such is the name given to this low ground, affords pasturage for immense herds of cattle of all sorts, and the herbage is so fine as to lead one to wonder what becomes of all the *fat* beef and mutton in Spain.

The post road from Xeres to Seville, as I have already mentioned, is very circuitous, increasing the distance from forty-three to fifty-six miles — reckoned fifteen and a half post leagues.

For the first thirteen miles, that is, to the post house of *La Casa real del Cuervo*, the road traverses a country rich in corn and olives, but skirting for some considerable distance the western limits of a vast heath, called the *llanura de Caulina*, whereon even goats have difficulty in finding sustenance. The first league of the road is perfectly level, the rest hilly. A little beyond the post house of El Cuervo, a road strikes off to the left to Lebrija. The *arrecife*, proceeding on towards Utrera, crosses numerous gulleys by which the winter torrents are led down from the side of the huge *Sierra Gibalbin*, which, here raising its head on the right, stretches to the north for a mile or two, keeping parallel to the road, and then again sinks to the plain. This passed, the remainder of the road to Utrera is conducted along what may be termed the brow of a wide tract of low table land, which, extending to the foot of the distant *Serranía de Ronda* on the right, breaks in the opposite direction into innumerable ramifications, towards the plain of the Guadalquivír.

In the entire distance to Utrera, (twenty-four miles from *El Cuervo*) there is not a single village on the road, and but very few farms or even cottages scattered along it. It is plentifully furnished with bridges for crossing the various *barrancas* [42] that drain the mountain ravines in the winter, and by means of these bridges the chaussée is kept nearly on a dead level throughout. About midway there is another post house. This road is so perfectly uninteresting, that, availing myself of the earliest opportunity of quitting it and proceeding to Seville by a more direct, if not a more diversified route, I will strike into a well-beaten track that presents itself, edging away to the left, about three miles beyond *El Cuervo*, and is directed on Las Cabezas de San Juan, distant about six miles from the post road.

Las Cabezas de San Juan is a wretched little village, which inscriptions found in its vicinity have decided to be the *Ugia* [43] of the Romans. It is situated on a knoll, commanding an extensive view over the circumjacent flat country, and some years since contained a population of a thousand or twelve hundred souls. But, having been the hotbed wherein Riego's conspiracy was brought to unnatural maturity, it was razed to the ground during the short contest that restored Ferdinand to a despotic throne, and "all its pleasant things laid waste."

From hence to *Los Palacios* is ten miles. The country is flat, and but partially cultivated. A short league before reaching *Los Palacios*, a long ruined bridge, called *El Alcantarilla*, is seen at a little distance off the road on the right. In the time of Swinburne, this bridge appears to have been passable, and an inscription was then sufficiently perfect to announce its Roman origin. It was probably raised to carry a road from Lebrija to Utrera across a marshy tract, which in winter is apt to be flooded by the *Salado de Moron*; or perhaps the road over it may have been directed on *Dos Hermanos*, which is known to be the Roman town of Orippo.

Los Palacios is a clean compact village, of about 1,000 inhabitants. A plain extends for many miles on all sides of it, but a slight, perhaps artificial, mound rises slightly above the general level of the place on its eastern side, and bears the weight of its ruined castle: the walls of the village itself are also fast crumbling to the dust. The inns are miserable; but a Spanish nobleman, with whom we had become acquainted at Xeres, had obligingly furnished us with a letter of introduction to a gentleman of the place, who entertained us most hospitably, and very reluctantly—for he wished much to detain us—gave orders to the *dueña* of his household to have the usual breakfast of chocolate and bread fried in lard prepared for us by daybreak on the following morning.

From Los Palacios to Seville the distance is reckoned five "*leguas regulares*," but it is barely fifteen miles. The country to the north of the village is very fruitful, and becomes hilly as one proceeds. At about nine miles there is a solitary venta, on the margin of a stream that comes down from *Dos Hermanos*; which village is situated about a league off on the right.

It is a matter of some little difficulty to make any of the roads between Cadiz and Seville (that is, from Port St. Mary's onwards) agree with the route laid down in the Itinerary of Antoninus. The distance of the *Portus Gaditanus* from *Hispalis* is therein stated to be seventy-six Roman miles, [44] or, according to Florez, sixty-eight; [45] which miles, if computed to contain eight *Olympic* stadia each, are equal to seventy, and sixty-three British statute miles respectively; the actual distance from Puerto Santa Maria to Seville being, by the chaussée, sixty-six miles; by Lebrija and the marshes, fifty-two.

On comparing these distances, therefore, one would naturally be led to suppose that the Roman military way followed the circuitous line of the existent chaussée, but that monuments and inscriptions, which have been found at Las Cabezas de St. Juan and Dos Hermanos, prove those places to be the towns of *Ugia* and *Orippo*, mentioned in the Itinerary as lying upon the road. We are under the necessity, therefore, of adopting a line which reduces the distance from the *Portus Gaditanus* to *Hispalis* far below even that given by Florez.

The only way of meeting all these difficulties and premises seems to be by taking a smaller stadium than the *Olympic*. That of 666⅔ to a degree of the meridian [46] I have generally found to agree well with the actual distances of places in Spain, and it is a scale which we are warranted in adopting, since it is sometimes used by Strabo on the authority of Eratosthenes, and Pliny admits that no two persons ever agreed in the Roman measures.

Taking this scale, therefore (though a yet smaller would agree better), I fix the first station, *Hasta*, at a small table hill, even now called by the Spaniards *La Mesa de Asta*, lying N.N.W. of Xeres; [47] making the distance from the *Portus Gaditanus* sixteen miles, as in the Itinerary, instead of eight, as altered by Florez: a number, by the way, which scarcely agrees better with the actual distance from Port St. Mary's to Xeres—at which latter place he fixes Hasta—than the sixteen miles of the original.

The next place mentioned in the Itinerary is *Ugia*; determined, as has been already stated, to have stood where Las Cabezas de San Juan is now situated; and the distance from the *Mesa de Asta* to this place, passing through *Nebrissa* (Lebrija—omitted in the Itinerary, as not being a convenient halting-place for the troops), agrees tolerably well with that specified, viz., twenty-seven Roman miles. The remaining distances, viz., twenty-four miles to *Orippo* (Dos Hermanos), and nine to *Hispalis* (Seville), agree yet better, though still somewhat below the scale I have adopted.

The appearance of Seville, approaching it on the side of the *Marisma*, is by no means imposing. Stretching as the city does along the bank of the Guadalquivír, its least diameter meets the view; and, from its standing on a perfect flat, the walls by which it is encircled conceal the most part of the houses, and take off from the height of the hundred spires of its churches—the lofty *Giralda* being the only conspicuous object that presents itself above them.

The wide avenue which, after crossing the river *Guadaira*, leads up to the city gate, is, however, prepossessing; a spacious botanical garden is on the left hand, and, in advance of the city walls, are the Amphitheatre, the Royal Snuff Manufactory, and several other handsome public buildings.

Seville is generally considered,—at all events by its inhabitants,—the largest city of Spain. It is of an oval shape, two miles long, and one and a quarter broad; and, washed by the Guadalquivír on the eastern side, is enclosed on the others by a patched-up embattled wall, the work of all ages and nations.

The city is tolerably free from suburbs, excepting at the Carmona and *Rosario* gates on its western side; but numerous extramural convents, hospitals, barracks, and other public edifices, are scattered about in different directions, which, with the town of Triana, on the opposite bank of the river, materially increase the size of the place, and swell the amount of its population to at least 100,000 souls.

Seville cannot be called a handsome city, for it contains but one tolerable street; the houses, however, are lofty, and generally well built, the shops good, and the lamps within sight of each other, which is not usually the case in Spanish towns. Most of the houses in the principal thoroughfares are built with an edging of flat roof overlooking the street. This part of the house is called the *Azotea*, and, with the lower orders, serves the manifold purposes of a dormitory in summer, a place for washing and drying clothes in winter, and a place of assignation at all seasons.

In hot weather awnings are spread from these *azoteas* across the streets, rendering them delightfully cool and shady; the canvass covering, fanned by the breeze, sending down a refreshing air, whilst it serves at the same time as a shelter from the sun. Even in the most sultry days of summer, I have never found the streets of Seville *impracticable.*

There are several spacious squares in various parts of the city; in the largest, distinguished by the extraordinary, though, perhaps, not *unsuitable* name of *La Plaza de la Incarnacion*, the market is held. This is abundantly supplied with bread, meat, fish, poultry, and all sorts of vegetables and fruits, and is, perhaps, the cheapest in Andalusia; it certainly is the cleanest.

The *Alamedas*, of which there are two, are equally as well taken care of as the market, though in point of beauty they are not quite deserving of the praise which has been bestowed upon them. One is in the interior of the city, and becomes only a place of general resort when the weather is unsettled. The other more commonly frequented walk is between the walls of the town and the Guadalquivír, extending nearly a mile along the bank of the river, from the *Torre del Oro* to the bridge of boats communicating with Triana. It is well sheltered with trees, and furnished with seats, and is indeed a most delightful and amusing promenade, being nightly crowded with all descriptions of people, from the grandee of the first class to the goatskin clad swineherd, who visits the city for a *sombrero* of the *ultima moda*, or a fresh supply of *bacallao.*

The carriage drive round the walk is generally thronged with equipages of all sorts and ages, any one of which, shown as a *spectacle* in England, would most assuredly make the exhibitor's fortune. The *blazon* on the pannels, and venerable cocked hats and laced coats of the drivers and attendants, bespeak them, nevertheless, to belong to *sons of somebody*; and the wives and daughters of somebody seated therein, seem not a little proud of possessing these indubitable proofs of the antiquity of their houses. Few of these distinguished personages, however, excepting such as labour under the infliction of gout, rheumatism, or the indelible marks of old age, are satisfied to remain quiet spectators of the gay scene; but, after driving once or twice round the *paseo* to see *who* has arrived, alight, and join the flutter of their fans, and, with grief I say it, their loud laugh and conversation to the already over-powering din of the "promiscuous multitude."

This scene of gaiety is prolonged until long after the sun has ceased to gild the mirror-like surface of the Guadalquivír. The walk, indeed, is still in its most fashionable state of throng, when a tinkling bell, announcing the elevation of the Host, marks the concluding ceremony of the vesper service in a neighbouring church. At this signal the motley crowd appears as if touched by the wand of an enchanter. Each devout Romanist either reverentially bends the knee, or stands statue-like on the spot where the homage-commanding sound first reached the ear. The men take off their hats—the ladies drop their fans. The coachmen check their hacks—the hacks hang down their heads—not a whisper is heard, not an eye is raised. The bell sounds a second time, and animation returns, the breast is marked with repeated crosses, the dust brushed off the knees, "*conques*" innumerable take up the interrupted conversation, and once more

"Soft eyes look love to eyes which speak again."

So ludicrously observant are the Spaniards of this ceremony, that, on the ringing of the bell, I once remarked a water-carrier stop in the midst of his sonorous cry, "*A....*" and devoutly uncovering his head, and crossing himself, wait until the second tinkle permitted him again to open his mouth; when, with most comical gravity, he finished the wanting syllable "*gua! Agua fres—ca!*"

The Guadalquivír is about 200 yards wide at Seville, where it forms a kind of basin, and is navigable for vessels of 150 tons burthen. It is so liable to be swollen by the freshes poured down from the mountains in the upper part of its course, that a permanent bridge has never been attempted; and the banks are so low, that the floods have frequently reached to the very gates of the city. The influence of the tide is felt some little distance above Seville, rendering the water of the river unfit for general purposes. The water of the wells, on the other hand, is considered unwholesome, so that the city is, in a great measure, dependent for its supply of this most necessary article on an aqueduct, that brings a stream from *Alcalà de Guadaira*, a distance of about nine miles.

The populous town of Triana is still worse off than Seville, for, as the expedient of a leather pipe has not yet been thought of, the "essential fluid" has to be carried across the river on men's or asses' backs, rendering it a most expensive article of consumption; a circumstance that accounts, in a great measure, for the very Egyptian complexion of the inhabitants.

The public buildings of Seville fully entitle the city to its boasted title of the Western Capital of Spain. It contains no less than sixty convents and nunneries, besides numerous other religious establishments and hospitals. The Archiepiscopal Church is the largest in Spain, [48] its dimensions being 450 feet by 260; and it is one of the most splendid piles in the universe. The architecture of the exterior is heavy and tasteless, so that one is but little prepared for the striking change which meets the eye on drawing aside the ponderous leathern curtain that closes the portal, and entering the vast vaulted interior.

It is built in the gothic style, not of a florid kind, however, but simple, aërial, and imposing. The colour of the free stone used in its construction is a subdued white; the pavement is laid in squares of black and white marble, and the stained glass windows, which are of extreme beauty, shed a warm, variegated glow throughout the building, that produces an effect well suited to its character. Indeed, no cathedral that I have any where seen either presents a more striking coup d'œil, or draws forth, in a greater degree, that instinctive feeling of devotion implanted in the human breast. The walls, too, are not so disfigured with tawdry chapels, as those of most Roman Catholic churches, and the few paintings with which they are decorated are *chef d'œuvres* of the best Spanish masters.

One modern painting has, however, been admitted to the collection, rather, I should think, out of compliment to the ladies of Seville, than on account of its own merit. It represents two maidens of this saintly city, who, "*mucho tiempo hay,*" [49] to use our conductor's expression, having been accused of some heretical practices, were exposed to be devoured by a ferocious lion. The gallant sovereign of the woods and forests, instead, however, of making a meal of these tempting morsels of human flesh and imagined frailty, "*se echó à sus pies,*" and began caressing them after his feline fashion, to the great astonishment of all beholders! This miraculous want of appetite on the part of the lion, making the innocence of the damsels evident, led, of course, to their liberation, and their names are now enrolled upon the long list of saints of Seville.

The tower of the cathedral, commonly called *La Giralda*, from a colossal statue of *Faith*, at its summit, which, with strange inconsistency of character, wheels about at every change of wind, is by no means a handsome structure. It was built by the Moors, about 250 years before the city was captured by San Fernando, and originally was only 280 feet in height; but a belfry has since been added, which makes it altogether 364 feet high. The tower is fifty feet square, and the ascent is effected by an inclined plane, by means of which, some queen of Spain is rumoured to have ridden on horseback to the gallery under the belfry.

The view from the summit of the tower fully repays one, even for the labour of ascending it on foot, and I am not quite sure but that the inclined plane rather increases than lessens the fatigue of mounting. From hence alone can a correct idea be formed of the size and splendour of Seville. The eye, from this elevation, embraces the whole extent of the city, its long narrow streets, wide circuit of walls, its gateways, magnificent public buildings, and spacious plazas, its verdant orangeries, and its house-top flower-gardens. Beyond the busy city, a fruitful plain extends for several miles in every direction; on one side bearing luxuriant crops of corn and olives, on the other, giving pasture to countless herds of cattle; the lovely Guadalquivír winding through and fertilizing the whole.

The Archiepiscopal palace occupies one side of a small square, that is immediately under the *Giralda*; the façade of this building is handsome, but we had not an opportunity of seeing the interior, as its worthy occupier was unwell. Near the cathedral, but on the opposite side to the Archbishop's residence, is the *Lonja*; a splendid edifice, which (as the name implies) was originally built for an exchange. But, though the lower suites of apartments are still set apart for the use of the merchants, the building is so inconveniently situated, that no commercial business is transacted there, and the whole of the upper story has been fitted up as a repository for the "American archives." These records are most voluminous, and are preserved with as much care, and ticketed with as great regularity, as if Spain shortly intended to resume the sovereignty over her former vast transatlantic possessions.

As a mark of especial favour, the tip of my little finger was permitted to rest upon the edge of the first letter written from the *other world*; the keeper of the archives requesting me, at the same time, not to press too hard upon the valuable MS., and assuring us, that most persons were obliged to be satisfied with looking at the precious document bearing the signature of the adventurous Columbus, in its glass case.

The whole of the shelves, drawers, &c., are of cedar; a wood which has the property of preserving the papers committed to their charge from all descriptions of insects. The floors are laid in chequers of red and blue marble, and the grand staircase is composed of the same, which is highly polished and remarkably handsome. One of the apartments of the vast quadrangle contains two original paintings of Columbus and Hernan Cortes.

A little removed from the *Lonja*, is the *Alcazar*, or Royal Palace. This is kept up in a kind of half-dress state, and has a governor appointed to its peculiar charge, who usually resides within its precincts. It is built in the Moorish style, and is generally supposed to have been the work of Moorish hands, though raised only—so at least a Gothic inscription on its walls is said to state—by "the puissant King of Castile and Leon, Don Pedro."

There is probably some little exaggeration in this, and, in point of fact, perhaps, the mighty monarch only repaired and added to the palace of the Moorish kings, which the neglect of a hundred years had, in his time, rendered uninhabitable. It is a very inferior piece of workmanship to the Alhambra, but, nevertheless, contains much to admire, particularly the ceilings of the apartments (of which there are upwards of seventy), and the walls of one of the courts.

The different towers command very fine views over the city and adjacent country, and the gardens are delightful, though of but small extent. The walks are laid with tiles, between which little tubes are introduced vertically, that communicate with waterpipes underneath, and, by merely turning a screw, the whole of the valves of these tubes are simultaneously opened, and each shoots forth a diminutive stream of water. This plan was adopted, as being an improvement on the tedious method usually practised in watering gardens. It affords the facetiously disposed a glorious opportunity of inflicting a practical joke upon unwary visiters to the Alcazar; who, conducted to the garden, and then and there seduced, out of mere politeness, to join in the complaint expressed of a want of rain, suddenly find themselves *over* a heavy shower, and under the necessity of laughing at a piece of wit from which there is no possibility of escape.

The *Casa Pilata* is another of the sights of Seville. It is a private house, said to be built on the exact model of that of the Roman governor of Jerusalem. It is fitted up with much taste, but its chief beauty consists in a profusion of glazed tiles, which give it actual coolness, as well as a refreshing look.

Most of the other subjects worthy of the traveller's notice are situated without the walls of the city. The first in order, issuing from the Xeres gate, is the *Plaza de los Toros*, or amphitheatre, an immense circus, one half built of stone, and the other half of wood, and capable of accommodating 14,000 persons. The next remarkable object is the *Royal Tobacco Manufactory*, (the term seems rather absurd to English ears,) a huge edifice, so strongly built, and jealously defended by walls and ditches, as to appear rather a detached fort, or citadel, raised to overawe the turbulent city, than an establishment for peacefully grinding tobacco leaves into snuff, and rolling them into cigars. The manufactory employs 5000 persons, and of this number 2600 are occupied solely in making cigars. But, as I have elsewhere shown, even with the assistance of the Royal Manufactory lately established at Malaga, the supply of *lawful* cigars is not equal to one-tenth part of the consumption of the country.

The demand for snuff may probably be fully met by the Royal Manufactory; for the Spaniards are not great consumers of tobacco through the medium of the nose; and most of the snuffs prepared at Seville are extremely pungent, so that "a little goes a great way." There is a coarse kind, however, called, I think, "Spanish bran," which is much esteemed by *connoisseurs*.

The Royal Cannon Foundry is in the vicinity of the Tobacco Manufactory, and though this establishment for furnishing the means of consuming powder is not in such activity as its neighbour employed in supplying food for smoke, yet it is in equally good order, and, on the whole, is a very creditable national establishment. The brass pieces made here are remarkably handsome, and very correctly bored, but they want the lightness and finish of our guns—qualities in which English artillery excels all others. Two of the "monster mortars," cast by the French for the siege of Cadiz, are still preserved here.

The Cavalry Barracks, Royal Saltpetre Manufactory, Military Hospital, and various other edifices, planned on a scale proportioned to Spain's *former* greatness, together with numerous convents, equally disproportioned to her present wants, follow in rapid succession in completing the circuit of the walls. The most interesting amongst the religious houses is a convent of Capuchins, situated near the Cordoba gate. It contains twenty-five splendid paintings by Murillo, "any one of which," as a modern writer has justly remarked, "would suffice to render a man immortal."

Murillo was certainly a perfect master of his art. His style is peculiar, and in his early productions there is a coldness and formality that partake of the school of Velasquez; but the works of his maturer age are distinguished by a boldness of outline, a gracefulness of grouping, and a depth and softness of colouring, which entitle him to rank with Rubens and Correggio.

The paintings of Murillo, though met with in all the best collections of Europe, where they take their place amongst the works of the first masters, are, nevertheless, valued by foreigners rather on account of their rarity than of their execution. The fact is, those of his paintings which have left

Spain are nearly all devoted to the same subject—the Madonna and Child; and, even in that, offer but little variety either in the disposition, or in the colouring of the figures. The Spanish artist is, consequently, accused of want of genius and self-plagiarism. Nor does Murillo receive due credit for the pains he took in finishing his paintings; for, amongst those of his works which have found their way into foreign collections, there are few which have not received more or less damage, either in the transport from Spain, or by subsequent neglect; and, in many instances, the attempts made to restore them by cleaning or retouching have inflicted a yet more severe injury upon them.

Those persons only, therefore, who have visited Spain, and, above all, Murillo's native city—Seville—can fully appreciate the merits of that wonderful artist. The vast number of master-pieces which he has there left behind him, and the variety of subjects they embrace, sufficiently prove, however, that, whilst in versatility of talent he has been equalled by few, in point of *industry* he almost stands without a rival.

Besides the twenty-five paintings in the Capuchin convent, already noticed, the *Hóspital de la Caridad* contains several of Murillo's master-pieces; two, in particular, are deserving of notice—the subjects are, the miracle of the loaves and fishes, and Moses striking the rock. The great size of these two paintings saved them from a journey to Paris, but the French, in their zeal for the encouragement of the fine arts, stripped the chapel of all the other works of Murillo that enriched it—only a few of which were restored at the peace of 1815.

Other paintings of the Spanish Rafael are to be found in the various churches of Seville, and every private collector (of whom the city contains many,) prides himself on being the possessor of at least one *original* of his illustrious fellow-citizen.

The theatre of Seville has ever held a comparatively distinguished place in the dramatic annals of Spain; and, lamentable as is the condition to which the national stage has been reduced, the capital of Andalusia may still be considered as one of the most *playgoing* places in the kingdom. This may, perhaps, partly be accounted for by the number of dramatic authors to whom the city has given birth, partly by the peculiar disposition of the inhabitants of the province, who are deeper tinged with romance, and have more imagination than the rest of the natives of the Peninsula.

The deplorable atrophy under which the drama has of late years been languishing in every part of Europe [50] had, aided by various predisposing circumstances, long been undermining the at no-time very robust constitution of the Spanish theatre; which, like a condemned criminal, existed only from day to day, at the will and pleasure of a despotic sovereign; and had, moreover, constantly to combat the hostility of the priesthood: a bigoted race, prone at all times to discourage an art, which, by enlarging the understandings of the community, tended to diminish the respect with which their own profane melo-dramatic mysteries were regarded. The priests, in fact, have always been, and ever will be, averse to their flock being fleeced by any other shears than their own.

Considering, therefore, the obstacles which the Spanish theatre has had to contend against, obstacles which were yet more formidable in that country in times past than they are at the present day, it cannot but be admitted that the drama was cultivated in Spain with a degree of success which could little have been expected.

Our own early dramatists, indeed, drew largely from the prolific sources opened by Lope de Vega, Calderon, and other Spanish writers of the sixteenth century; and, perhaps, to the example set by those authors is our stage indebted for its release from the thraldom in which others are yet held, by a preposterous, though *classic,* adherence to the preservation of the unities.

The drama (in the strict sense of the term) never, however, became a popular amusement with the Spaniards generally. The legal disabilities imposed upon the performers by the intrigues of the Romish church brought the profession of an actor into disrepute, and, as a natural consequence, checked the progress of the histrionic art. The stage had no door opening to preferment, and the knight of the buskin (to whom, by the way, the *Don* was interdicted), though endowed with the talents of a Talma or a Kemble, of a Liston or a Potier, ranked below the lowest of the train of bullfighters, and could never expect to amass a fortune, or hope to be considered otherwise than as a "diverting vagabond." A Spanish actress was yet more discouragingly circumstanced, as, however irreproachable her character, she held only the same grade in society as the frail Ciprian whose beauty gained her livelihood.

Labouring under such disadvantages, it is not surprising, therefore, that Thalia and Euterpe should eventually have been driven from the Spanish stage, and a licentious monster—the illegitimate offspring of Comus and Impudicitia—have been crowned with the palm-wreath snatched from the brows of the immortal Parnassides.

The modern Spanish dramatic authors—if it be not profanation so to call them—pandering to the vitiated taste of the day, indulge in all the licence of Aristophanes, without varnishing their obscenities with the brilliancy of his wit. They write, in fact, for auditors, who, whilst endowed with a quick perception of the ridiculous, are too ignorant to discriminate between right and wrong, and cannot perceive where legitimate satire ends, and libertinism commences; who, possessing a vast stock of native wit, inherit with it a coarse, degenerate taste. The human frailties of the monastic orders are, consequently, the favourite subjects now held up to ridicule on the stage, as if to prove the truth of Voltaire's lines,

"*Les prêtres ne sont point ce qu'un vain peuple pense,*
Notre credulité fait toute leur science;"

and no modern *saynete* [51] is considered perfect, unless some member of their church is brought forward to serve as a recipient for the ribald jokes of an Andalusian *majo*, or to become the amatory dupe of an intriguing *graciosa*.

These pieces are not suffered to appear in print; or rather, I should say, perhaps, would not *sell* if they were printed, for the press of the day has far exceeded the bounds of decorum in giving light to many of the somewhat less objectionable productions of *Sotomayor*, *Comella*, and other prolific scribblers of Vaudevilles. The only modern dramatic writers who have been at all successful in obtaining public favour on worthier grounds, are *Iriate*, *Martinez de la Rosa*, and *Moratin*, but their writings are by no means numerous.

The plays of the last-named (who is considered the Terence of Spain) are always well received at Seville, where the dramatic taste is somewhat more refined than in the minor provincial towns. They are full of incident, without being encumbered with plot, like those of the old Spanish school; and the dialogue is natural and sprightly, without falling into licentiousness or vulgarity. This author's translation of Shakspeare's Hamlet is lamentably weak, however, for his language is not sufficiently elevated for tragedy. To Molière he has done more justice.

The Spanish language is remarkably well adapted to the stage, being not less melodious than emphatic and dignified; and there is a raciness about it well suited to comedy, though, on the whole, I should say, it is better adapted for tragedy. The national taste is, however, in favour of comedy, which, besides being more congenial to the character of the people, speaks more intelligibly to their uncultivated understandings. And, indeed, it must be confessed, that but for the infinite superiority of the language, the long speeches of the heroes of Spanish tragedy would be yet more wearying to listen to, than even the jingling, rhymed declamations of the French drama.

It is not surprising, therefore, that the impatient *Andaluzes*,—whose whole thoughts are bent upon the coming Bolero and laughter-causing farce,—should complain of the interminable "*platicas importunas*" of their tragedies, and even of their *serious* comedies; especially since they are delivered in a diction which to the lower orders is almost unintelligible, the dialogue being generally carried on in the second person plural, *vos*: a style which is never now heard in common parlance, and is, therefore, quite unnatural to them.

I will, however, draw the curtain upon Spanish tragedy, and bring the graceful *Baylarinas* upon the stage; at the first click of whose castañets, whilst even yet behind the scenes, every bright eye sparkles with animation, and every tongue is silenced.

The Bolero, which is the favourite national dance, admits of great variety as well of figures as of movements, for it may be executed by any number of persons, though two or four are generally preferred. It is a purified kind of *Fandango*, and, when danced by Spaniards, is as graceful and pleasing an exhibition as can be imagined. It is altogether divested of those dervish-like gyrations, and other wonderful displays of limbs and under-petticoats, that are so much the vogue on the boards of London and Paris, and on which, in fact, the reputation of a *Ballerina* seems to depend. In Spain the taste in dancing has not yet reached this pitch of refinement; for, even in the *Cachucha*, when the dancer turns her back upon the spectators, a Spanish lady deems it necessary to turn her face from the stage.

The castañets, though furnishing but little to the entertainment in the way of music, afford the performers the means of displaying their figures to advantage; and are yet further useful, by giving employment to the hands and arms; which, with most dancers, public as well as private, are generally found to be very much in the way.

There are other dances of a less *modest* character than the *Bolero*, which are performed at the minor theatres; but it may be said of Spanish public dancing generally, that it is light, spirited, and *poetic*, and admits of the display of considerable grace without being *indecent*.

Although of all modern languages—that of dulcet Italy alone excepted—the Spanish is the best adapted to song, yet the Spaniards have little or no relish for musical entertainments. The truth is, they are not a musical nation. In expressing this opinion, I am aware that I declare war against a host of preconceived notions; but in proof of my assertion I will ask, what country possesses so little national music as Spain? Has a single *known* opera ever been produced there? Is not her church music all borrowed? Is not the trifling guitar the only instrument the Spaniard is really master of? Is not the *Sostenuto* bellow of the *arriero* almost the only approach to melody that the peasant ever attempts?

Spanish music consists of a few simple airs, which are probably heir-looms of the Saracens; and a medley of *Boleros*, that may be considered mere variations of one tune. Neither their vocal nor instrumental performances ever reach beyond mediocrity, and in concert they invariably sing and play *a faire casser la tête*.

A fine climate and a gregarious disposition lead the peasantry to assemble nightly, and amuse themselves by dancing and singing to the monotonous thrumming of a cracked guitar; and this habit has earned for the nation the character of being musical—a character to which the Spaniards are little better entitled than the *Tom Tom*-loving black *apprentices* of our West India islands.

There are exceptions to every rule, and I willingly admit that I have heard an opera of Rossini very well performed by Spanish "*artists.*" But that they do not *pride themselves* on being a musical nation is evident from their always preferring Italian music to their own, though they like to sing Spanish words to an Italian opera.

The Theatre is a place of fashionable resort at Seville. It fills up a vacuum between the Paseo and the Tertulia. And when the times are sufficiently quiet to warrant the outlay, a sufficient sum is subscribed to bribe a second-rate Italian company to expose their melodious throats to the baneful influence of the sea breezes. The house is large and rather tastily decorated, but so ill-shaped that, unless one is close to the stage, not a word can be heard; and if there, the prompter's voice completely drowns those of the performers. The fall of the curtain at the conclusion of the *Bolero* is generally the signal for the *beau monde* to retire, leaving the highly seasoned *Saynete* to the enjoyment of the "*gente baja y desreglada.*" [52]

This breaking up is not the least amusing part of the play. The antediluvian carriages are again put in requisition; and now, besides the cocked-hatted attendants, each vehicle is accompanied by two or more torch-bearers on foot; so that the blaze of light on first issuing from the Theatre is most dazzling and astounding,—astounding, because it is only on walking into the gutter, or over a heap of filth in the first cross street one has occasion to enter, that the want of lamps in these minor avenues renders the utility of this extraordinary illumination apparent.

Each carriage, after "taking up," moves majestically off, its torch-bearers running ahead to show the way, scattering long strings of sparks, like comets' tails, amongst the humble pedestrians.

The Tertulias commence after the families have supped at their respective houses, that is to say, at about eleven o'clock; and are generally kept up until a late hour.

CHAPTER V

THE society of Seville is divided into nearly as many circles as there are degrees in the Mohammedans paradise. In former days, the bounds of each were marked with *heraldic* precision, and those of the innermost were guarded as jealously from trespass as the precincts of a royal forest, but of late years politics have materially injured the fences. The fine edged bridge of *Sirat* is no longer difficult of passage, and a foreigner, in especial, provided some mufti of the Aristocracy but holds out his hand to him, may reach the seventh heaven without the slightest chance of stumbling over his pedigree.

The English, above all other foreigners, are favourably received at Seville, for the nobles of the South of Spain, not being so much under court influence as those of the provinces lying nearer the capital, are by no means distinguished for their love of *absolutism*. With some few, indeed, the want of courtly sunshine has engendered excessive liberalism; but the nobles of Andalusia generally may be considered as favourably disposed towards a limited monarchy—that is, are of moderate, or what they term *English*, politics.

Of persons of such a political bias is the first circle of the society of Seville composed, and it is, perhaps, in every respect, the best in the kingdom. It is adorned by many men of highly cultivated talents, and much theoretical information, who, with a sincere love of country at their hearts, are yet not arrogantly blind to the faults of its former and present institutions; and who, removed to a certain extent from the baneful influence of a corrupt court, are proportionally free from the demoralising vices which distinguish the society of the upper classes in the capital.

The ladies of the *exclusive* circle are, it must needs be confessed, deficient in education: but they possess great natural abilities, a wonderful flow of language, and—excepting that they will pitch their voices so high—peculiarly fascinating manners.

The morals of Spanish women have usually been commented upon with unsparing severity; it strikes me, however, that the moral *principle* is as strong in them as in the natives of any other country or climate. The constancy of Spanish women, when once their affections have been placed on any object, is, indeed, proverbial, and if they are but too frequently faithless to the marriage vow, the source of corruption may be traced, *first*, to the lamentable religious education they receive—since the demoralizing doctrines of the efficacy of penance and absolution in the remission of sins furnish them at all times with a ready palliative; and, *secondly*, to the habit of contracting early marriages, and, especially, *marriages de convenance*, by which, in their anxiety to see their daughters well established, parents—and above all Spanish parents—are apt to sacrifice, not only their children's happiness, but their honour.

Of all the evils under which Spanish society labours, this last is the most serious as well as most apparent. A marriage of this kind, in nine cases out of ten, tends to demorality. It is followed by immediate neglect on the part of the husband, whose affections were already placed elsewhere when he gave his hand at the altar; and is soon regarded by the wife merely as a civil compact, to which the usages of society oblige her to subscribe. With *her*, however, this state of things had not been anticipated. The innate, all-powerful feeling, *love*, had, up to this period, lain dormant within her breast—for in Spain, if the extremely early age at which females marry did not of itself warrant this supposition, the little intercourse which, under any circumstances, an unmarried woman (of the upper classes of society) has with the world, naturally leads to the conclusion that her affections had not previously been engaged; she expects, therefore, to receive from her husband the same boundless affection that her inexperienced heart is disposed to bestow on him;—and what is the inevitable consequence? Disappointed in her cherished hope of occupying the first place in her husband's affections, her innocence is tarnished at the very outset, by thus acquiring the knowledge of his turpitude; she turns from him with disgust; and her better feelings, seared by jealousy and wounded pride, seeks out some other object on whom to bestow the love slighted by him, who pledged himself to cherish it.

Thrown thus at an early age upon the world, without the least experience in its ways, with strong passions to lead, and evil examples to seduce her, is it surprising that a Spanish wife should wander from the path of virtue, and that she should hold constancy to her lover more sacred than fidelity to a husband who quietly submits to see another possess her affections?

The understanding once established, however, that jealousy is not to disturb the ménage, the parties live together with all the outward appearances of mutual esteem, and inflict the history of their private bickerings only upon their favoured friends.

The Spaniards of all classes have great conversational powers, but even those of the upper are sadly deficient in general information. Their knowledge of other nations is picked up entirely from books, and those books mostly old ones; for few works are now written in their own language, and still fewer are translated from those of other countries; so that what little knowledge of mankind they possess is of the last century.

Cards help out the conversation at the Tertulias of the first circle. Dancing, forfeits, and other puerile games, are the resources of the rest. Balls and suppers are *funciones* reserved for great occasions, and dinner parties are of equally rare occurrence.

In the entertainments of the nobility, the French style prevails even to the wines, but the national dish, the *olla*, generally serves as a prelude, and may be considered the *"piece de resistance"* of the interminable dinner. Toothpicks (!!) and coffee are handed round, and the party breaks up, to seek in the *siesta* renewed powers of digestion.

To those, however, who think exercise more conducive to health, the environs of Seville hold out plenty of attractions; and, if the weather be too hot for either walking or riding, the city contains hackney coaches and *calesas* without number, by means of which (most of the roads in the vicinity being level) the various interesting points may be reached without difficulty or inconvenience.

The places most deserving of a visit in the immediate environs of Seville, are the villages of *San Juan de Alfarache* and *Santi Ponce;* near the latter of which are the ruins of Italica.

Both these places are situated on the right bank of the Guadalquivír; the former, about three miles below Seville, the latter a little more distant, up the stream. The road to both traverses the long town of Triana, which contains nothing worthy of observation but a sombre gothic edifice, where the high altar of Popish bigotry, the Inquisition, was first raised in the Spanish dominions. It has long, however, been converted to another purpose, never, let us hope, to be again applied to that which for so many ages disgraced Christianity.

By many Triana is supposed to be the Osset of Pliny, but I think without sufficient reason, as it does not seem probable that a place merely divided from Seville by a narrow river should have been distinguished by him as a distinct city. The words of Pliny, *"ex adverso oppidum Osset,"* imply certainly that Osset stood on the opposite bank of the river to Hispalis, but not that it was situated *immediately opposite*, as some authors have translated it. It is yet more evident that Alcalà de Guadaira cannot be Osset, as supposed by Harduin, since that town is on the *same* side of the Guadalquivír as Seville.

Florez imagines Osset to have been where San Juan de Alfarache now stands, [53] near which village traces of an ancient city have been discovered; and the position occupied by an old Moorish castle, on the edge of a high cliff, impending over the river, and commanding its navigation, seems clearly to indicate the site of a Roman station, since the Saracens usually erected their castles upon the foundations of the dilapidated fortresses of their predecessors. The village of San Juan de Alfarache stands at the foot of the before-mentioned cliff, compressed between it and the Guadalquivír; which river, making a wide sweep to the north on leaving Seville, here first reaches the roots of the chain of hills bounding the extensive plain through which it winds its way to the sea, and is by them turned back into its original direction.

Of the Moorish fortress little now remains but the foundation walls; the stones of the superstructure having probably been used to build the church and convent that now occupy the plateau of the hill. The view from thence is quite enchanting, embracing a long perspective of the meandering Guadalquivír and its verdant plain, the whole extent of the shining city, and the distant blue outline of the Ronda mountains.

The hills rising at the back of the convent are thickly covered with olive trees, the fruit of which is the most esteemed of all Spain: and, indeed, those who have eaten them on the spot, if they like the flavour of olive rather than of salt and water, would say they are the best in the world. The fruit is suffered to hang upon the tree until it has attained its full size, and consequently will not bear a long journey. For the same reason, it will not keep any length of time, as the salt in which it is preserved cannot penetrate to a sufficient depth in its oily flesh to secure it from decay. Let no one say, however, that he dislikes *olives*, until he has been to San Juan de Alfarache.

Retracing our steps some way towards Seville, we reach the great road leading from that city into Portugal by way of Badajoz; and, continuing along the plain for about five miles, we arrive at the priory of Santi Ponce, situated on the margin of the Guadalquivír, and close to the ruins of Italica. So complete has been the destruction of this once celebrated city, the birthplace of three Roman Emperors, that, but for the vestiges of its spacious amphitheatre, one would be inclined to doubt whether any town could possibly have stood upon the spot; the more so as the vicinity of Seville seems, at first sight, to render it improbable that two such large cities would have been built within so short a distance of each other.

Opinions on the subject of the relative antiquity of these two cities are, however, very various; for, whilst some Spaniards are to be found, who maintain that Hispalis was founded long before Italica, and some who, declaring, on the other hand, that the two cities never existed together, insist on calling Italica, *Sevilla la Vieja*; [54] others there are who suppose that the two cities flourished contemporaneously for a considerable period, and that Hispalis (the more modern of the two) eventually caused the other's destruction.

This last hypothesis might readily be received, since, from the influence of the tide being felt at Seville and not at Santi Ponce, the situation of the former is so much more favourable for trade than that of the latter; but that, setting aside the traditionary authority of Seville having been founded by *Hispalis*, one of the companions of Hercules, we have the testimony of several writers to prove that Hispalis was a place of consequence when Italica must have been yet in its infancy. For the antiquity of this latter is never carried further back than the 144th Olympiad, i.e. 200 B.C. Now, Hispalis is mentioned by Hirtius, at no very great period after that date, as a city of great importance; whereas, Italica is noticed by him (proving it to have been a *distinct* place) merely as a walled town in the vicinity. [55]

The two places are again mentioned separately by Pliny; the one, however, as a large city, giving its name to a vast extent of country—the *Conventus Hispalensis*—the other as one of the towns within the limits of that city's jurisdiction.

The foundation of Italica being fixed, therefore, about two hundred years before the Christian era, and attributed to the veteran soldiers of P. C. Scipio; that is to say, immediately after the expulsion of the Carthagenians from the country; it may naturally be concluded that the Romans, who had not come to Spain merely to drive out their rivals, would, with their usual foresight, have planted a colony of their own people to overawe the *principal city* of a country they intended to bring under subjection; and hence, that Seville existed long before Italica was founded.

The amphitheatre, which alone remains to prove the former grandeur of Italica, is of a wide oval shape. The dimensions of its arena are 270 feet in its greatest diameter, 190 in its least. It rests partly against a hill, a circumstance that has tended materially to save what little remains of it from destruction; but, nevertheless, only nine tiers of seats have offered a successful resistance to the encroachments of the plough. Few of the vomitorios can be traced, but it would appear that there were sixteen. Some of the caverns in which the wild beasts were confined are in tolerable preservation.

From the ruined amphitheatre we were conducted to a kind of pound, enclosed by a high mud wall, and secured by a stout gate, wherein we were informed other reliques of Italica were preserved. There was some little delay in obtaining the key of this *museo*, the *custodio* being at his *siesta*; and, hearing the grunting of pigs within, we began to doubt whether it could contain any thing worth detaining us under a broiling sun to see. Unwilling, however, to be disappointed, we clambered with some little difficulty to the top of the wall, and, *horresco referens!* beheld an old sow rubbing her back against that of the Emperor Hadrian, whilst the profane snouts of her young progeny were grubbing at the tesselated cheeks of Clio and Urania, the only two of the immortal Nine whose features could be distinctly traced in an elaborate mosaic pavement that covered the greater part of the court.

Several fragments of statues were strewed about; but all were in too mutilated a state to excite the least interest. The feeling with which we contemplated the beautiful, outraged pavement, was one of unmitigated disgust; for the workmanship of such parts of it as remained intact was of the most delicate description, the stones not being more than one fifth of an inch square, and, as far as we could judge, put together so as to form a picture of great merit. I fear that this valuable specimen of the art has long since been altogether lost, for, at the time of which I write, the stones were lying in heaps about the yard, and the pavement seemed likely to be subjected to a continuance of the mining operations of the "swinish multitude," as well as to exposure to the destructive ravages of the elements.

I could not refrain from expostulating with the owner of the piggery (when he at length made his appearance) at this, in the words of Don Quijote, *puerco y extraordinario abuso*. He was a wag, however, and answered my "Why do you keep your pigs here?" precisely in the words that an Irish peasant replied to a very similar question, viz., "But am I to have the company of the pig?" put to him by a friend of mine, who had a billet for a night's lodging on his cabin: to wit, "*No hay toda comodidad?*" "Isn't there every convey'nance?"

We then attempted to persuade him that the pigs being young and inexperienced would probably kill themselves by swallowing the little square stones piled up against the walls, when the supply of Indian corn failed them. "No, Señor," he replied; "*el Puerco es un animal que tiene mas sesos que una casa.*" "The hog is an animal that has more (sesos) brains (or bricks) than a house." And, indeed, the discrimination of the animal is wonderful, for, whilst we were yet arguing the case, one of the little brutes grubbed up the entire left cheek of Calliope, to get at a grain of corn that had fallen into one of the numerous crow's feet with which unsparing Time had furrowed the Muse's animated countenance. Without further observation, therefore, we abandoned the chaste daughters of Mnemosyne to their ignominious fate, remounted our horses, and bent our steps homewards.

The foreigner who visits Seville, under any circumstances, cannot but find it a most delightful place, and our short sojourn at it was rendered particularly agreeable by the kindness and hospitality of the *Marques de las Amarillas*, who, independent of the pleasure it at all times affords him to show his regard for the English, whom he considers as his old brothers in arms, was pleased to express peculiar gratification at having an opportunity of evincing his sense of some trifling attentions that it had been in my power to pay his only son, when, as well as himself, driven by political persecution to seek a refuge within the walls of Gibraltar.

The life of this distinguished nobleman, now Duke of Ahumado, has been singularly varied by the smiles and frowns of fortune, and furnishes a melancholy proof of the little that can be effected by talents, however exalted, and patriotism, however pure, in a country writhing, like Spain, under the combined torments of religious and political revolution. For, the more sincere a lover of his country he who puts himself forward, *having aught to lose*, may be, the more he becomes an object of distrust and envy to *the many*, who seek in change but their own aggrandizement. To him who would take the helm of affairs in times of revolution, an unscrupulous conscience is yet more necessary than the possession of extraordinary talents.

The Marques de las Amarillas, well known in the "Peninsular War" as General Giron, was appointed minister at war in the first cabinet formed by Ferdinand VII. after he had sworn to the Constitution. A sincere lover of rational liberty, and a strong advocate for a mixed form of government, the Marques, himself a soldier, saw the danger of permitting the very existence of the government to be at the mercy of the undisciplined rabble army, that, seduced by its democratic leaders for their own private ends, had effected the revolution; and had projected a plan for its partial reduction and entire reorganization.

The *Exaltados*, however, fearful lest the establishment of a *rational* form of government should result from a project which certainly would have had the effect of allaying the existing agitation, accused the Marques of a plot to subvert the constitution, and restore Ferdinand to a despotic throne; and he was obliged to save himself from the impending danger by a rapid flight, and to take refuge within the walls of Gibraltar. There he remained during the period of misrule that preceded the invasion of the country by the Duc d'Angoulême in 1823; suffering, during the feeble struggle that ensued, from the most painfully conflicting feelings that could possibly enter a patriot's breast. For, aware that his unhappy country had but the sad alternative of a continuance in anarchy and misery, or of bending the neck to foreign dictation, and receiving back the cast-off yoke of a despot, he could take no active part in a struggle which, end as it would, was fraught with mischief to his native land.

It ended, as he had always foreseen, in the restoration of the despicable monarch, who possessed neither the courage to draw the sword in defence of what he conceived to be his *rights*, nor the virtue to adhere to the word pledged to his people; who by his contemptible intrigues exposed, and by his vacillating plans sacrificed, his most devoted adherents; who with his dying breath bequeathed the scourge of civil war to his wretched country; whose very existence, in fine, was as hurtful to Spain, as is the odour of the upas-tree to the incautious traveller who rests beneath its shade.

The contemptible Ferdinand, restored to his throne, forbade the *Marques de las Amarillas* to present himself in the capital—the crime of having held office in a constitutional cabinet being considered quite sufficient to warrant the infliction of such a punishment. Some ten years afterwards, however, he was, through the influence of his relatives, the Dukes of Baylen and Infantado, appointed captain-general of Andalusia, and on the death of Ferdinand was called to Madrid, to form one of the Council of Regency.

He again held a distinguished post in the Torreno administration, and again fell under the displeasure of the anarchists—his talents had less influence than the halbert of Serjeant Gomez.

These are not merely *"cosas de España,"* however, but have been, and will be, those of every country where the hydra, democracy, is cherished. God grant that our own may be preserved from the many-headed monster!

We quitted Seville only "upon compulsion" (our leave of absence being limited), making choice of a road which, though, by visiting Moron and Ronda, it proceeds rather circuitously to Gibraltar, traverses a more romantic and picturesque portion of the Serranía than any other. The most direct of the numerous roads that offer themselves between Seville and the British fortress, is by way of Dos Hermanos, Coronil, Ubrique, and Ximena.

The first place lying upon the road we selected is Alcalà de Guadaira. This town is distant about eight miles from Seville (though generally marked much less on the maps), and is the first post station on the great road from Seville to Madrid.

For the first five miles from Seville the road traverses a gently undulated country, that is chiefly planted with corn; but, on drawing near Alcalà, the features of the ground become more strongly marked, and are clothed with olive and other trees; and amongst the hills that encompass the town rise the copious springs which, led into a conduit, supply Seville with water. Alcalà administers to yet another of the great city's most material wants, for it almost exclusively furnishes Seville with bread, whence it has received the agnomen of "*de los panaderos*" (of the bread-makers), as well as that of "*de Guadaira,*" which it takes from the river that runs in its vicinity. The numerous mills situated along the course of this stream, by furnishing easy means of grinding corn, probably led the inhabitants of Alcalà to engage in the extensive kneading and baking operations which are carried on there.

The immediate approach to the town is by a narrow gorge between two steep hills; that on the right, which is the more elevated of the two, and very rugged and difficult of access, is washed on three sides by the Guadaira, and crowned with extensive ruins of a Moorish fortress. The town itself is pent in between these two hills and the river, and, there can be but little doubt, occupies the site of some Roman city, its situation being quite such as would have been chosen by that people.

That it is not on the site of Osset is, as I have before observed, quite evident, and its present name, being completely Moorish, furnishes no clue whatever to discover that which it formerly bore. Some have supposed it is Orippo; but inscriptions found at Dos Hermanos determine that place to be on the ruins of the said Roman town. Possibly—for such a supposition accords with the order in which the towns of the county of Hispalis are mentioned by Pliny—Alcalà may be Vergentum.

It is a long dirty town, full of ovens and charcoal, and contains a population of 3000 souls. The chaussée to Madrid, by Cordoba, here branches off to the left; whilst that to Xeres and Cadiz, crossing the Guadaira, is directed far inland upon Utrera, rendering it extremely circuitous. A more direct road strikes off from it immediately after crossing the river, proceeding by way of Dos Hermanos.

We still continued to pursue the great road, which, after ascending a range of hills that rises along the left bank of the Guadaira, traverses a perfectly flat country, abounding in olives, that extends all the way to Utrera, a distance of eleven miles.

Utrera thus stands in the midst of a vast plain, that may be considered the first step from the marshes of the Guadalquivír, towards the Ronda mountains, which are yet twelve miles distant to the eastward. A slight mound, that rises in the centre of the town, and is embraced by an extensive circuit of dilapidated walls, doubtless offered the inducement to build a town here; and these walls, some parts of which are very lofty, and in a tolerably perfect state, appear to be Roman, though the castle and its immediate outworks are Moorish.

What the ancient name of the town was would, without the help of monuments or inscriptions, be now impossible to determine, but it certainly did not lie upon either of the routes laid down in the Itinerary of Antoninus, between Cadiz and Cordoba, though some have imagined it to be Ilipa. [56] Others have supposed it to be Siarum; but adopting Harduin's reading of Pliny—"Caura, Siarum," instead of Caurasiarum—it seems more likely that Utrera was Caura, and that Moron, or some other town yet more distant from Seville, was Siarum.

By its present name it is well known in Moorish history, its rich *campiña* having frequently been ravaged by the Moslems, after they had been driven from the open country to seek shelter in the neighbouring mountains.

At the present day, it is celebrated only for its breeds of saints and bulls, the former ranked amongst the most devout, the latter the most ferocious, of Andalusia. The town is large, and not walled in; the streets are wide and clean, and a plentiful stream rises near and traverses the place—remarkable as being the only running water within a circuit of several miles. It contains 15,000 inhabitants, mostly agriculturists, and a very tolerable inn.

Utrera, as has already been observed, is situated on the *arrecife*, or great road, from Cadiz to Madrid, which *arrecife* makes two considerable elbows to visit this place and Alcalà. Now from Utrera there is a cross-road to Carmona (which town is also situated on the great route to the capital), that, by avoiding Alcalà, reduces the distance between the two places from seven to six leagues; and from Utrera there is also another cross-road (by way of Arajal) to Ecija, which, by cutting off another angle made by the *arrecife*, effects a yet greater saving in the distance to that city, and consequently to Cordoba and Madrid. From these circumstances, Utrera becomes, in military phrase, an important *strategical* point; and as such, the French, when advancing upon Cadiz in 1810, attempted to gain it by the cross-road from Ecija, ere the Duke of Albuquerque, who had taken post at Carmona, with the view of covering Seville, could reach it by the *arrecife*. The duke, however, with great judgment, abandoned Seville to what he well knew must eventually be its fate, and by a rapid march saved Cadiz, though not without having to engage in a cavalry skirmish to cover his retreat.

What important consequences hung upon the decision of that moment; for how different might have been the result of the war, had the important fortress of Cadiz fallen into the enemy's hands, and given them 30,000 disposable troops at that critical juncture! [57]

On issuing from Utrera, we once more quit the chaussée (which is henceforth directed very straight upon Xeres), and, taking an easterly course, proceed towards a lofty mountain, that, seemingly detached from the serrated mass, juts slightly forward into the plain.

At the distance of six miles from Utrera, the ground, which thus far is quite flat and very barren, begins to be slightly undulated, and is here and there dotted with *cortijos* and corn fields; and, at eight miles from Utrera, a road crosses from Arajah to Coronil; the first-named town being distant about two miles on the left, the latter half a league on the right. For the next league the country is one waving corn-field. At the end of that distance we reached the steep banks of a rivulet, which here first issues from the mountains, and is called *El Salado de Moron*. The road crosses to the right bank of this stream, on gaining which it immediately turns to the north (keeping parallel to the ridge of the detached mountain, upon which, as I have already noticed, it had previously been directed), and ascends very gradually towards Moron. The country, during this latter portion of the road, is partially wooded. The total distance from Utrera to Moron is about sixteen miles.

Moron is singularly situated, being nestled in the lap of five distinct hills, the easternmost and loftiest of which is occupied by an old castle, a mixed work of the Romans and Moors.

According to La Martinière, Moron is on the site of Arunci; and this opinion seems to rest on a better foundation than that of other authors, who maintain that Arcos occupies the position of the above-named ancient city; for it is natural to suppose that the territory of the *Celtici* (amongst whose towns *Arunci* is enumerated by Pliny) did not extend beyond the intricate belt of mountains known at the present day as the *Serranía de Ronda*. Now, Moron commands one of the principal entrances to the Serranía, whereas Arcos is situated far in the plains of the Guadalete towards Xeres, and would seem rather to have been one of the cities of the "county of Cadiz."

Moron is a strong post, for though raised but slightly above the great plain of Utrera, it commands all the ground in its immediate neighbourhood; and, standing as it does in a mountain gorge, by which several roads debouch upon Seville from various parts of the *Serranía*, it occupies a military position of some consequence. The French guarded it jealously during the war, and placed the castle in a defensible state. Since those days its walls have again been dismantled; but the strength of its position tempted Riego (1820) to try the chances of a battle with the royal army, commanded by General Josef O'Donnel, ere he finally abandoned the mountains.

In vain, however, Riego pointed out to his men the far distant hill of *Las Cabezas*, where they had first raised the cry of "Constitution, or death;" their *exaltacion* had abandoned them, and they in turn abandoned their exaltation, leaving their strong position after a very slight resistance. A few days afterwards, at *Fuente Ovejuna*, they were entirely dispersed.

The successful general, ready to march either against the insurgents of the Isla de Leon, or upon the capital, wrote to the king, announcing that the army of Riego was no more, and requesting to know his commands: but *"eheu! quam brevibus pereunt ingentia causis!"* a few weeks after this letter was penned, the victor was a prisoner at Ceuta, and the vanquished general (without doing any thing in the meanwhile to retrieve his character) had become the hero of hymns and ballads! The imbecile Ferdinand, fearful lest, by further delay in accepting the Constitution he should lose his crown, had despatched orders to those generals who remained faithful to him, to give up their respective commands, just as the tide of affairs seemed to be turning in favour of a continuance of his despotic reign.

The dispersion of the constitutional army proved two things, however; the first, that Riego was no general; the second, that he and his party had deceived themselves as to the political feeling of the inhabitants of the province. In the course of his rambling operations, Algeciras and Malaga were the only places where Riego was at all well received. In vain he tried to maintain himself in the latter city; driven out of it at the point of the bayonet, he attempted to regain Cadiz, the head-quarters of the revolt; but, closely pressed by the royal army on his retreat through the Serranía, was obliged, as I have stated, to receive battle at Moron, where the disorganization of his force was completed.

Moron contains a population of 8,000 souls, and is a well built town, with wide streets, and good shops. There is a mountain road from hence to Grazalema (seven leagues) by way of Zahara. The road from Moron to Ronda passes by Olbera. The distance between the two places is thirty-one miles. The country, immediately on leaving Moron, becomes rough and desolate, and the road, (a mere mule-track,) traverses a succession of strongly marked ridges, which, though not themselves very elevated, are bounded on all sides by bare and rocky mountains. The numerous streams which cross the stony pathway all flow to the south, uniting their waters with the *Salado de Moron*. On penetrating further into the recesses of the *Serranía*, the valleys become wider, and are thickly wooded, and the luxuriant growth of the unpruned trees, the absence of houses, bridges, and all the other signs of the hand of man, offer a picture of uncultivated nature that could hardly be surpassed even in the interior of New Zealand.

At nine miles from Moron is situated the solitary venta of *Zaframagon*, and, a mile further on, descending by a beautifully wooded ravine, we reached an isolated rocky mound, under the scarped side of which, embosomed in groves of orange and pomegranate trees, stands a picturesque water-mill. From hence to Olbera is seven miles. The country is of the same wild description as in the preceding portion of the route, but gradually rises and becomes more bare of trees on drawing near the little crag-built town. An execrable pavé, which appears to have remained intact since the days of the Romans, winds for the last two miles under the chain of hills over whose narrow summit the houses of Olbera are spread, rising one above another towards an old castle perched on the pinnacle of a rocky cone.

By some Spanish antiquaries, Olbera has been supposed to be the *Ilipa* mentioned in the Roman Itinerary, as being on the *second* route laid down between Cadiz and Cordoba, passing by Antequera. This route, by the way, is not a less strange one to lay down between the two cities, than a post road from London to Dover *by way of Brighton* would be considered by us; but the fancy of winding it through the least practicable part of the mountains of Ronda, from Seville (if, as some imagine, it first went to that city) to Antequera, is even yet more strange, since a nearly level tract of country extends between those two cities in a more direct line.

Considering it, however, merely as a military way, made by the Romans to connect the principal cities of the province, and serving in case of need as a communication between Cadiz and Cordoba, *avoiding Seville*; a much more probable line may be laid down, on which the distances will be found to agree infinitely better. [58]

Olbera is a wretched place, containing some 3,000 or 4,000 of the rudest looking, and, if report speak true, of the least scrupulous, inhabitants of the Serranía. Their lawless character has already been alluded to, and, in Rocca's Memoirs, a most interesting account is given of their reception of him, when, with a party of dragoons, he was on the march from Moron to Ronda.

His description of the rickety old town-house, wherein he saved his life from an infuriated mob by making a fat priest serve as a shield, is most correctly given, and, in the present dark, suspicious-looking, cloak-enveloped inhabitants, one may readily picture to one's-self the descendants of the men who skinned a dead ass, and gave it to the French troopers for beef; ever after jeering them by asking *"Quien come carne de burra en Olbera? Who eats asses'-flesh at Olbera?"*

Carula (Puebla de Santa Maria)	24
Ilipa (Grazalema)	18
Ostippo [59] (La Torre de Alfaquime)	14
Barba (Almargen)	20
Anticaria (Antequera)	24
Angellas	23

Ipagro	20
Ulia	10
Cordoba	18
Total	[60] 294

The view from the old castle is very commanding; the outline of the amphitheatre of mountains is bold and varied, and the valleys between the different masses are richly wooded. To the south may be seen the rocky little fortress of Zahara, sheltered by the huge *Sierra del Pinar*; and only about two miles distant from Olbera to the north, is the old castle of Pruna, similarly situated on a conical hill that stands detached from a lofty impending mountain.

Olbera is fourteen miles from Ronda. At the distance of rather more than a mile, a large convent, *N. S. de los Remedios*, stands on the right of the road, and a little way beyond this, the road descends by a narrow ravine towards *La Torre de Alfaquime*, and, after winding round the foot of the cone whereon that little town is perched, reaches and crosses the Guadalete. This point is about four miles from Olbera. The stream issues from a dark ravine in the mountains that rise up on the left of the road, and serves to irrigate a fertile valley, and turn several mills that here present themselves.

A road to Setenil is conducted through the narrow gorge whence the little river issues, but that to Ronda, ascending for three quarters of an hour, reaches the summit of a lofty mountain on whose eastern acclivity are strewed the extensive ruins of Acinippo.

The view is remarkably fine; to the westward, extending as far as Cadiz, and in the opposite direction looking down upon a wide, smiling valley, watered by the numerous sources of the Guadalete, and upon the little castellated town of Setenil, perched on the rocky bank of the principal branch of that river. This place was very celebrated in the days of the Moslems, having resisted every attack of the Christians, [61] until the persevering "*Reyes Catolicos*" brought artillery to bear upon its defences.

The road to Ronda descends for two miles, and then keeps for about the same distance along the banks of the Guadalete, crossing and recrossing it several times. The surrounding country is one vast corn-field. Leaving, at length, this rich vale, the road ascends a short but steep ridge, whence the first view is obtained of the yet more lovely basin of Ronda, which, clothed with orchards and olive grounds, and surrounded on all sides by splendid mountains, is justly called the pride of the Serranía.

A good stone bridge affords a passage across the *Rio Verde*, or of Arriate, about a mile above its junction with the Guadiaro; and the road falls in with that from Grazalema on reaching the top of the hill whereon the town stands.

CHAPTER VI

RONDA and the road from thence to Gaucin have been already fully described; I will, therefore, pass on, without saying more of either than that, if the road be one of the *worst*, the scenery along it equals any to be met with in the south of Spain. The road was formerly practicable for carriages throughout, but it is now purposely suffered to go to decay, lest it should furnish Gibraltar with greater facilities than that great commercial mart already possesses, for destroying the manufactures of Spain—such, at least, is the excuse offered for the present wretched state of the road.

From the rock-built castle of Gaucin we will descend—by what, though called a road, is little more than a rude flight of steps practised in the side of the mountain—to the deep valley of the Genal, and, crossing the pebbly bed of the stream, take a path which, winding through a dense forest of cork and ilex, is directed round the northern side of the peaked mountain of *Cristellina*, to a pass between it and the more distant and wide-spreading *Sierra Bermeja*.

The scenery, as one advances up the steep acclivity, is remarkably fine. I do not recollect having any where seen finer woods; and the occasional glimpses of the glassy Genal, winding in the dark valley below; the numerous shining little villages that deck its green banks; the outstretched town of Gaucin and ruined battlements of its impending castle covering the ridge on the opposite side, and backed by the distant mountains of Ubrique, Grazalema, &c., furnish all the requisites for a perfect picture.

Soon after gaining the summit of the wooded chain, the road branches in two, that on the left hand proceeding to Estepona, the other to Casares. Taking the latter, we emerged from the forest in about a quarter of an hour, and found ourselves at the head of a deep and confined valley, which, overhung by the scarped peaks of Cristellina on one side, is bounded on the other by a narrow ridge that, stretching several miles to the south, terminates in a high conical knoll crowned by the castle of Casares.

The road, which is very good, keeps under the crest of the left-hand ridge, descending for two miles, and very gradually, towards the town. The view on approaching Casares is remarkably fine, embracing, besides the picturesque old fortress, an extensive prospect over the apparently champaign country beyond, which (marked, nevertheless, with many a wooded dell and rugged promontory,) spreads in all directions towards the Mediterranean; the dark, cloud-capped rock of Gibraltar rising proudly from the shining surface of the narrow sea, and overtopping all the intervening ridges.

Before reaching Casares, the mountain, along the side of which the road is conducted, falls suddenly several hundred feet, and a narrow ledge connects it with the conical mound more to the south, whereon the castle is perched. The town occupies the summit of this connecting link—which in one part is so narrow as to afford little more than the space sufficient for one street—but extends, also, some way round the bases and up the rude sides of the two impending heights, thus assuming the shape of an hour-glass.

Having reached the *Plaza*,—and a tolerably spacious one it is considering the little ground the town has to spare for embellishments,—we looked about for the usual signs of a *venta*, but, failing in discovering any, applied to the bystanders for information, who, pointing to a wretched hovel, on the wall of which was painted a shield, bearing, in heraldic language, gules, a bottle sable, told us it was the only *Ventorillo* [62] in the town.

Now, though it is a common saying that "good wine needs no bush," we had yet to learn that dirty floors need no broom; and, unwilling to be the first to gain experience in the matter, we determined, after a minute examination of the house, to present ourselves to the *Alcalde*, and, in virtue of our passports, ask his "aid and assistance" in procuring better quarters.

The unusual sight of a party of strange travellers had brought that important personage himself into the market-place, who, collecting round him the principal householders of the town, forthwith laid our distressing case before them, and, in his turn, asked for aid and assistance in the shape of advice.

Our papers were accordingly handed round the standing council, and, having been minutely inspected, turned upside down, the lion and unicorn duly admired, the great seal of the Governor of Gibraltar examined with eyes of astonishment, and the question asked "*Son Ingleses?*" [63] (which was excusable, considering the absurdity of giving passports in *French* to English travellers in *Spain*) a shrug of the shoulders seemed all that the *Alcalde* was likely to get in the way of advice, or we in the lieu of board and lodging.

Guessing at last, by the oft-repeated question concerning our nationality, "*De que pie cojeaba el negocio*"; [64] we took occasion to signify to the conclave, that a few dollars would most willingly be paid for any inconvenience the putting us up for the night might occasion. Our prospects immediately brightened; each had now "*una salita,*" that he could very well spare for a night or so ... "we had our own *mantas,* so that we should require but mattresses to lie down upon—and as for stabling, that there was no loss for"—in fact, the only difficulty appeared to be, how the Alcalde should avoid giving offence to a dozen, by selecting *one* to confer the favour of our company upon.

He saw the delicacy of his position, and hesitated—"he himself, indeed, had a spare room, but ..." here a portly personage, clothed in a black silk cassock, and sheltered by an ample shovel hat, stepped forward to relieve the embarrassed functionary from his dilemma; and giving him a nod, and us a beckon, drew his *toga* up behind, and walked off at a brisk pace towards the castle hill.

The claims of *El Señor Cura*—for such our conductor proved to be—no one presumed to dispute; so making our bow to the *Alcalde,* who assured us that

> *Quien a buen arbol se arrima*
> *buena sombra le cobija,* [65]

we followed the footsteps of the worthy member of the Church Hospitaliar, without further colloquy.

Our conductor stopped not, and spoke not, until we had reached the very top of the town, and then, leading our horses into a commodious stable, he ushered us into his own abode; wherein he assured us, if the accommodation he could offer was suitable, "we had but to *mandar.*" It consisted of a large *sala* and an *alcoba,* or recess, for a bed; the latter scrupulously clean, the former lofty and airy. We, therefore, expressed our entire satisfaction, requesting only that a couple of mattresses might be spread upon the floor; a friend, who had joined us at Gaucin, rendering this increase of accommodation necessary.

Having given instructions to that effect, Don Francisco Labato—for such our host informed us were his *nombre y appellido,* [66] not omitting to add, that he was a *clerigo beneficiado* [67] —proposed to accompany us, to cast an ojeada [68] upon the curious old town, from the ruined battlements of its ancient fortress; observing that there was yet abundance of time to do so, "ere Phœbus took his evening plunge into the western ocean."

We gladly accepted the proffered ciceroneship of our classical host, and, mounting the rugged pathway up the isolated crag, in a few minutes reached the plateau at its summit. It would be hardly possible to select a less convenient site for a town than that occupied by Casares. Pent in to the north and south between impracticable crags, and bounded on the other two sides by deep ravines; it can, in fact, be reached only, either by describing a wide circuit to gain the mountains, rising at its back; or, by ascending a rough winding path, practised in the side of the castle hill.

The principal part of the town is clustered round the base of the old fortress, the houses rising one above another in steps, as it were, and occupying no more of the valuable space than is necessary to give them a secure foundation. The streets, which are barely wide enough to allow a paniered donkey to pass freely, are formed out of the live rock, and, here and there, are cut in wide steps, to render the ascent less difficult and dangerous. These flat slabs of native limestone, when heated by a summer sun, though passable enough by unshod animals, afford but a precarious footing to a horse's iron-bound hoofs.

The castle can only be approached through the town, and although its walls have long been in ruins, yet, so strong are its natural defences, that the muzzles of a few rusty old guns, propped up by stones, and protruded from the prostrate parapets, were sufficient to deter the French from making any attempt upon the place during the war of independence:—such, at least, is the version of the inhabitants.

That Casares was a Roman town is almost proved by the name it yet bears; but the matter is placed beyond a doubt on examining the old foundations of the castle, which are clearly of a date anterior to the occupation of Spain by the Saracens.

The name it anciently bore strikes me as being equally obvious, viz., *Cæsaris Salutariensis*; so designated from the mineral waters in its neighbourhood, which, though *now* known by the name of the modern town of Manilba, are within the *termino* of Casares. For, not only were the valuable properties of these springs well known to the Romans, but, according to the common belief in the country, they performed a wonderful cure on one of the emperors—Trajan, I think.

Cæsaris Salutariensis is mentioned by Pliny, amongst the Latin towns of the *conventus gaditanus*; the limits of which country may, at first sight, appear to be somewhat stretched to include Casares; but Barbesula, which stood at the mouth of the river Guadiaro, at an equal distance from Cadiz, (as is clearly proved by inscriptions found there,) is also mentioned by that excellent authority as one of the stipendiary towns of the same county; and the order in which they are enumerated, viz., those first which were nearest to the capital, tends to confirm my supposition.

On our return from the old castle, which commands a splendid view, we were not displeased to find that our host was no despiser of the good things of this world, much as he gave us to understand that all his thoughts were directed towards the never-ending joys of that which is to come. Every thing bespoke a well-conducted *ménage*; the house, besides being clean and tastily decorated with flowers, was provided with some solid comforts. The *Cura's niece*—his housekeeper, butler, and factotum—was pretty, as well as intelligent and obliging. His *cuisine* was tolerably free from garlic and grease, his wine from aniseed. Our horses were up to their knees in fresh straw; and three clean beds were prepared for ourselves.

Our host excused himself from partaking of our meal, he having already dined, and, whilst we were doing justice to his good catering, paced up and down the room pretending to read, but in reality watching our movements, and, as it at first struck us, looking after his silver spoons: but divers testy hints given to his bright-eyed niece that her constant attendance upon us was unnecessary, soon made it evident that *she* was the object of his solicitude; as, judging from the occasional direction of our eyes, he rightly conjectured what was the subject of our conversation. Anon, however, he would approach the table, thrust the volume of Homilies under his left arm, and, taking a pinch of snuff, (which he said was *"bueno para el estudio"* [69]) ask our way of thinking on various subjects, political and theological, always prefacing his interrogatories by some observation, either on his passion for study, the cosmopolitan bent of his mind, or the superiority his learning gave him over the vulgar prejudices of the age. And, at length, when the table was cleared, the niece gone, and he had elicited from us that we were all three *English*, he observed, without further circumlocution, *"Pues Señores*, you are not members of the *Santa Iglesia, Catolica Romana?"*

"No," we replied, "*Catolica* but not *Romana*."

"That is to say, you are heretical Christians."

"That is to say, we differ with you as regards the corporeal nature of the elements partaken of in the Eucharist; we deny the efficacy of masses; the power of granting indulgences; and the necessity for auricular confession:— and so far certainly we are heretics in the eyes of the church of Rome."

The worthy *Cura*—much as he had studied—was by no means aware that our pretensions to Catholicism were so great as, on continuing the controversy, he discovered them to be. [70] He made a stout stand, however, for the absolute necessity of auricular confession; maintaining that we, by dispensing with it, deprived the poor and ignorant of a friend, a counsellor, and an intercessor;—stript our church of the power of reclaiming sinners, and checking growing heresies;—and our government of the means of anticipating the mischievous projects of designing men.

It was in vain we urged to our host that, in our favoured country, education had done away with the necessity for strengthening the hands of government by such means; that the poor were provided for by law; and that the clergy were ever ready to counsel and assist those who stood in need of spiritual consolation. But, before leaving us for the night, the *Padre* admitted that *we* were certainly Christians, and that many of the mysteries and practices of the Church of Rome were merely preserved to enable the clergy to maintain their influence over the people;—an influence which we deemed quite necessary for the well-being of the state.

Rising betimes on the following morning, we set off on foot to clamber to the lofty peak of the *Sierra Cristellina*; and regular climbing it was, for all traces of a footpath were soon lost, and we then had to mount the precipitous face of the cone in the best way we could. The magnificence of the view from the summit amply repaid us for the fatigue and loss of shoe-leather we had to bear with; for, though scarcely 2000 feet above the level of the sea, the peak stands so completely detached from all other mountains, that it affords a bird's eye view which could be surpassed only by that from a balloon. The entire face of the country was spread out like a map before us. To the north, penned in on all sides by savage mountains, lay the wide, forest-covered valley of the Genal, its deeply furrowed sides affording secure though but scanty lodgment to the numerous little fastnesses scattered over them by the persecuted *Mudejares*, when expelled from the more fertile plains of the Guadalquivír and Guadalete; and on which castellated crags the swarthy descendants of these "mediatised" Moors still continue to reside and bid defiance to civilization.

These little strongholds stand for the most part on the summit of rocky knolls that jut into the dark valley; and round the base of each a small extent of the forest has in most cases been cleared, serving, in times past, to improve its means of defence, and, at the present day, to admit the sun to shine upon the vineyards, in the cultivation of which the rude inhabitants find employment, when, obliged for a time to lay aside the smuggler's blunderbuss, they take to the axe and pruning-knife. Behind, serving as a kind of citadel to these numerous outworks, rises the huge *Sierra Bermeja*, which afforded a last refuge to the persecuted Moslems; and at its very foot, about five miles up the valley of the Genal, are the ruins of *Benastepar*; the birth-place of the Moorish hero, *El Feri*, whose courage and address so long baffled the exterminating projects of the Spaniards.

Turning now round to the south, a totally different, and yet more magnificent, view meets the eye. Gibraltar,—its lovely bay,—the African mountains, rising range above range,—and the distant Atlantic, successively present themselves: whilst, from the height at which we are raised above the intermediate country, the courses of the different rivers, that issue from the gorges of the sierras at our back, may be distinctly followed through all their windings to the Mediterranean, the features of the intervening ground appearing to be so slightly marked as to lead to the supposition that the country below must be perfectly accessible;—but, as one of our party drily observed, those who, like himself, had followed red-legged partridges across it could tell a different story.

We returned to Casares by descending the eastern side of the mountain, which is planted with vines to within a short distance of the summit. In fact, wherever a little earth can be scraped together, a root is inserted. The wine made from the grapes grown on this bank is considered the best of Casares; it is not unlike Cassis—small, but highly flavoured. The town, looked down upon in this direction, has a singular appearance, seeming to stand on a high cliff overhanging the Mediterranean shore, though, in reality, it is six or seven miles from it.

We amused ourselves during the rest of the afternoon in taking sketches of the town from various points in the neighbourhood, and excited the wrath of some passers-by to a furious degree. They swore we were *mapeando el pueblo*, [71] and that they would have us arrested; but we were strong in our innocence, and turned a deaf ear to their menaces. It is, however, a practice that is often attended with annoying consequences; for I have known several instances of English officers having been taken before the military authorities for merely sketching a picturesque barn or cork tree—so great is the national jealousy.

At our evening meal, our host, as on the former occasion walked book-in-hand up and down the room, but was evidently less watchful of his pretty niece and silver spoons. His attention, indeed, appeared to be entirely given to the state of the mercury in an old barometer, which, appended to the wall at the further end of the room, he consulted at every turn, putting divers weatherwise questions to us as he did so. And at last, he asked in plain language, whether our church ever put up prayers for rain, and if they ever brought it.

The occasion of all this *pumping* we found to be, that the country in the neighbourhood having long been suffering from drought, the husbandmen, apprehensive of the consequences, had for some days past been urging him to pray for rain, but the state of the barometer had not hitherto, he said, warranted his doing so, and he had, therefore, put them off, on various pretences. "Yesterday, however," he observed, "seeing that the mercury was falling, I gave notice that I should make intercession for them; and, I think, judging from present appearances, that my prayers are likely to be as effectual as those of any bishop could possibly be." And off he started to church, giving us, at parting, a very significant, though somewhat heterodoxical grin.

Nevertheless, not a drop of rain fell that night; the barometer was at fault; and the only clouds visible in the morning were those gathered on the brow of the *Cura*. They dispersed, however, like mist under the sun's rays; when, bidding him farewell, and thanking him for his hospitable entertainment, we slipped a *doublon de à ocho* into his hand; which, pocketing without the slightest hesitation, he assured us, with imperturbable gravity, should be applied to the services of the *church*—"as, doubtless, we intended."

Threading once more the rudely *graduated* streets of the town, we took the stony pathway, before noticed, which winds down under the eastern side of the castle hill, and in rather more than half an hour were again beyond the limits of the Serranía, and in a country of corn and pasture.

At the foot of the mountain two roads present themselves, one proceeding straight across the country to San Roque and Gibraltar (nineteen and twenty-five miles), the other seeking more directly the Mediterranean shore, and visiting on its way the sulphur-baths and little town of Manilba.

The *Cura* had spoken in such terms of commendation of the *Hedionda* (fetid spring)—claiming it jealously as the property of Casares—that we were tempted to lengthen our journey by a few miles to pay it a visit.

The road to it follows the course of the little stream that flows in the valley between the Cristellina mountain and Casares, which, escaping by a narrow rocky gorge immediately below the town, winds round the foot of the castle crag, and takes an easterly direction to the Mediterranean. The country at first is open, and the stream flows through a smiling valley, without encountering any obstacle; but, at about two miles from Casares, a dark and narrow defile presents itself, which, the winding rivulet having in vain sought to avoid, finally precipitates itself into, and is lost sight of, under an entangled canopy of arbutus, lauristinus, clematis, and various creepers. So narrow and overshadowed is the chasm, so high and precipitous are its bank—themselves overgrown with coppice and forest-trees, wherever the crumbling rocks have allowed their roots to spread—that even the sunbeams have difficulty in reaching the foaming stream, as it hurries over its rough and tortuous bed; and the pathway, following the various windings of the narrow gorge,—now keeping along the shady bank of the rivulet, now climbing, by rudely carved zig-zags, some little way up the precipitous sides of the fissure,—is barely of a width to admit of the passage of a loaded mule.

So wildly beautiful is the scenery, so free from artificial embellishments,—for the low moss-grown water-mills which are scattered along the course of the stream, and here and there a rustic bridge, owe their beauty rather to nature than art—so *romantic*, in fine, is the spot, that, if in the vicinity of a fashionable *baden*, it could not fail of being a little fortune to all the ragged donkey-drivers within a circuit of many leagues, and of proving a mine of wealth to the surveyors of *tables d'hôtes*, and *restaurans*, and keepers of billiard and faro tables.

The amusements of the frequenters of the humble *Hedionda* are, however, very different, and the sequestered dell is visited only by chanting muleteers, driving their files of laded animals to or from the mills; or, perchance, by some sulphurated old lady, who, ensconced in a pillowed *jamuga*, [72] is bending her way, with renovated health, towards Casares or Ximena: to which places the narrow fissure offers the nearest road from the baths.

After proceeding about a mile down the dark ravine, its banks, crumbling down in rude blocks, recede from each other, and a huge barren sierra is discovered rising steeply along the southern bank of the stream, to which the road now crosses. It greatly excited our surprise how this lofty and strongly marked ridge could have escaped our observation from Casares, for it had seemed to us, that on descending from thence we should leave the mountains altogether behind us.

From the base of this barren ridge issues the *Hedionda*; still, however, about a mile from us; and ere reaching it, the hills retiring for a time yet more from the stream, leave a flat space of some extent, and in form resembling an amphitheatre, which is planted with all kinds of fruit-trees, and dotted with vine-clung cottages. This spot is called *La Huerta*—the orchard; and these comfortless looking little hovels—pleasing nevertheless to the eye— we eventually learnt are the lodging-houses of the most aristocratic visiters of the baths.

Traversing the fruitful little dell, and mounting a low rocky ledge that completes its enclosure to the east, leaving only a narrow passage for the rivulet, we found ourselves close to the baths; our vicinity to which, however, the offensive smell of the spring (prevailing even over the strong perfume of the orange blossoms) had already duly apprized us of.

The baths are situated almost in the bed of the pure mountain stream, whose course we had been following from Casares; and a short distance beyond, and at a slight elevation above them, stands a neat and compact little village.

The season being at its height, we found the place so crowded with visiters, that it would have been impossible to procure a night's lodging, had such been our wish. All we required, however, was information concerning the place; for which purpose we repaired to the *Fonda*,—a kind of booth, such as is knocked up at fairs in England for the sale of gin, "and other cordials,"—and ordered such refreshment as it afforded, asking the *Moza* [73] if she could tell us whether any of the houses were vacant, &c.

She replied, that the Fonda was provided with every thing necessary for travellers of distinction, being established on the footing of the hotels "*de mas fama*" of Malaga and San Roque; and that El *Señor Juan*, the "*intendente*" [74] of the place,—who, doubtless, on hearing of our arrival, would forthwith pay his respects to us,—could furnish every sort of information respecting it.

Oh! a master of the ceremonies, with his book, thought we—well, this will be amusing: some urbane "captain," no doubt, all smiles to all persons!— and whilst we were yet picturing to ourselves what this Spanish Beau Nash could possibly be like, a tall ungainly personage, with a considerable halt in his gait, a fund of humour in his long leathern countenance, and a paper cigar screwed up in the dexter corner of his mouth, presented himself, and placed his services at our disposition.

He held a huge pitcher of the fragrant water in one hand, which, when he was in motion, gave him a "lurch to starboard;" a stout staff in the other, by means of which he established an equilibrium when at rest. His body was coatless, his neck cravatless, his shirt sleeves were rolled up to the elbow, leaving his brown sinewy arms bare; his trowsers hung in braceless negligence about his hips; his large bare feet were thrust into a pair of capacious shoes; and his head was covered with a high-crowned, narrow-brimmed, Frenchified hat, which had evidently browned under the heat of many summers, and bent to the storms of intervening winters. Round his neck hung a stout silver chain (which the fumes of the sulphur-spring had turned as black as Berlin iron), whence was suspended a ponderous master-key.

"He must be the prison-keeper," said we, "carrying the daily allowance of water to the incarcerated malefactors!"

"This is *Señor Juan, el intendente*," said our smirking attendant, placing a bottle of wine upon the table before us.

"Oh! this is *Señor Juan*, the master of the ceremonies!—Then pray be seated, *Señor Juan*; and bring another wine-glass, *Mariquita*."

Our requests were instantly complied with; and in half an hour we had disengaged from the numberless "*por supuestos, conques*," and "*pues*," with which Señor Juan interlarded his conversation, and from the smoky exhalations in which he enveloped it, all the information we required concerning the baths, though by no means so full an account of them as the gossip-loving *Tio* seemed disposed to give us. So pleased were we, however, with his description of the amusements of the place, and of the valuable properties of its waters, that, assuring him we should take an early opportunity of renewing his acquaintance, and commending him to the care of *San Juan Nepomaceno*, we arose, and took our departure.

I was not long in performing my promise. Indeed, I became an annual visiter to the baths for a few days during the shooting season; and will devote the following chapter to a more particular description of the *Hedionda*, and the manner of life at a Spanish watering-place.

The mule-track from the baths to Gibraltar—for during the first few miles it is little else—keeps down the valley for some little distance, and then, ascending a steep hill, joins at its summit a road leading to Casares from Manilba; which latter little town is seen about three-quarters of a mile off, on the left. This road to Casares turns the *sierra* overhanging the baths on its western side, where it meets with some flat, nearly table-land; but our route to Gibraltar, after keeping along it a few hundred yards, strikes off to the left, and, traversing a wild and very broken country, in something more than three miles forms its junction with the road from the town of Manilba to San Roque and Gibraltar, which again, half a mile further on, falls into the road from Malaga to those two places. This spot is distant five miles from the baths, and rather more than two from the river Guadiaro.

Near some farm-houses on the left bank of this river, and about a mile from its mouth, are ruins of the Roman town of *Barbesula*. Some monuments and inscriptions found here, many years since, were carried to Gibraltar.

The bed of the Guadiaro is wide but shallow, and offers two fords, which are practicable at most seasons. There is a ferry-boat kept, however, at the upper point of passage, for cases of necessity. A venta is situated on the right bank of the stream, whereat a bevy of custom-house people generally assemble to levy contributions on the passers-by. It is a wretched place of accommodation, though better than another, distant about a mile further, on the road to Gibraltar, and well known to the sportsmen of the garrison by the name of *pan y agua*—bread and water—those being the only supplies that the establishment can be depended upon to furnish. Its vicinity to some excellent snipe ground occasions it to be much resorted to in the winter.

At the first-named venta, two roads present themselves, that on the right hand proceeding to San Roque, (eight miles,) the other seeking the coast and keeping along it to Gibraltar—a distance of twelve miles.

The country traversed by the former is very rugged, but the path is, nevertheless, unnecessarily circuitous. In various places—but a little off the road—are vestiges of an old paved route, which, it is by no means improbable, was the Roman way from *Barbesula* to *Carteia*, of which further notice will be taken, when the coast road from Malaga to Gibraltar is described.

CHAPTER VII

THE baths of Manilba lie about seventeen miles N.N.E. of Gibraltar, and four, inland, from the sea-fort of Savanilla. The town, from which they take their name, is about midway between them and the coast; and, standing on a commanding knoll, is a conspicuous object when sailing along the Mediterranean shore.

The virtues of the sulphureous spring have long been known; but it is only within the last few years that the increasing reputation of the medicated source led a company of speculators to build the village which now stands in its vicinity; the scattered cottages of the *Huerta* having been found quite incapable of lodging the vast crowd of valetudinarians, annually drawn to the spot. The same parties have yet more recently erected a chapel, and also the *Fonda*, mentioned in the preceding chapter.

The little village is built with the regularity of even Wiesbaden itself, but nothing can well be more different in other respects than it is from that, or any other watering-place, which I have ever visited. It consists of five or six parallel stacks of houses, forming streets which open at one end upon the bank overhanging the now sulphurated stream, that flows down from Casares; and which abut, at the other, against the side of the lofty mountain whence the medicated spring issues. These streets are covered in with trellis-work, over which vines are trained, rendering them cool, as well as agreeable to the sight. The houses are all built on a uniform plan, namely, they have no upper story, and contain but *one room each*; which room is furnished with the usual Spanish kitchen-range—that is, with three or four little bricked stoves built into a kind of dresser. By this arrangement, every room is, of itself, capable of forming a *complete establishment*; and in most cases, indeed, it does serve the triple purposes of a kitchen, a refectory, and a dormitory, to its frugal inmates. When a family is large, however, an entire lareet must be hired for its accommodation.

The principal speculator in the joint-stock village is a gentleman of Estepona; and *El Señor Juan*—or *Tio Juan*, as he is familiarly called by those admitted to his intimacy—is a poor relative, who, for the slight perquisites of office, readily undertook the charge of the infant establishment.

The choice of the *Tio* was, in every respect, a judicious one; for, having drunk himself off the crutches on which he hobbled down to the baths, he has become a kind of walking advertisement of the efficacy of the waters. He is not, however, like the unsightly fellows who perambulate the streets of London with placards, a silent one; for I know of no man more thoroughly versed in the art of *viva voce* puffing than *Tio Juan*; and then he has stored his memory with such a fund of useful watering-place information, that he is a perfect guide to the *Hedionda* and its environs.

The *Tio* and I soon became wonderful cronies; I derived great amusement from his *cuentas*—he, much gratification from my nightly whisky-toddy. In fact, the two dovetailed into each other in a most remarkable manner; for, when once the *Tio* had attached one of his long stories to a (*pint*) bottle of "poteen," there was no possibility of separating them—they drew cork and breath together, and together only they came to a conclusion.

He knew every body that visited the baths, and every thing about them; could point out those who came for health, and those who were allured by dissipation; could tell which ladies and gentlemen were looking out for matrimony, which for intrigue; whether the buxom widow had fruitful vineyards and olive grounds with her weeds; whether the young ladies had shining *onzas* to recommend them as well as sparkling eyes.

Then the Tio knew where every medicinal herb grew that was suited to any given case—could point out the haunt of every covey of red-legged partridges in the vicinity—could tell to an hour when a flight of quail would cross from the parched shores of Africa—when the matchless *becafigos* would alight upon the neighbouring fig-trees—and, as the season advanced, he would mark the time to a nicety when the first annual visit of the woodcocks might be looked for to the wooded glens beyond the baths.

As the historian of the wonder-working spring, the *Tio* was not less valuable; though, it must be confessed, the terms in which he conveyed the idea of its vast antiquity were any thing but prepossessing; viz., "*Pues! saben ustedes, que esa hedionda es mas vieja que la sarna.*" "Know then, gentlemen, that this fetid spring is older than the itch." In other respects, however, the information he had collected, besides being most rare, possessed a freshness that was truly delightful; "*Siglos hay,* [75] " he would continue, "the spring was *endemoniado,* for *Carlomagno,* or some other great hero of the most remote antiquity, drove an evil spirit into the mountain, which said spirit, to be revenged on mankind, poisoned the source whence the stream flows. Saint James, however, arriving in the country soon after—having taken Spain under his especial protection—determined to expel this imp of Satan. This was done accordingly, and the devil went over into Barbary, (where he eventually stirred up the Moors against the adopted children of *Santiago*—the story of *Don Rodrigo* and *La Cava* being all a fable,) leaving nothing but his sulphur behind."

"The good saint, to perpetuate the fame of the miracle he had wrought, next determined to endue the spring with extraordinary curative properties; not depriving it, however, of the unusually bad smell left by the devil, that the marvellous work he was about to perform might be the more apparent to future generations."

"Some years after this, the baths were visited by '*muchos emperadores de Roma;*' [76] amongst others, Trajan and Hercules; as also by the famous Roland; and, '*segun dicen,*' by *un Ingles, llamado Malbrù, y otra gente muy principal.*" [77] "In those days," continued the Tio, "there were *palathios, posa'a, y to'o,* [78] but then came the Moors (with the devil in their train), and laid every thing waste. They had not the power, however, to deprive the stream of its virtues; and great they are, and most justly celebrated *por todo la España.*" [79]

In detailing the wonderful properties of the spring committed to his charge, *Tio Juan* would enter with all the minuteness of an Herodotus. By his account, there was no ailment to which suffering humanity is exposed that it would not reach. It was a "universal medicine"—a Hygeian fountain that bestowed perpetual youth—a Styx that rendered mankind invulnerable. It gave strength to the weak, and ease to those who were in pain—rendered the barren fruitful, and the splenetic, good-humoured—made the fat, lean, and the lean, fat. By it the good liver was freed from gout, and the bad liver from bile. The sores of the leper were dried up, and the lungs of the asthmatic inflated—it made the maimed whole, and patched up the broken-hearted. He had known many instances of its curing consumption, and had seen it act like a charm in cases of tympany.

"In fact," said old Juan—"*para todo tiene remedio.—Mir' usted* [80] —I, who on my arrival here could not put a foot to the ground, now, as you may perceive, walk about like a *Jovencito;* [81] and, under proper directions, I have no doubt it would make a man live for ever." [82]

Nor did the long list of the water's valuable qualities end here. It was good for all the common purposes of life—for stewing and for boiling—for washing and for shaving;—and, to wind up all, as we go on sinning, until, by constant repetition, crime no longer pricks one's conscience, so, the *Tio* declared, one went on drinking this devilish water until it positively became palatable. "*Jo no bebo otra,*" he concluded, "*nunca bebo otra—guiso y to'o con ella.*" [83]

Now, though the Tio painted the yellow spring thus *couleur de rose*, and his account of its wonderful properties, like his system of chronology, must be received with caution, yet I must needs confess that the *Hedionda* seemed to perform extraordinary cures; and, even in my own case, I ever fancied that after a few days passed at the baths, I returned to Gibraltar with invigorated powers of digestion. I could by no means, however, bring myself to submit to the *Tio's* discipline, and he was wont to shake his head very seriously, when, returning from a hard day's shooting, I used to request him to open a bath for me after sunset—Hercules, himself, he thought could not have stood that.

That this spring was known to the Romans there can be no manner of doubt, since the public bath, which still exists, is a work of that people. The source is very copious, and the water of an equal temperature throughout the year, viz., 73 to 75 degrees of Fahrenheit's thermometer.

On analysis it is found to contain large quantities of hydrogen and carbonic acid gases, and the following proportions of fixed substances in fifty pounds of water, viz., six grains of muriate of lime; fifty-six of sulphate of magnesia; thirty-five of sulphate of lime; ten of magnesia; and four of silica. The quantity of sulphur it holds in solution is so great, that the vine-dressers in the neighbourhood make themselves matches, by merely steeping linen rags in the waste water of the baths.

The use of the bath has been found very efficacious in the cure of all kinds of cutaneous diseases, ulcers, wounds, and elephantiasis; and taken inwardly, the water is considered by the faculty as extremely beneficial in cases of gout, asthma, scrofula, rheumatism, dyspepsia, and, as the Tio said, in fact, in almost every disorder that human nature is subject to.

The season for taking the waters is from the beginning of June to the end of September; and it is astonishing during those four months what vast crowds of persons, of every grade and calling, are brought together. Nobles, priests, peasants, and beggars—the gouty, hypochondriac, lame, and blind— all flock from every part of the kingdom to the famed Hedionda. It was ever a matter of surprise to me where such a host can find accommodation.

The same regimen is prescribed at this as at other watering places; viz., plenty of the spring, moderate exercise, and abstemious diet; and in this latter item, at least, the injunctions are as generally disregarded at Manilba as at the Brunnens of Nassau: that is, comparatively speaking, for it must be borne in mind that a German's daily food would support a Spaniard for a week.

The principal bath is open to the public, and, being very large and tolerably deep, is by far the pleasantest, when one can be sure of its entire possession. Those which have been built by the company of speculators are too small, though convenient in other respects. The charge for the use of these is moderate enough, viz., one real and a half each time of bathing; which includes a trifling gratuity to *Tio Juan*.

The source from which the drinkers fill their goblets is open to all comers, and any one may bottle and carry off the precious water *ad libitum*. A considerable quantity is sent in stone jars to the neighbouring towns; but Tio Juan maintained—and I believe not without good reason—that it lost all its properties on the journey *"amen del mal olor."* [84]

The situation of the new village would have been more agreeable had it been built somewhat higher up the side of the sierra, instead of on the immediate bank of the rivulet, where it is excluded from the fine view it might otherwise command, and is sheltered from every breath of air. It is not, however, so sultry as might be expected, considering its confined situation; for the mountain behind screens it from the sun's rays at an early hour after noon, and the opposite bank of the ravine, by sloping down gradually to the stream, and being clothed to the water's edge with vines, fig, and other fruit-trees, throws back no reflected heat upon the dwellings.

The manner of life of the visiters of the *hedionda* is not less different from that of the watering places of other countries, than the place itself is from Cheltenham or Carlsbad. They rise with the sun; drink their first glass of water at the spring on their way to chapel; a second glass, in returning from their devotions; and then take a *paseito* [85] in the *huerta*: but not until after the third dose do they venture on their usual breakfast of a cup of chocolate. The bath and the toilette occupy the rest of the morning. Dinner is taken at one or two o'clock; the *Siesta* follows, and before sunset another bath, perhaps. The *Paseo* comes next—that is quite indispensable—and the *Tertulia* concludes the arrangements for the day.

This, at the baths, is a kind of public assembly held in the open air, and generally in one of the vine-sheltered streets of the modern village. A guitar, cards, dancing, and games of forfeit, are the various resources of the *réunion*; which breaks up at an early hour.

Tio Juan, in his shirt-sleeves and slippers, is a constant attendant at the *Tertulia*, usually looking on at the sports and pastimes with becoming gravity, but occasionally taking a hand at *Malilla*, [86] or joining the noisy circle playing at *El Enfermo*; [87] in which, when the usual question is asked, "What will *you* give the sick man?" he invariably answers, *"El Agua—nada mas que el agua—que no hay cosa mas sano en el mundo,"* [88] puffing away at his paper cigar all the while with the most imperturbable gravity, and casting a side glance at me, as much as to say—"not a word of our nightly *symposium*, if you please."

The company on these occasions is, as may be supposed, of a very mixed kind. Let it not be imagined, however, that because *"Señor Juan"* presents himself with bare elbows, that it is altogether of a secondary order—far from it—for such is the caprice of fashion, such the love of change, that even the noblest of the land are ofttimes inmates of the little inconvenient hovels that I have described; but *Tio Juan* is a privileged person—every body consults him, every one makes him his or her confidant. And so curiously is Spanish society constituted, that though considered the proudest people in the world, yet, on occasions like this, Spaniards lay aside the distinction of rank, and mix together in the most unceremonious manner. Indeed, no people I have ever seen treat their inferiors with greater respect than the Spanish Nobles. They enter familiarly into conversation with the servants standing behind their chair; and, strange as it may appear, this freedom is never taken advantage of, nor are they less respected, nor worse served in consequence.

The custom of kneeling down in common at their places of public worship may have a tendency to keep up this feeling, warning the rich and powerful of the earth that, though placed temporarily above the peasant in the world's estimation, yet that he is their equal in the sight of the Creator of all; an accountable being like themselves, and deserving of the treatment of a human being.

The Spanish nobles certainly find their reward in adopting such a line of conduct, for they are served with extraordinary fidelity; and the horrors which were perpetrated *through the instrumentality of servants*, during the French revolution, is little to be apprehended in this country; perhaps, indeed, this good understanding between master and man has hitherto saved Spain from its reign of terror.

The chapel of the bathing village is generally thronged with penitents; for people become very devout when they have, or fancy they have, one foot in the grave. The little edifice may be considered the repository of the *archives* of *the Hedionda*, for countless are the legs, arms, heads, and bodies, moulded in wax, or carved in wood, and telling of wondrous cures, that have been offered at the shrine of Our Lady of *Los Remedios*.

Leaving the good Romanists at their devotions within the crowded chapel, and *Tio Juan*, with one knee and his pitcher of water on the ground, and his staff in hand, offering a passing prayer behind the throng collected outside the open door, we will devote the morning to a scramble to the summit of the steep mountain that rises at the back of the baths.

The *Sierra de Utrera*, by which name this rugged ridge is distinguished, is of very singular formation. Its eastern base (whence the *hedionda* issues) is covered with a crumbling mass of schist, disposed in laminæ, shelving downwards, at an angle of 25 or 30 degrees with the horizon. This sloping bank reaches to about one third the height of the mountain, when rude rocks of a most peculiar character shoot up above its general surface, rising pyramidically, but assuming most fantastic forms, and each pile consisting of a series of huge blocks (sometimes fourteen or fifteen in number), resting loosely one upon another, and seemingly so much off the centre of gravity as to lead to the belief that a slight push would lay them prostrate.

At first these detached pinnacles rise only to the height of fifteen or twenty feet, but, on drawing near the crest of the ridge, they attain nearly twice that elevation. The general surface of the mountain, above which these piles of rocking stones rise, is rent by deep chasms, as if the whole mass of rock had, at some distant period, been shaken to its very foundation by an earthquake. In these rents, soil has been gradually collected, and vegetation been the consequence; but the general character of the mountain is arid and sterile.

The ascent becomes very difficult as one proceeds, and, in fact, it requires some little agility to reach the crest of the singular ridge. Its summit presents a very rough, though nearly horizontal surface, varying in width from 300 to 400 yards; and, looking from its western side, the spectator fancies himself elevated on the walls of some vast castle, so precipitously does the rocky ledge fall in that direction, so level and smiling is the cultivated country spread out but a couple of hundred feet below him.

This rocky plateau appears to have been covered, in former days, with the same singularly formed pyramids that protrude from the eastern acclivity of the mountain; but they have probably been hewn into mill stones, as many of the rough blocks strewed about its surface are now in process of becoming. The plateau extends nearly two miles in a parallel direction to the rock of Gibraltar, that is, nearly due north and south by compass; and, when on its summit, the ridge appears continuous; but, on proceeding to examine the southern portion of the plateau, I found myself suddenly on the brink of a chasm, upwards of a hundred feet deep, which, traversing the mountain from east to west, cuts it completely in two. This cleft varies in width from 50 to 100 feet; and in winter brings down a copious stream, being the drain of a considerable extent of country on the western side of the ridge. It is partially clothed with shrubs and wild olive-trees, and a rude pathway leads down the dark dell to the *hedionda*, which issues from the base of the mountain, about 200 yards to the north of the opening of the chasm.

This remarkable gap, though not distinguishable from the baths situated immediately below it, is so well defined, and has so peculiar an appearance at a distance, that it is an important landmark for the coasting vessels.

The southern portion of the Sierra is far less accessible than that which has been described; in fact, access to its summit can be gained only by means of a ramped road, which, piercing the rocky precipice on its western side, has been made to facilitate the transport of the millstones prepared there. In other respects, this part of the plateau is of the same character as the other.

Wonderful are the tales of fairies, devils, and evil spirits, told by the goatherds and others who frequent this singular mountain; and *Tio Juan*, who never would suffer himself to be outdone in the marvellous, told us that *"un Ingles,"* who, about two years before, had been on a visit to the baths, had disappeared there in a most mysterious way. A goatherd of his acquaintance had seen him descend into a cleft in search of some herb, but out of it he had never returned. *"Se dicen,"* he concluded, *"que era uno de esos Lores, de que hay tantos en Inglaterra;* [89] but I can hardly believe, if he had possessed such *'montones de oro'* [90] as was represented, that he would have been going about like a pedlar, with a basket slung to his back, picking up all sorts of herbs, and drying them with great care every day when he returned home, spreading them out between the leaves of a large book. *'A me mi parece,'* [91] that he was gathering them to make tea with; but I know an herb which grows on that Sierra, which is worth all the medicines [92] in the world: ay! and in some cases it is yet quicker, though not more effectual, in its cure, than even the waters of the *hedionda*; and some day, *Don Carlos*, I will walk up and show you the cleft wherein it grows."

The *Tio's* occupations were, however, too constant to allow of his accompanying me in search of this wonderful plant, and, consequently, my curiosity concerning it was never gratified.

The district of Manilba is celebrated for the productiveness of its vineyards, and the undulated country between the baths and the southern foot of the *Sierra Bermeja* is almost exclusively devoted to the culture of the grape. That most esteemed is a large purple kind. It is highly flavoured, and makes a strong-bodied and very palatable wine, though, in nine cases out of ten, the wine is spoilt by some defect of the skin in which it has been carried.

The husks of the Manilba grape, after the juice has been expressed, enjoy a reputation for the cure of rheumatism, scarcely less than that of the sulphureous spring itself. The sufferer is immersed up to the neck in a vat full of the fermenting skins, and, after remaining therein a whole morning, comes forth as purple as a printer's devil. I have met with persons who declared they had received great benefit from this vinous bath; but I question whether interment in hot sand (a mode of treatment, by the way, which has been tried with great success) would not have been found more efficacious, without subjecting the patient to this unpleasant discoloration.

Several interesting mornings' excursions may be made from the baths. The village of Manilba (about two miles distant) is situated on a high, but narrow ridge, that protrudes from the south-eastern extremity of the Sierra de Utrera. It is a compactly built place, and commands fine views: towards the mountains on one side, and over the Mediterranean on the other. The population amounts to about 3000 souls, principally vinedressers and husbandmen.

On one occasion—having found all the lodging-houses at the *hedionda* occupied, I established myself for a few days at the posada at Manilba, where a singular adventure befel me. Mine host entered my room on the evening of my arrival, and very mysteriously informed me, that a certain person—a friend of his—a Spanish officer "*por fin*," who had distinguished himself greatly under the constitutional government, and was a *caballero de toda confianza*, [93] wished very much to have the honour of paying me a visit, if I were agreeable, which, hearing I was alone, he thought it possible I might be; and, before I had time fully to explain that I was quite tired from a long day's shooting, and must beg to be excused, the *Lismahago* himself walked in—as vulgar, off-handed, free-and-easy a gentleman as I ever came across.

Having expressed unbounded love for the English nation, and stated his conviction—drawn from his intimate knowledge of the character of British officers—that they were, one and all, well disposed to assist in the grand work of regenerating Spain, he proceeded to state, that the "friends of liberty," in various towns of that part of the Peninsula, had entered into a plot to subvert the existing government of the country, and having many friends in Gibraltar, wished, through the medium of an officer of that garrison, to communicate with them; that, understanding I was, &c. &c. &c.

I had merely acknowledged that I comprehended what he was saying, by bowing severally to the numerous panegyrics on liberty, and compliments to myself and nation, with which he interlarded his discourse—for the above is but the skimmed milk of his eloquent harangue; but, finding that he had at length concluded, I expressed the deep regret I felt at not being able to meet his friendly proposal in the way he wished, from the circumstance of my time being fully occupied in preparing a deep-laid plot against my own government—nothing less, in fact, than to give up the important fortress of Gibraltar to the Emperor of Morocco, until we had established a republic in England. When this grand project was accomplished, I added, I should be quite at leisure, and would most willingly enter into any treasonable designs against any other government; but, at present, he must see it was quite out of the question.

My visiter gazed on me "with the eyes of astonishment," but I kept my countenance. He rose from his seat—I did the same.

"Are you serious?" asked he.

"Perfectly so," I replied; "but, of course, I reckon on your maintaining the strictest secrecy in the matter I have just communicated," I added earnestly.

"You may rely in perfect confidence upon me."

"Do you smoke? Pray accept of a Gibraltar cigar. I regret that I cannot ask you to remain with me, but I have letters of the utmost importance to write, which must be sent off by daybreak." He accepted my proffered cigar, begged I would command his services on all occasions, and walked off.

I made sure he was a government spy, and in a towering rage sent for the innkeeper. He protested such was not the case, adding, "but, to confess the truth," he was a poor harmless fellow,—a reduced officer of the constitutional army,—who was very fond of the English, not less so of wine; talked a great deal of nonsense, which nobody minded; and hoped I would take no notice of it.

I reminded mine host, that he had said he was a "*distinguished officer*," and had called him "*his friend.*"—"*Si, señor, es verdad;* [94] but the fact is, he followed me up stairs, and I knew he was at the door, listening to what I might say."

I very much doubted the truth of his asseverations, and my doubts were confirmed by my never afterwards seeing the constitutional officer about the premises; but, to prevent a repetition of such introductions, I begged to be allowed the privilege of choosing my own associates, telling him, indeed, that my further stay at his house would depend upon it. I still, however, continued to look upon the fellow as a spy, until the mad attempt made by Torrijos to bring about a revolution, not very long afterwards, led me to think that my visiter's overture might really have been seriously intended.

Manilba is distant about seven miles from Estepona. The first part of the road thither lies through productive vineyards; the latter along the sea-shore, on reaching which it falls into the road from Gibraltar to Malaga.

Not many years since Estepona was a mere fishing village, built under the protection of one of the *casa fuertes* that guard the coast; but the fort stands now in the midst of a thriving town, containing 6000 inhabitants.

The fish taken here finds a ready sale in the Serranía, whither it is conveyed in a half-salted state, on the backs of mules or asses. The *Sardina* frequents this coast in great numbers; it is a delicious fish, of the herring kind, but more delicately flavoured.

The environs of Estepona are very fruitful; and oranges and lemons are exported thence to a large amount—the greater portion to England. The place is distant twenty-five miles from Gibraltar (by the road), and sixteen from Marbella. To the latter the road is very good.

A most delightful ride offers itself to return from hence to the baths of Manilba, by way of Casares. The road, for the first few miles, keeps under the deeply seamed and pine-clad side of the *Sierra Bermeja*, and then, leaving the mountain-path to Gaucin (mentioned in a preceding chapter) to the right, enters an intersected country, winding along the edge of several deep ravines, shaded by groves of chesnut-trees, and reaches Casares very unexpectedly; leaving a large convent, situated on the side of a steep bank, on the left, just before entering the narrow, rock-bound town.

The road from Casares to the baths has already been described, but two other routes offer themselves from that town to reach Manilba. The more direct of these keeps the fissure in which the *hedionda* is situated on the right; the other makes a wide circuit round the *Sierra de Utrera*, and leaves the baths on the left. By the former the distance is five and a half, by the latter seven miles.

CHAPTER VIII

IN the wildest part of the mountainous belt that, stretching in a wide semicircle round Gibraltar, cuts the rocky peninsula off, as it were, from the rest of Spain, is situated the *Casería de Sanona*; a lone house, now dwindled down to a mere farm; but, as both its name implies, and its appearance bespeaks, formerly a place of some consequence.

It was brought to its present lowly state during the last war, when its inhabitants were so reduced in number, as well as circumstances, that hands and means are still equally wanting for the proper looking after, and attending to, the vast herds and extensive *dehesas* [95] and forest-lands belonging to it. The consequence is, that the wolves and wild boars, from having been so long permitted to roam about in undisputed possession of the woods, have in their turn, from being the persecuted, become the aggressors, and are now in the habit of making nightly predatory visits to the cattle folds and plantations of the *Casería*, carrying off the farmer's sheep and heifers, and destroying his winter stock of vegetables, whenever, by any neglect or remissness of the watch, an opportunity is afforded them.

Besides the animals above mentioned, deer, and, in the winter, woodcocks, find the unfrequented ravines in the vicinity of the *Casería* equally well suited to their secluded habits; and, tempted by the promising account of the sport the place afforded, a party was formed, consisting of three of my most intimate friends, myself, and a piqueur, to proceed thither for a few days' shooting.

Sending forward a messenger to the Casería, as well to go through the form of asking its proprietor to "put us up," during our proposed visit, as to request him to have a sufficient number of beaters collected—on which the quality of the sport mainly depends—we provided ourselves with a week's consumption of provisions and ammunition, and, leaving Gibraltar late in the afternoon, proceeded to Los Barrios; whence, we could take an earlier departure on the following morning than from the locked-up fortress.

The *Piqueur* who usually accompanied us on these shooting excursions was a personage of some celebrity in the Gibraltar *sporting world*, and his name—Damien Berrio—will doubtless be familiar to such of my readers as may have resided any time on "the rock." By birth a Piedmontese, a baker by profession, Damien's bread—like that of many persons in a more elevated walk of life—was not to his taste. At the very mention of a *Batida*, he would leave oven, home, wife, and children; shoulder his gun, fill his *alforjas*—for he was a provident soul, and, though a baker, ever maintained that man could not live on bread alone—borrow a horse, and, in half an hour, "be ready for a start."

Possessing a perfect knowledge of the country, a quick eye, an unerring aim, and a nose that could wind an *olla* if within the circuit of a Spanish league, Damien was, in many respects, a valuable acquisition on a shooting party. And to the aforesaid qualifications, befitting him for the *staff*, he added that of being an excellent *raconteur*. In this he received much assistance from his personal appearance, which, like that of the inimitable Liston, passed off for humour that which, in reality, was pure nature.

His person was much above the common stature, erect, and well-built, but his hands and feet were "prodigious." His face—when the sun fell directly upon it, so as to free it from the shadow of his enormous nose—was intelligent, and bespoke infinite good nature, though marked, nevertheless, with the lines of care and sorrow. His costume was that of a French sportsman, except that he wore a high-crowned, weather-beaten old hat, placed somewhat knowingly on one side of his head, and which, of itself alone, marked him as "*a character.*"

To those who have not had the pleasure of his acquaintance, a *precis* of his early history may not be unacceptable; those who already know it will, I trust, pardon the short digression.

Born on the sunny side of the Alps, some fifteen years before the breaking out of the French revolution, Damien, at a very early age, was called upon to defend his country against the aggression of its Gallic neighbours. He was draughted accordingly to a regiment of grenadiers of the Piedmontese army commanded by General Colli; and, in the short and disgraceful campaign of 1796, was made prisoner with the brave but unfortunate Provèra, at the Castle of Cosséria.

On the formation of the Cisalpine republic soon afterwards, our grenadier, released, as he fondly imagined, from the necessity of any further military service, purposed returning to his family and regretted agricultural pursuits; but, on applying for his discharge, he found that he had quite misunderstood the meaning of the word *freedom*. "What!" said the regenerator of his oppressed country; "what! return home like a lazy drone, when so much still remains to be done! No, no, we cannot part with you yet; we are about to give liberty to the rest of Italy; you must march; can mankind be more beneficially or philanthropically employed? *Allons!*

en avant! vive la liberté!"—"And so," said Damien, "off we were marched, under the tail of the French eagle, to give freedom to the *Facchini of Venice,* and *Lazzaroni* of Naples; and to spoil and pillage all that lay in our way."

This marauding life was ill-suited either to our hero's taste or habits, and accordingly he embraced the first favourable opportunity of quitting the service of the "Regenerator of Italy." How he managed to effect his liberation I never could find out, it being one of the very few subjects on which Damien was close; but I suspect—much as he liked shooting—that the love of the smell of gunpowder was not a *natural* taste of his. Be that as it may, he made his way to Spain—took to himself a Spanish wife—and settled at Gibraltar.

His language, like the dress of a harlequin, was made up of scraps,— French, Spanish, English, and Italian, joined in angularly and without method or regularity; and all so badly spoken, as to render it impossible to say which amongst them was the mother-tongue. Nevertheless, Damien got on well with every body, and his *bonhommie* and good nature rendered him a universal favourite. In other respects, however, he was not so favoured a child of fortune; for, though no idle seeker of adventures, in fact, he was wont to go a great way to avoid them, yet, as ill luck would have it, adventures very frequently came across him. And it generally happened, as with the famed Manchegan knight, that Damien, in his various encounters, came off "second best." That is to say, they usually ended in his finding himself *minus* his gun, or his horse, or both, and, perhaps, his *alforjas* to boot.

By his own account, these untoward events invariably happened through some want of proper precaution—either whilst he was indulging in a *Siesta*, or taking a snack by the side of some cool stream, his trusty gun being out of his immediate reach, or when committing some other imprudent act. So it was, however, and these *"petits malheurs,"* as he was in the habit of calling them, had generated a more than ordinary dread of robbers, which, in its turn, had produced in him a disposition to be gregarious whenever he passed the bounds of the English garrison.

In travelling through the mountains, we always knew when we were approaching what Damien considered a likely spot for an ambuscade, by his striking up a martial air that he told us had been the favourite march of the regiment of grenadiers in which he had served; giving us from time to time a hint that it would be well to be upon the look-out by observing to the person next him, *"Hay muchos ladrones par ici, mon Capitaine—el año pasado (maledetti sian' ces gueux d'Espagnols!) on m'a volé une bonne escopète en este maldito callejon* [96] *—Il faut être preparé, Messieurs!"* and then the Piedmontese march was resumed with increased energy, growing *piu marcato e risoluto*, as the banks of the gorge became higher and the underwood thicker.

On regaining the open country, the air was changed by a playful *Cadenza* to one of a more lively character, and, after a *Da Capo*, generally ended with *"n'ayez pas peur, Messieurs—questi birbánti Spagniuoli"* [97] (he seldom abused them in their native language, lest he should be over-heard) *"n'osent pas nous attaquer à forces égales."*

Poor *Damien!* many is the good laugh your fears have unconsciously occasioned us—many the joking bet the tuning up of the Piedmontese grenadiers' march has given rise to—and every note of which is at this moment as perfect in my recollection as when we traversed together the wild *puertas de Sanona*.

The town of Los Barrios, where we took up our quarters for the night, is twelve miles from Gibraltar. It is a small, open town, containing some 2000 souls, and, though founded only since the capture of Gibraltar, already shows sad symptoms of decay.

Being within a ride of the British garrison, it is frequently visited by its inmates, and two rival *posadas* dispute the honour of possessing the *golden fleece.* One of them, for a time, carried all before it, in consequence of the beauty of the *Donzella de la Casa*: [98] but beauty *will* fade, however unwillingly—as in this case—its possessor admits that it does; and the "fair maid of Los Barrios," who, when I first saw her, was really a very beautiful girl, had, at the period of my last visit, become a coarse, fat, middle-aged, *young woman*; and, as the charges for looking at her remained the same as ever, I proved a recreant knight, and went to the rival posada.

Nothing could well be more ludicrous than the contrast, in dress and appearance, between the beauty's mother and the beauty herself—unless, indeed, the visiter arrived very unexpectedly,—the one being dirty, slatternly, and clothed in old rags; the other, *muy bien peynado,* [99] and pomatumed, and decked in all the finery and ornaments presented by her numerous admirers. The old lady was excessively proud of her daughter's beauty and wardrobe; and in showing her off always reminded me of the *sin-par* [100] Panza's mode of speaking of his *Sanchita, una muchacha a quien crio para condesa.* [101]

The father of "the beauty" was a notorious *liberal*; and, having outraged the laws of his country on various occasions, was executed at Seville some years since. He was, I think, the most thorough-going leveller I ever met with—one who would not have sheathed the knife as long as any individual better off than himself remained in the country. Boasting to me on one occasion of the great deeds he had done during the war, he said that in one night he had despatched eleven French soldiers, who were quartered in his house. He effected his purpose by making them drunk, having previously drugged their wine to produce sleep. He put them to death with his knife as they lay senseless on the floor, carried them out into the yard, and threw them into a pit. The monster who could boast of such a crime would commit it if he had the opportunity; and though I suspect the number of his victims was exaggerated, yet I have no doubt whatever that he did not make himself out to be a murderer without some good grounds; and, I confess, it gave me very little regret to hear, a year or two afterwards, that he had perished on the scaffold.

The road to Sanona enters the mountains soon after leaving Los Barrios, ascending, for the first few miles, along the bank of the river Palmones. The scenery is very fine; huge masses of scarped and jagged sierras are tossed about in the most fantastic irregularity, whilst the valleys between are clad with a luxuriance of foliage that can be met with only in this prolific climate.

Looking back, the silvery Palmones may be traced winding between its wooded banks towards the bay of Gibraltar, which, viewed in this direction, has the appearance of a vast lake; the African shore, from Ape's Hill to the promontory of Ceuta, seeming to complete its enclosure to the south.

After proceeding some miles further, the road becomes a mere mule-track, and the country very wild and barren. The Piedmontese march had been gradually *crescendo* ever since leaving the cultivated valley of the Palmones, and Damien, as he rode on before us, had already given sundry yet more palpable intimations of impending danger, — firstly, by examining the priming of his old flint gun, — secondly, by trying whether the balls were rammed home, — and, lastly, by producing a brandy bottle from his capacious pocket; when, arrived at the foot of a peculiarly dreary and rocky pass, pulling up and dismounting from his horse, under pretence of tightening the girths of his saddle, he exclaimed, "*à present, Messieurs, es preciso cargar — ces lâches d'Espagnols viennent toujours a l'improviste, et se non siamo apparecchiati sarémo tutti inretati come tanti uccellini. — Somos todos muy bien armados con escopetas à dos cañones; y con juicio, no tendremos que temer — ma ... bisogna giudizio!*" [102] and in accordance with his wishes thus clearly expressed, we all loaded with ball, and, pushing on an advanced guard, boldly entered the rugged defile, joining our voices in grand chorus in the inspiriting grenadier's march.

On emerging from this rocky gorge, we entered a peculiarly wild and secluded valley, which, so completely is it shut out from all view, one might imagine, but for the narrow path under our feet, had never been trodden by man. The road winds round the heads of numerous dark ravines, crosses numberless torrents, that rush foaming from the impending sierra on the left, and is screened effectually from the sun by an impenetrable covering of oak and other forest-trees, festooned with woodbine, eglantine, and wild vines; whilst the valley below is clothed, from end to end, with cistus, broom, wild lavender, thyme, and other indigenous aromatic shrubs.

At the end of about three leagues, we reached the head of the valley, where one of the principal sources of the Palmones takes its rise. The neck of land that divides this stream from the affluents to the Celemin, is the pass of Sanona. From hence the *Casería* is visible, and a rapid descent of about a mile brought us to the door of the lone mansion.

Our arrival was announced to the inmates by a general salute from the countless dogs that invariably form part of a Spanish farmer's establishment. The horrid din soon brought forth the equally shaggy-coated bipeds, headed by a venerable-looking old man, who, with a slight recognition of Damien, stepped to the front, and, in a very dignified manner, announcing himself as the owner of the *Casería*, begged we would alight, and consider his house our own.

"My habitation is but a poor one, *Caballeros*; the accommodation it affords yet poorer. I wish for your sakes I had better to offer; but of this you may rest assured, that every thing *Luis de Castro* possesses, will ever be at the service of the brave nation who generously aided, and by whose side I have fought, to maintain the independence of my country." — "*Bravo, Don Luis!*" ejaculated Damien, which saved us the trouble of making a suitable speech in return.

We were much pleased with our host's appearance: indeed the shape of his cranium was itself sufficient to secure him the good opinion of all disciples of Spurzheim; but this feeling of gratification was by no means called forth by his *Casería*, from the outward inspection of which we judged the organ of accommodation to be wofully deficient.

The house and out-buildings formerly occupied a considerable extent of ground, but at the present day they are reduced to three sides of a small square, of which the centre building contains the dwelling apartments of the family, and the wings afford cover to the retainers, cattle, and farming implements. A stout wall completes the enclosure on the fourth side, wherein a wide folding gate affords the only means of external communication.

The *Casería* has long been possessed by the family of its present occupant, but, losing something of its importance at each succeeding generation, has dwindled down to its present insignificant condition. Don Luis strives hard, nevertheless, to keep up the family dignity of the De Castros, though joining with patriarchal simplicity in all the services, occupations, and pastimes, of his dependents.

The portion of the house reserved for himself and family consists but of two rooms on the ground-floor. The outer and larger of these serves the double purpose of a kitchen and refectory; the other is appropriated to the multifarious offices of a chapel, dormitory, henroost, and granary. In this inner room we were duly installed,—the lady de Castro, and other members of the family, removing into a neighbouring *choza* during our stay: and a sheet having been drawn over the Virgin and child, the cocks and hens driven from the rafters, and the Indian corn swept up into a corner, we found ourselves more *snugly* lodged than outward appearances had led us to expect.

Leaving our friend Damien to make what arrangements he pleased as to dinner—a discretional power that always afforded him infinite gratification—we proceeded to examine the "location," with a view of obtaining some notion of the country which was to be the scene of our next day's sporting operations.

The situation of the *Casería* is singularly romantic; to the north it is backed by a richly wooded slope, above which, at the distance of about half a mile, a rocky ledge of sierra rises perpendicularly several hundred feet, its dark outline serving as a fine relief to the rich and varied green tints of the forest. In the opposite direction, the house commands a view over a wide and partially wooded valley, along the bed of which the eye occasionally catches a glimpse of a sparkling stream, that is collected from the various dark ravines which break the lofty mountain-ridges on either side. A wooded range, steep, but of somewhat less elevation than the other mountains that the eye embraces, appears to close the mouth of this valley; but, winding round its foot to the right, the stream gains a narrow outlet to the extensive plain of Vejer, and empties itself into the *Laguna de la Janda*—a portion of which may be seen; and over this intermediate range rise, in the distance, the peaked summits of the *Sierra de la Plata*, whose southern base is washed by the Atlantic.

The beauty of the scenery, heightened by the broad shadows cast upon the mountains, and the varied tints that ever attend upon a setting sun in this Elysian atmosphere, had tempted us to continue roaming about, selecting the most favourable points of view, without once thinking of our evening meal; and when, at length, the sun disappeared behind the mountains, we found we had, unconsciously, wandered some considerable distance from the *Casería*. We forthwith bent our steps homewards, and, on drawing near the house, were not a little amused at hearing Damien's stentorian halloos to draw our attention, which were sent back to him in echoes from all parts of the *Serranía*. He was right glad to see us, though vexed at our extreme imprudence in wandering about the woods without an *escopeta*, or defensive weapon of any sort amongst us.

"*Messieurs, quand vous connoitrez ces gens çi aussi bien que moi— —!*"

We referred to Don Luis (who had come out with the intention of proceeding in search of us), whether there were any *mala gente* in the neighbourhood. A faint smile played about the old man's mouth as he looked towards Damien, as if guessing the source from which our interrogation had sprung, and, then waving his right hand to and fro, with the forefinger extended upwards, he replied, "*Por aqui Caballeros no hay mala gente alguna; esa Canalla conoce demasiado quien es Luis de Castro!*" [103]

On entering the house, we found a large party assembled round the charcoal fire, preparing to take their evening *gazpacho* [104] *caliente*; and, hot as had been the day, we gladly joined the circle, until our own more substantial supper should be announced. The group consisted of the wife, son, and daughter-in-law of our host, and several of his friends, who, living at a distance, had come overnight, to be ready to take part in the *batida* on the following morning.

A *batida* bears so strong a resemblance to the same sort of thing common in Germany, and indeed in some parts of Scotland, that a very detailed account of one would be uninteresting to most of my readers. We turned out at daybreak, and, recruited by the neighbouring peasantry, found that we mustered twenty-three guns, and dogs innumerable, mostly of a kind called by the Spaniards *podencos*, for which the most appropriate term in our language is lurcher; though that does not altogether express the strong-made, wiry-haired dog used by the Spaniards on these occasions.

As the *camas* [105] about Sanona are very wide, and require a number of guns to line them, only eleven of the men could be spared for beaters. These were placed under the direction of Alonzo, our host's son, whilst Don Luis himself took command of the sportsmen in the quality of *capitan*; and his first order was to prohibit all squibbing off of guns, by which the game might be disturbed.

The two parties, on leaving the house, took different directions. Our's, after proceeding about a mile, was halted, and enjoined to form in rank entire, and keep perfectly silent. We then ascended a steep, thickly coppiced hill, and were placed in position along its crest, at intervals of about a hundred yards, with directions to watch the openings through the underwood in our front—to screen ourselves from observation as well as we could—not to stir from the spot until the signal was made to retire—and to observe carefully the position of our fellow sportsmen on either side, to prevent accidents.

We were much amused at the manner in which Don Luis—to whom we were all perfect strangers—selected us to occupy the different approaches to the position. Scanning us over from right to left, and from head to foot, he seemed to pick and choose his men as if perfectly aware of the peculiar qualities each possessed, befitting him for the situation in which he purposed placing him; and, beckoning the one selected out of the rank, without uttering a word he led him to the assigned post, pointed out the various openings in the underwood, and gave his final instructions in a low whisper.

On leaving me he pointed to a narrow passage between two huge blocks of rock, and in a low voice said "*Lobo;*" [106] which, I must confess, made me look about for a tree, as a secure position to fall back upon, in the event of my fire failing to bring the expected visiter to the ground.

The position we occupied had a deep ravine in front, a wide valley on one flank, and a precipitous wall of rock on the other; but, as the event proved, it was far too extended. Thus posted, we remained for a considerable time, and I began to think very meanly of the sport, especially as I did not much like to withdraw my eyes from the rocky pass where the wolf was to be looked for; but at length the distant shouts of the beaters resounded through the mountains, and a few minutes after, the faint but true-toned yelp of one of the hounds put me quite on the *qui vive*; and when, in a few seconds, other dogs gave tongue, and several shots were fired by the beaters (who are furnished with blank cartridge), giving the assurance that game had been sprung, a feeling of excitement was produced, that can, I think, hardly be equalled by any other description of sport.

The first gun from our own party almost induced me to rush forward and break the line; but, just at the moment, a rustling in the underwood drew my attention, and, looking up, I saw a fine buck "at gaze," as the heralds say, about thirty yards off, and exactly in the direction of the spot where I had seen my friend G—— posted.

The animal, with ears erect, was listening, in evident alarm, to the barking of the dogs; yet, from the shot just fired in his front, scarcely knowing on which side danger was most imminent. I was so screened by the underwood that he did not perceive me, and I could have shot him with the greatest ease—that is to say, had my nervous system been in proper trim,—but that the fear of killing my neighbour withheld me; so there I stood, with my gun at the first motion of the present, and there stood the deer, in just as great a *quandary*.

At length, losing all patience, I hallooed to my neighbour by name, hoping by his reply to learn whereabouts he was (for that he had moved from his post was evident), and, if possible, get a shot at the deer as he turned back, which I doubted not he would do. But, alas! my call produced no response, and the fine animal bounded forward, breaking through our line, and rendering it too hazardous for me to salute him with both barrels, as I had murderously projected.

Soon after the horn sounded for our reassembly. The *cama* [107] had been very unsuccessful. One deer only, besides that which visited me, had been driven through our line; the rest of the herd, and several wild boars, turned our position by its right, which was too extensive for the small number of guns. One of the Spaniards had shot a fox, which was all we had to show; and his companions shook their heads, considering it a bad omen, and that it was, indeed, likely to turn out "*una dia de zorras.*" [108]

On my relating the tantalizing dilemma in which I had been placed, old *Luis*, who felt somewhat sore at the signal failure of his generalship, declared we should have no sport if I stood upon such ceremony; adding, with much energy of manner, and addressing himself to the assembled party, "As soon as ever you see your game, *carajo! candela!*" [109] —a speech that reminded us forcibly of Suwarrow's reply to his Austrian coadjutor, when urging the prudence of a *reconnoissance* before undertaking some delicate operation, viz.—"*Poussez en avant—chargez à la bayonette—voilà mes reconnoissances.*"

The beaters were now directed to make a "wide cast," and, if possible, head the game that had escaped us, whilst we moved off to a fresh position, about half a mile in rear, and perpendicular to the former. This plan was pretty successful: we killed a wolf and two deer, but Don Luis was by no means satisfied.

It was now noon-day, and, ascending a rocky ledge that projects into the wide valley, already described as lying in front of the house, we obtained a splendid panoramic view of the whole wooded district of Sanona. We found, on gaining the summit, that the provident Damien had directed a *muchacho* to meet us there, with a mule-load of provender, which he was pleased to call "*un petit peu de rafraichissement.*" We were quite prepared to acknowledge our sense of his foresight and discretion in the most unequivocal manner; for the exertion of climbing the successive mountain-ridges, and forcing our way through the underwood, as well as the excitement of the sport, had given a keen edge to our appetites.

Whilst seated in a convivial circle, smoking our cigars at the conclusion of our repast, we observed that poor Alonzo—who, though a stoutly built, was a very sickly-looking man—appeared to be quite exhausted from the heat and fatigue of the day, and that poor old Luis looked from time to time on his son, as he lay full-length upon the ground, with a heart-rending expression of grief.

One of our party remarked to him, that Alonzo did not appear to be well, and suggested that he had better not exert himself further. Don Luis shook his head. "Alas! señor!" he replied, "my poor Alonzo is as well as ever he again will be. But do not suppose that he is a degenerate scion of the De Castros; nor even that I regret seeing him in his present state. No: much as I once wished to see the family name handed down to another generation—of which there is now no chance—I would rather, much rather, that he should have sacrificed his health—his life indeed—for his country, than that any vain wish of mine should be gratified."

Our curiosity excited by the words, and yet more by the manner of the old man, we ventured, after some little preamble, to ask what had occasioned the change in his son that his speech implied.

"It is a long story, *caballeros*," he answered; "but, as the sun is now too powerful to allow us to resume our sport, I will, if you feel disposed to listen to a garrulous old man, relate the circumstances that led to my son's being reduced to the lamentable state in which you see him." We contracted the circle round Don Luis, the Spaniards, apparently, quite as intent on hearing the thrice-told tale as ourselves; and Damien, though still busily occupied at his "*rafraichissement*," also lending an attentive ear.

The fine old man was seated on a rock, elevated somewhat above the rest of the party, holding in his right hand his uncouth-looking fowling-piece, whilst the other rested on the head of a favourite dog, that came, seemingly, to beg his master to remonstrate with Damien for using his teeth to tear off the little flesh that remained on a ham-bone.

Don Luis, after patting the impatient favourite on the head and bidding him lie down, thus began his story.

CHAPTER IX
LUIS DE CASTRO

"Tiene este caso un no sé que de sombra de adventura de Caballeria." —Don Quijote.

I need not tell enlightened Englishmen—commenced Don Luis—that the name I bear is no common one. The Casería which you there see, and all the shady glens we here look down upon, were granted to the renowned De Castro, whose valour so materially aided the Catholic kings, of blessed memory, in the pious work of extirpating the vile followers of the Arabian Impostor from the soil of Spain; and the patrimony thus acquired by my ancestor's sword has been handed down from generation to generation to me,—too likely, alas! to be the last of the race to inherit it.

I married early in life, and was blessed with several children. Alonzo, the first-born, was the only one permitted to reach maturity,—but I repine not. They were all healthy, and every thing a parent could wish. Years rolled on unmarked by any events of importance. Our days were passed in attending to our herds; our evenings, in singing and dancing to the notes of the wild guitar. Our festivals were devoted to the exhilarating sport we have this morning been following; nor did we, amidst our happiness, neglect to offer up our thanks to the Omnipotent Deity, who,—through the propitiating influence of our patron saints—was pleased to pour his blessings upon us.

But a storm arose, which, for a time, shook our happy country to its foundation. Spain became the object of a vile tyrant's insatiable ambition. The perfidious Corsican, under the specious plea of friendship, marched his licentious legions into our devoted country: and having, by shameless deceit, first possessed himself of all our strongholds, threw off the mask, and treated us as a conquered nation.

This favoured province was, for some considerable time saved from the desolation that wasted the rest of Spain, by the heroism of one of her sons:—the brave Castaños hastened to place himself at the head of the national troops, and in the defiles of the Sierra Morena, captured a whole French army. But jealousy and intrigue—the greatest enemies our country had to contend against—caused his services to be requited with ingratitude.

Another French army advanced, but we had not another Castaños to oppose it. The enemy forced the barriers with which nature and art had defended the province, and, like a swarm of locusts, spread over and consumed the rich produce of its fertile fields.

The mountaineers of Ronda and Granada, engaged in the vile contraband trade which the disorganized state of the country favoured, were slow to take up arms against the invaders, but "*Io y mi gente*" (I and my people) were early in the field, harassing their parties conveying supplies to the siege of Cadiz, as well as protecting the surrounding country from their predatory visits; and our secluded *Casería* afforded a secure retreat to the inhabitants of the plain, when forced to abandon their hearths.

I will not take up your time with the account of the various encounters we had with the enemy—they are well known throughout the Serranía—but will confine my narrative to what more particularly concerns my son.

On one occasion, fortune presented him with an opportunity of saving a party of the king's troops, who had got entangled in the intricacies of the Serranía; his knowledge of the country having enabled him to lead them clear of their pursuers, and bring them safely to the *Casería*.

Disappointed of the prey they had so confidently calculated upon, and uneasy at a body of disciplined troops being added to our *guerilla*, and established so close to them, the enemy determined on sending a large force to root us out of our fastness. We, on our parts, hoping that the French were unconscious of the place where the troops had found a refuge, were meditating an attack upon their post of Alcalà, when the storm burst suddenly upon our heads, and, but for the devotedness and presence of mind of my gallant son, would have involved us all in one common destruction.

Alonzo had gone off to reconnoitre in the direction of Tarifa, a rumour having reached us that the enemy had invested that place; and we were anxiously awaiting his return to decide upon our plans, when, soon after nightfall, a lad belonging to the *Venta de Tabilla* arrived at the *Casería* on my son's horse, and in hurried words, informed me that a large body of French troops was advancing upon the house.

The enemy had forced this lad,—who alone had been left in charge of the *Venta*,—to be their guide, and he had already conducted them across the swamps at the head of the *Laguna de la Janda*, and was within a hundred yards of the road leading from Tarifa to Casa Vieja—by keeping along which to the left, he purposed gaining the shortest road into our sequestered valley—when Alonzo crossed the path immediately in front of them.

From what we learnt afterwards it appeared, that he had been for some time watching the enemy's movements, and, guessing from the direction they had finally taken, whither they were bound, had thus purposely thrown himself in their way; resolved—cut off as he found himself from the shortest road to the *Casería*—to take this hazardous step to save us from a surprise.

On being questioned as to his knowledge of the country, he at once offered to guide them to the *Casería*. "This is your way," he said, pointing in the direction, whence he had just come, "but yonder is my house," motioning with his head towards the *Cortijo de le las Habas*; which, though about half a mile off, was yet visible in the dusk; "I will send my jaded horse home by the boy, and accompany you on foot."

The commanding officer, to whom this was addressed, made no objection; in fact, he probably thought that their guide would be more in their power without his horse.

Alonzo gave his beast to the lad, saying significantly, "*Juanillo*, tell my father I have fallen in with some friends and shall not be at home for some little time; be quick; make your way back to the venta without delay, as soon as you have delivered my message; and, as you value your life,—no babbling."

My son then turned off to the right, taking the best but far the most circuitous route into the valley of Sanona, whilst *Juanillo*, putting his horse into a canter, proceeded in the direction of the *Cortijo de las Habas*, but, ere reaching it, struck into the difficult pass you see below there, whence a rude foot-path leads direct to the *Casería*, and by which he had intended to conduct the enemy.

It seemed to us—what indeed proved to be the case—that my son's message was intended to hint to us the necessity for flight, and *Juanillo's* account of the number of the enemy, would fully have warranted our avoiding an encounter; but, thinking Alonzo's life would surely pay the forfeit of our escape, we determined to anticipate their attack and give him a chance of saving himself.

Prudence suggested the propriety of sending away our women and children. Mounting them, therefore, on *borricos*, we hurried them off by the mountain path to the *Casa de Castañas*, or *de las Navas*, as it is otherwise called, from the name of its proprietor—a solitary house, situated in a wooded valley, several miles to the north of Sanona.

The women had scarcely left the *Casería*, ere we heard the distant tramp of horses in the valley below. Leaving a part of the soldiers to defend the house, I led the rest, and my own people, out as silently as possible, and posted them on the upper side of the path by which the French were advancing. The enemy halted directly under the muzzles of our guns, and a corporal and two dragoons were sent on to the house to ask for a night's lodging.

Nothing could be more favourable than the opportunity now presented for attacking them, but I hesitated to give the word until I had discovered my son, anxious as well to give him a chance of escape, as to save him from our own fire. At last I recognised him: he was standing at the side of the commander of the party, who, with a pistol in his hand, was questioning him in a low tone of voice.

The corporal now thundered at the gate of the *Casería*. "*Quien es?*" demanded the soldiers from within. I listened to no more; for, observing that the commander's attention was for the moment attracted to the proceedings of his advanced guard, and that Alonzo, in consequence, was comparatively out of his reach, "*Candela!*" I cried out to my people, directing, at the same time, my own unerring rifle at the head of the French captain.

Twenty guns answered to the word. The commander of the enemy fell headlong to the earth; his horse sprung violently off the ground, reared, staggered, and fell back; a dozen Frenchmen bit the dust; the rest turned and fled, ere we could reload our pieces.

I pressed forward to embrace my brave son, but saw him not. I called him by name, but a faint groan was the only reply I received. I turned in the direction of the sound, and found the Frenchman's horse, struggling in the agonies of death, upon the bleeding body of my Alonzo. He had been wounded in the breast by the Frenchman's pistol, the trigger of which had, apparently, been pressed in the convulsive movement occasioned by his death-wound. The horse had been shot by one of our men, had fallen upon Alonzo, and broken several of his ribs. We conveyed him to the house, without a hope of his recovery.

In the excess of my grief, I thought not of sending after the women. Alonzo was the first to bring me to a sense of my remissness, by enquiring for his wife and child. I expressed my joy at hearing him speak, for he had lain many hours speechless. He pressed my hand, and added, "Father, I wish to see them once again before I die—to have a mother's blessing also—for I feel my end approaching."

I instantly despatched four of my people to the *Casa de Castañas* to escort them back, for I recollected that the three Frenchmen who had been sent forward to demand admission to the house, had effected their escape, and must be, wandering about the mountains.

The sun had risen some hours, and yet no tidings reached us of them. I began to feel very uneasy. A terrible presentiment disturbed me. I went to the iron cross that stands on the mound in front of our house, whence a view is obtained of the pass leading to *Las Navas*. I heard a wild scream, that pierced my very soul, and the moment after, caught a glimpse of a female figure, hastening with mad speed down the rocky path leading to the *Casería*. It was my daughter-in-law, Teresa!

"See," she exclaimed, with frantic exultation, showing me her hands stained with blood, "see—I killed him! my knife pierced the heart of the murderer of my child! I killed the vile Frenchman! The wife of a De Castro ever carries a knife to avenge her wrongs—to defend her honour!"

That some terrible catastrophe had happened was too evident, but from the unhappy maniac it was impossible to gather any thing definite.

I mounted my horse, and rode with the speed of desperation towards the *Casa de Castañas*, but had not proceeded far ere I met my people returning, bearing my wife on a litter, and accompanied by two only of the women who had accompanied her, mounted on *borricos*.

"Dead?" I asked. It was the only word I could utter.

"No, Luis," replied one of my faithful followers, "not dead, and, we hope, not even seriously hurt; but evil has befallen your house—your three young children and your grandson are lost to you for ever."

"Lost! murdered? This is, indeed, a heavy blow, a severe trial. Perhaps I am now childless;—God's will be done."

"Proceed gently to the *Casería* with your burthen; I will hasten forward, and send assistance, and such cordials as may be required to restore my Ana."

On my return I was surprised to see Alonzo sitting up, and his wife at his bedside. I cannot describe the joy of that moment; but there was a fearful expression of determination in my son's contracted brows, that almost led me to fear for his mind. He turned to me for explanation, but as yet I could give him none. The party shortly arrived, however, and the women gave us a full account of the overwhelming disaster that had befallen us.

On leaving the *Casería* they had proceeded with such speed as the darkness of the night permitted, towards the *Casa de Castañas*, and had reached within a quarter of a league of the house, when the trampling of horses behind them, spread the greatest alarm amongst these defenceless females. It was clear that those who were in pursuit could not be their friends, otherwise they would call to them to return; and concluding therefore, that the enemy had prevailed at the *Casería*, naturally considered their danger imminent.

My wife and daughter-in-law, with their children, and three of the women, being well mounted, pressed forward to the solitary house for shelter; the others, finding the Frenchmen—whom they could now hear conversing—gaining rapidly upon them, with more good fortune took to the woods; and, as we eventually learnt, reached Los Barrios in safety.

On arriving at the *Casa de Castañas*, it was found to be totally abandoned. They had barely time to close the outer gate, and shut themselves up in a loft,—that could be ascended only by a ladder, and through a trap-door, which they let fall—before their pursuers rode up to the house. At first the Frenchmen civilly demanded admission; but this being refused, they—guessing, probably, how the case stood, from none but female voices replying to their demands—proceeded to threaten to force an entrance.

My daughter-in-law, who speaks a few words of French, then appeared at the window; told them it was an abandoned house, and contained absolutely nothing, not even refreshment for their horses; that, by keeping down the valley to the left, they would, in less than an hour, reach the *Hermita of El Cuervo*, where they would find all they might stand in need of.

The beauty of her who addressed them—for in those days my daughter-in-law was a lovely young woman of eighteen—awakened the most lawless of passions in these ruthless profligates. Affecting, however, to disbelieve her statement of the unprovided condition of the house, they forced open the outer gate, and, after vainly endeavouring to persuade the terrified females to descend from their place of refuge, collected all the straw and other combustible articles that were scattered about the premises, in the apartment beneath, and threatened to set fire to the house.

In vain was appeal made to their clemency, to the boasted gallantry of their nation, to every honourable feeling that inhabits the breast of man. And at length, exasperated at the determination of these devoted women, and possibly—it is a compliment I am willing to pay human nature—thinking that a little smoke would soon induce them to descend, the reckless monsters fired the straw. The whole building was quickly enveloped in flames.

For some minutes the unhappy beings above thought that the straw, being damp, would not ignite so as to communicate with the wooden rafters of the floor which supported them, and hoped that they were free from danger; but the smoke which ascended soon, of itself, became intolerable.

Two of my children dropped on the floor from the effects of suffocation; and one of women, taking her infant in her arms, jumped from the window and was killed on the spot.

My daughter-in-law, seeing that for herself there was but a choice of death,—for the flames had now burst through the crackling floor,—determined to make an effort to save her child. Pressing him to her bosom, and covering him with her shawl to protect him from the flames in her descent, she lifted the trap-door and placed her foot upon the ladder. The fire had yet spared the upper steps, but ere she reached the bottom the charred wood gave way, and she fell. The child escaped from her arms and rolled amongst the blazing straw; she started upon her feet to save him, but the rude hand of one of the ruffians seized and dragged her from the flames into the court-yard. Vainly she implored to be allowed to go to the rescue of her helpless infant; the monster—even at such a moment looking upon his victim with the eyes of lust—would not listen to her heart-rending appeals. The agonizing screams of her writhing offspring gave her superhuman strength; she seized her knife; plunged it deep in the Frenchman's breast; and, released from his paralyzed arms, rushed back into the flames.

Alas! it was too late—nothing but the blackened skeleton now remained of her darling child.

She darted, with the fury of a tigress robbed of its young, upon one of the other Frenchmen, but he disarmed her, and, with a returning feeling of humanity, forbore inflicting any further injury upon the frantic woman; and, after some apparent altercation with his companion, both mounted their horses and rode away. They were just in time to make their escape, as the four men I had despatched rode up to the front gate of the house, as they went off by the other.

One of my people was an inhabitant of the *Casa de Castañas*, and knowing the premises, quickly brought a ladder from a place of concealment, and applied it to the window of the burning portion of the building. My wife and the other two women were brought down safely, though all more or less scorched, but the floor gave way before the children, who were lying in an insensible state from suffocation, could be removed.

I despatched an indignant remonstrance to the French general, on the inhuman conduct of his troops towards helpless women and children; and threatened, if the perpetrators were not signally punished, to hang every one of his countrymen that might fall into my hands, but he never deigned to answer my letter.

Some weeks elapsed after these events, ere Alonzo could leave his couch; and the enemy seemed now so fully occupied in pressing the siege of Cadiz, that we were led to believe they entertained no idea of paying the *Casería* a second visit.

Want of provisions, and still more of ammunition, had hitherto prevented our being of much service, in harassing the enemy during their operations; but, having obtained supplies from Algeciras, I determined to follow up my remonstrance with a blow, and mustering all our strength, to make an attempt to carry the enemy's post at *Casa Vieja*.

For this purpose I fixed on the *Casa de Castañas* for the general rendezvous; that spot being more conveniently situated than Sanona, for those who were to join our ranks from Castellar, Ximena, and other places, and equally as near the projected point of attack.

At the appointed day, I proceeded with my people to the place of concentration. Alonzo had insisted on accompanying us, though yet hardly able to cross a horse; but he thirsted for the blood of the destroyers of his child and brothers. On reaching the *Casa de Castañas*, however, his strength failed him, and he was obliged to remain there.

Leaving *Pepito*, who sits there, then a beardless boy, to tend upon Alonzo, and accompany him back to Sanona on the morrow, we departed on our expedition.

The chapel and few houses which compose the village of *Casa Vieja*, are situated on the brow of a high hill overlooking a wide plain, watered by the river Barbate. Not a bush interrupts the view for several miles in any direction, so that to approach the place some circumspection was requisite. I halted my men in the woods bordering the Celemin—on the very spot, perhaps, where Muley Aben Hassan, King of Granada, fixed his camp, when he sallied forth from Malaga to plunder the estates of the Duke of Medina Sidonía—and sent one of my most trustworthy followers on to reconnoitre, purposing, if a favourable report was received, to make an attack at the point of day, trusting to the shadows of night to conceal our march across the open plain.

Our scout returned only a couple of hours before dawn. He had experienced much difficulty in fording the Barbate, which was swollen by recent rains. He brought us the startling news, that a considerable French force had left Alcalá de los Gazules, the preceding day, to penetrate into the mountains, and was now probably in our rear, either at the *Casa de Castañas* or at Sanona.

It was necessary to fall back immediately. We were at the fork of the roads leading from those two places to *Casa Vieja*, but on which should we direct our march? My heart whispered, to the former, where my Alonzo, the last of my race, was left defenceless; but the wives and families of my companions were all at Sanona, and duty bade me hasten thither for their protection. The struggle of my feelings was severe, but short. I sent a trusty friend on a swift horse to save Alonzo, if time yet permitted, and hurried the march of my troop to the *Casería*. We reached it in three hours.

We found every thing as we had left it. Those who had remained there had neither seen nor heard anything of the enemy, but my son had not returned home. I now regretted not having proceeded to the *Casa de Castañas*, and proposed to my wearied men to march on and attack the *Gavachos* in their passage through the passes, fully expecting they would now direct their steps to the *Casería*. They acceded to my proposal with *vivas*. A cup of wine and a mouthful of bread were given to each, and we were off.

We had not yet gained the pass yonder, at the back of the house, when we met the man I had sent to the *Casa de Castañas*, coming towards us at full speed. He informed us that he had encountered the French when on his way to *Las Navas*, directing their march towards *Casa Vieja*. Fortunately escaping their observation, he had concealed himself in a thicket whilst they passed. *Pepito*—whom, it will be recollected, I had left with Alonzo—was walking by the side of one of their officers, undergoing a strict examination respecting our movements, &c. They had several other prisoners in charge, who were tied together in couples, but he could not distinguish Alonzo amongst them. My son's favourite dog, *Hubilon*, however, brought up the rear, led by one of the marauders; and the faithful creature's oft-averted head and restive attempts to escape, sufficiently proved that his master had been left behind.

Under this conviction, he had pushed on to the *Casa de Castañas* as soon as the enemy were out of sight, and had thoroughly searched every part of the building; but not a living being did it contain. The pigeons even had deserted it, or, more probably, had been sacrificed, for feathers and bones were scattered about on all sides, the smoke of numerous fires darkened the white-washed walls, and the stains of wine were left on the stone pavement, proving that the house had lately been the scene of a deep carouse.

From this account, it was evident that the Frenchmen had marched upon our track in the hope of taking us between two fires, and it was most fortunate we had returned to Sanona, instead of falling back upon the *Casa de Castañas*; for the superiority of their number, in a chance encounter, would have given them every advantage.

It was probable that the enemy would now continue their pursuit in hopes of taking us by surprise at Sanona; we countermarched immediately therefore, and passing the *Casería*, took up a strong position about two miles beyond it, on the road to *Casa Vieja*, where we waited for the enemy.

We were not mistaken in our supposition, for scarcely were my men posted, when the French advance appeared in sight. I allowed them to approach to within pistol shot, and gave them a volley. My men were scattered among the bushes, so that the extent of our fire made our force appear much larger than it was in reality. We killed and wounded several.

The enemy paused, and seeing by their numbers that if they pushed boldly on, resistance on our parts would be vain, I determined to try and intimidate them; and taking for this purpose eight or ten active fellows, we made our way through the brushwood which covered the hill side on our left, and opened a flank fire upon the main body of the enemy; who, imagining a fresh column had come to take part in the action, fell back in some confusion to a place of greater security, and one where they had more space to deploy their strength.

We had effectually succeeded in frightening them, however, and no further attempt was made to force our position; but it was not until the next day that they finally left the mountains and retired to their fortified posts of Casa Vieja and Alcalà.

No sooner had I seen them fairly out of the Serranía, than I retraced my steps with all possible speed to Sanona; still indulging the fond hope that Alonzo might have made his escape and reached home; but, disappointed in this expectation, I proceeded on without loss of time to the *Casa de Castañas*.

I had scarcely entered the house ere I was greeted by "*Hubilon,*" — ay, my good dog, said Don Luis, caressing his pet, your grandsire — who evidently had come on the same errand as myself. But our search was fruitless. The well, the vaults, the lofts and out-houses, every place, was ransacked, but I discovered nothing to lead to the belief that Alonzo had either been left there or been murdered. I mounted my horse to return home, and had proceeded some little way, when I heard the howl of *Hubilon*. Thinking I had inadvertently shut him in the house, I sent back one of my companions to release him, but he returned, saying that the dog would not leave the spot. I returned myself, but the sagacious animal was not to be enticed away; he gave evident signs of pleasure at seeing me, and began scratching furiously at the boarded floor of one of the interior apartments. I approached to see what it was that excited his attention, and discovered a trap door. With some little difficulty I raised it up, and *Hubilon* instantly leapt into the dark abyss. His piteous whining soon informed me that he had found the body of his master; a light was struck; I let myself down, and on the stone floor of the cold, damp vault lay the body of my unfortunate son; his hands were tied behind his back, and a handkerchief was drawn across his mouth to stifle his cries!

To me it appeared that the spirit of my Alonzo had long left its earthly tenement, but the affectionate brute, by licking his master's face, proved that life was not yet entirely extinct. Assisted by my companions, I lifted my son out of the noxious vault, and, by friction, a dram of *aguadiente*, and exposure to the sun and a purer atmosphere, animation was gradually restored; and in the course of a few days he was able to bear the journey home; but from the effects of this confinement he has never recovered.

He had no recollection of any of the circumstances which preceded his incarceration. A raging fever, brought on by fatigue and exposure to the sun in his previously weak state, had affected his brain, as well as deprived him of all strength. But *Pepito* (who rejoined us a few days after,) stated, that Alonzo himself, in his delirium, had declared to the French on their arrival, who he was, and had besought them to put an end to his sufferings. The superior officer of the party had directed, however, that he should not be ill-treated; "what if he be the son of the *old wild boar*?" (the name by which they honoured me,) said he to his men; "we came not to murder our enemies in cold blood—carry him into the house and let him die in peace."

Pepito guessed by the malignant glance of one Italian-looking scoundrel— "I ask your pardon, Señor Damien," said Don Luis, in a parenthesis; "*servitore umilissimo*," replied he of the *Val d'Aosta.—Pépé* guessed, I say, by the look that he who stepped forward to execute the orders of his officer gave one of his companions, whom he invited to assist him, that their superior's humane intentions would not be fulfilled; he begged hard, therefore, to be allowed to remain and wait upon his young master. "Impossible," replied the officer, "you must be our guide."

The two men were absent but a few minutes, and then came out of the house and informed the officer that they had placed the rebel chief in the coolest place they could find; probably their fear of Alonzo's cries had deterred them from killing him outright.

The abominable cruelties of these dastards exasperated every one. The expedition which was at this time undertaken to raise the siege of Cadiz promised to afford us a favourable opportunity of taking vengeance; but the cowardice of a Spaniard—the cowardice, if not treason, of a Spanish general—marred our fair prospects. The glorious field of Barrosa decked with fresh laurels the brows of our brave allies; but, to this day, the very name fills the breast of every loyal Spaniard with shame. Oh! that I and my people had been thereto share the danger and glory of that day; but we fulfilled with credit the part allotted to us. In the plan adopted by the allied generals it was settled that the *Serraños*, should make a diversion in the direction of *Casa Vieja* and *Alcalà de los Gazules*, to draw the enemy's attention on that side, whilst their combined forces should proceed along the coast to Chiclana; accordingly *io y mi gente*....

CHAPTER X

THE old man, excited by the stirring recollections of the eventful times to which his narrative referred, his eyes sparkling with animation, and his words flowing somewhat more rapidly than in their wonted even current, had risen from his rocky seat, and, having transferred his fowling-piece to the left hand, was standing with his right arm extended in the direction of the scene of his former exploits, when he suddenly dropt his voice, and, after slowly, and, as it appeared to us, abstractedly, repeating his favourite expression, "*Io y mi gente,*" he ceased altogether to speak, and appeared transfixed to the spot. His right arm remained stretched out towards Cadiz, and his head was turned slightly to one side, but the only motion perceptible was a tightening of the fingers round the barrel of his long gun.

As if from the effect of sympathy, Damien's jaws—which for the last hour had been keeping *Hubilon* in a state of tantalization, threatening to produce St. Vitus's dance—suddenly became equally motionless; his huge proboscis was turned on one side for a moment to allow free access to his left ear, and then starting up he exclaimed, "*Javali! cospetto!*" [110]

"*Quiet ... o!*" said Don Luis, in an undertone, at the same time motioning Damien to resume his seat, "*Si, es una puerca.*" [111] And then making signs to his men, they rose without a word, and went stealthily off down the hill.

We now distinctly heard the grunting of a pig, and were hastily distributed in a semicircle, along the crest of the steep ridge we had selected for our resting-place. We had scarcely got into position before the cries of the beaters, and several shots fired in rapid succession, gave us notice that they had come in sight of the chase; but the sounds died away, and we were beginning to speak to each other in terms of disappointment, when a loud grunt announced the vicinity of a visiter. Hearing our voices, however, he went off at a tangent, and attempted to cross the ridge lower down; but this was merely, as the Spaniards say, "*Escapar del trueno y dar en el relampago:*" [112] a sharp fire there opened upon him, and after various trips he was fairly brought to the ground. Our *couteaux de chasse* were instantly brandished, but the grisly monster, recovering himself quickly, once more got into a long trot, and, most probably, would have effected his escape, but that he was encountered and turned back by some of the dogs. Finding himself thus pressed on all sides by enemies, he again attempted to force the line of sportsmen, and a second time was made to bite the dust. He managed, nevertheless, to recover himself once more, and might, even yet possibly, have got away from us but for the dogs, which hung upon and detained him until some of the beaters came up and despatched him with their knives; not, however, until he had killed one dog outright, and desperately gored two others. The dogs showed extraordinary *pluck* in attacking him.

On examining the huge monster, we found he had received no less than four bullets: two in the neck, and two in the body. A fire was immediately kindled, and, having been singed, to destroy the vermin about him, he was decorated with laurel and holly, placed on the back of a mule, and, with the rest of our spoils, sent off to the *Casería*.

The beaters informed us, that they had seen the wild sow and four young ones, which Don Luis had sent them after; but that they had made off through the wooded valley to the right, ere they could succeed in heading and turning them up the hill.

It was decided that we should proceed immediately after them, and leave the conclusion of Don Luis's tale for the charcoal fire-circle in the evening; but, as the rest of his story related principally to events that are well known, and was all "*Santiago y cierra España,*" [113] I will spare my readers the recital.

The rest of the day's sport was poor, but the grand and ever-varying mountain scenery was of itself an ample reward for the fatigue of scrambling up the steep braes. Towards sunset we retraced our steps, thoroughly tired, to the *Casería*. Damien, mounting a stout mule, rode on to prepare dinner, saying, "*Messieurs, sans doute, désireront goûter du chevreuil de Sanone; vado avanti con questo motivo, e subito, subito, all red-dy*"; [114] and, digging his heels into the animal's side, he thereupon started off at a jog-trot, his huge feet sticking out at right angles, like the paddle-boxes of a steamer, the smoke of a cigar rolling away from his mouth, like the clouds from the steamer's tall black funnel.

On the following morning we departed from Sanona, taking the road to Casa Vieja, and sending our game into Gibraltar.

Don Luis would on no account receive any remuneration for the use of his house, &c.; and a very moderate sum satisfied the beaters he had engaged for us.

The distance to Casa Vieja is about twelve miles, the country wild and beautiful; but the view, after gaining a high pass, about three miles from Sanona, is confined to the valley along which the road thenceforth winds, until it reaches the river Celemin. This stream is frequently rendered impassable by heavy rains. Emerging now from the woods and mountains, the road soon reaches the Barbate, which river, though running in a broad and level valley, is of a like treacherous character as the Celemin.

The little chapel and hamlet, whither we were directing our steps, now became visible, being situated under the brow of a high hill on the opposite bank of the river, and distant about a mile and a half. The road across the valley is very deep in wet weather, and the Barbate is often so swollen, as to render it necessary, in proceeding from Casa Vieja to the towns to the eastward, to make a wide circuit to gain the bridges of Vejer or Alcalà de los Gazules.

We "put up" at the house of the village priest, which adjoins the chapel. Indeed the portion of his habitation allotted to our use was under the same roof as the church, and communicated with it by a private door; and I have been credibly informed that, on some occasions, when the party of sportsmen has been large, beds have been made up within the consecrated walls of the chapel itself, whereon some of the visiters have stretched their wearied heretical limbs and rested their *aching* heads. In our case there was no occasion to lead the *Padre* into the commission of such a sin, since the small apartment given up to us was just able to contain four stretchers, in addition to a large table.

The priest was another "*amigo mio de mucha aprec'ion*" [115] of Señor Damien. Their friendship was based upon the most solid of all foundations — mutual interest; for, it being an understood thing that the accommodation, and whatever else we might require, was to be paid for at a fixed rate, both parties were interested in prolonging our stay: the *Padre*, to gain wherewith to shorten the pains of purgatory, either for himself or others; Damien, simply because he liked shooting better than even baking in this world.

To us also this was an agreeable arrangement, since it granted us a dispensation from all ceremony in ordering whatever we wanted, and gave us also the privilege of making the Padre's house our home as long as we pleased. Accordingly, finding the sport good, we passed several days here very pleasantly. The snipe and duck shooting in the marshes bordering the Barbate is excellent; francolins, bustards, plover, and partridges, are to be met with on the table-lands to the westward of the village; and the woods towards Alcalà and Vejer abound, at times, in woodcocks.

An adventure befel me during our short stay at Casa Vieja, which I relate, as affording a ludicrous exemplification of the power of flattery—an openness to which, that is to say, vanity, is certes the great foible of the Spanish character.

I had devoted one afternoon to a solitary ride to Vejer, (which town is about eleven miles from Casa Vieja,) and had proceeded some little distance on my way homewards, when, observing a very curious bird on a marshy spot by the road-side, I dismounted—knowing my pony would not stand fire—to take a shot at it. The gun missed fire, as I expected it would; for, in consequence of its owner not having been able to discharge it during the whole morning, I had lent him mine to visit the snipe-marsh, and taken his to bear me company on my ride. The explosion of the detonating cap was enough, however, to frighten my pony; he started—jerked the bridle off my arm—and, finding himself free, trotted away towards Casa Vieja.

I ran after him for some distance, fondly hoping that the tempting green herbage on the road-side would induce him to stop and taste, but my accelerated speed had only the effect of quickening his; from a trot he got into a canter, from a canter into a gallop; and, panting and perspiring, I was soon obliged to abandon the chase, and trust that the animal's natural sagacity would take him back to his stable.

I had long lost sight of the runaway—for a thick wood soon screened him from my view,—and had arrived within four miles of Casa Vieja, when I met a party of very suspicious-looking characters, who, under the pretence of being itinerant *wine-merchants*, were carrying contraband goods about the country. They were all very noisy; all, seemingly, very tipsy; and most of them armed with guns and knives.

The van was led by a fat Silenus-looking personage, clothed in a shining goatskin, and seated on a stout ass, between two well-filled skins of wine; who saluted me with a very gracious wave of the hand, evidently to save himself the trouble of speaking; but his followers greeted me with the usual *"Vaya usted con Dios;"* to which one wag added, in an undertone, *"y sin caballo,"* [116] —a piece of wit that put them all on the grin.

Regardless of their joke, I was about to make enquiries concerning my pony, which it was evident they knew something about, when I discovered a stout fellow, bringing up the rear of the party, astride of the delinquent. Considering the disparity of force, and aware of the unserviceable condition of my weapon, I thought it best to be remarkably civil, so informing the gentleman riding my beast that I was its owner, and extremely obliged to him for arresting the fugitive's course, I requested he would only give himself the further trouble of dismounting, and putting me in possession of my property.

This, however, he positively refused to do. "How did he know I was the owner? It might be so, and very possibly was, but I must go with him to Vejer, and make oath to the fact before *la Justicia*." This, I said, was out of the question: it was evident that the horse was mine, since I had claimed him the moment I had seen him; and as, by his own admission, he had found the animal, he must have done so out of my sight, since we were now in a thick wood. If, I added, he chose to return with me to Casa Vieja, the *Padre*, at whose house I was staying, would convince him of the truth of my statement, and I would remunerate him for his trouble. But I argued in vain! "If," he replied, "I felt disposed to give him an *onza*, [117] he would save *me* further trouble, but otherwise justice must take its course."

I remarked that the *haca* was not worth much more than a doubloon. "No!" exclaimed one of the party, jumping off his mule, thrusting his hand into his belt, and producing *two*, "I'll give you these without further bargaining."

This occasioned a laugh at my expense. I turned it off, however, by telling my friend, that if he would bring his money to Gibraltar we might possibly deal; but, as I had occasion for my pony to carry me back there, I could not at that moment conveniently part with him.

There seemed but slight chance, however, of my recovering my pony without trudging back to Vejer; and, probably, they would have ridden off, and laughed at me, after proceeding half way; or by paying a handsome ransom, which I was, in fact, unable to do, having only the value of a few shillings about me.

The dispute was getting warm, and my patience exhausted; for vain were my representations that the *haca could* belong to no one else—that the saddle, bridle, and even the very *tail* of the animal, were all English. The Don kept his seat, and coolly asked, whether I thought they could not make as good saddles, and cut as short tails, in Spain?

The party had halted during this altercation, and old Silenus, who, by his dress and position, seemed to be the head of the *firm*, had taken no part in the dispute. He appeared, indeed, to be so drowsy, as to be quite unconscious of what was passing. I determined, however, to make an appeal to him, and summoning the best Spanish I could muster to my aid, called upon him as a Spanish *hidalgo*, a man of honour, and a person of sense, as his appearance bespoke, to see justice done me.

He had heard, I continued, in fact he had *seen*, how the case stood; and was it to be believed that a foreigner travelling in Spain—perhaps the most enlightened country in the world—and trusting to the well-known national probity, should be thus shamefully plundered? An Englishman, above all others, who, having fought in the same ranks against a common enemy, looked upon every individual of the brave Spanish nation as a brother! Could a people so noted for honour, chivalry, gratitude, and every known virtue, be guilty of so bare-faced an imposition?

Oh, "flattery! delicious essence, how refreshing art thou to nature! how strongly are all its powers and all its weaknesses on thy side!"

"*Baj' usted!*" grunted forth Silenus to the man mounted on my pony, accompanying the words with a circular motion of his right arm towards the earth. "*Baj' usted luego!*" [118] repeated the irate leader in a louder tone, seeing that there was a disposition to resist his commands. "Mount your horse, caballero," he continued, turning to me, "you have not over-estimated the Spanish character."

I did not require a second bidding, but, vaulting into the vacated saddle, pushed my pony at once into a canter, replying to the man's application for something for his trouble, by observing, that I did not reward people for merely obeying the orders of their superiors; and, kissing my hand to the fat old Satyr, rode off, amidst the laughter occasioned by the discomfiture of the dismounted knight.

On the morning fixed for our departure from Casa Vieja, Damien came to us at a very early hour—a smile breaking through an assumed cloudy expression of countenance—to report that the Barbate was so swollen by the rain which had fallen without cessation during the night, as to be no longer fordable: "*Nous pouvons demeurer encore trois ou quatre jours,*" he added, "*car il nous reste de quoi manger—du thé, du sucre, du jambon, un bon morceau de bouilli de rosbif, et autres bagatelles; et comme il fait beau temps à présent, puede ser que havra una entrada de gallinetas esta noche—no es verdad Señor Padre?*" [119] turning to the priest, who had followed him into the room.

We were prepared for this contingency, however, and, stating that we *must* go, signified our intention of returning home by way of Alcalà de los Gazules. Damien was horror-struck. "*Corpo di Bacco! Messieurs, celle là est la plus mauvaise route du pays! è infestata di cattivissima gente, ad ogni passo. No es verdad, Don Diego, que esa trocha de Alcalà allà 'se llama el camino del infierno!*" "*Si, si,*" replied the priestly lodging-house keeper with a nod, "*tan verdad como la Santa Escritura.*" [120]

Finding, however, that we were bent on departing, Don Diego went to make his bill out; and Damien, now truly alarmed, proposed that, at all events, we should take the shorter and more practicable route homewards, by way of Vejer. But the name of the other had taken our fancy, and orders were given accordingly, our departure being merely postponed until the afternoon; for, as it would be necessary to sleep at Alcalà, which is but nine miles from Casa Vieja, we agreed to have another brush at the snipes ere leaving the place.

In the afternoon we set out. At two miles from Casa Vieja the road crosses a tributary stream to the Barbate, which reached up to our saddle-girths, and then traverses some wooded hills for about an equal distance. The rest of the way is over an extensive flat.

Little is seen of Alcalà but an old square tower, and the ruined walls of its Moorish castle, in approaching it on this side. The town is built on a rocky peninsulated eminence, which, protruding from a ridge of sierra that overlooks the place to the east, stretches about a mile in a southerly direction, and, excepting along the narrow neck that connects it with this mountain-range, is every where extremely difficult of access. A road, however, winds up to the town by a steep ravine on the south-eastern side of the rugged eminence; and a good approach has also been made, though with much labour, at its northern extremity. The river Barbate washes the western side of the mound, and across it, and somewhat above the town—which is huddled together along the northern crest of the ridge—a solid stone bridge presents itself, where the roads from Casa Vieja, Medina Sidonia, and Xeres, concentrate.

The ascent from the bridge, as I have mentioned, is good, but very steep. The position of the town is most formidable; its walls, however, are all levelled; and, of the castle, the square tower, or keep, alone remains. The streets are narrow, but not so steep as we expected to find them, and they are remarkably well paved. The houses are poor, though some trifling manufactories of cloths and tanneries give the place a thriving look. Its population amounts to about 9000 souls.

This Alcalà receives its distinctive name of *"los Gazules"* (i.e. the Castle of the Gazules), from a tribe of Moors so called; but what Roman city stood here is a mere matter of conjecture.

The inn afforded but indifferent accommodation; but our host and hostess were obliging people, and very good-naturedly made over to us the olla prepared for their own supper. It was a fine specimen of the culinary art; the savoury odour alone, that exuded from the bubbling stew, drew a smile from Damien's unusually lugubrious countenance; and, on afterwards witnessing the justice we did to its merits, he kindly wished—with a doubt-implying compression of the lips—that we might have as good an appetite to enjoy as good a supper on the following night.

We set out at daybreak, accompanied by a guide, though, I think, we could have dispensed with his services. The road enters the Serranía, immediately on leaving Alcalà, taking an easterly direction, and ascends for five miles by a rock-bound valley, partially under cultivation, and watered by several streams, along which mills are thickly scattered. On leaving them behind, the country becomes very wild and desolate; the mountains ahead appear quite impracticable; and, long ere we reached their base, the Piedmontese march had several times resounded through the rocky gorges that encompassed us.

At length we began to scramble up towards a conical pinnacle, called *El Peñon de Sancho*, [121] which presents a perpendicular face, to the south-west, of some hundreds of feet, and whose white cap, standing out from the dark sierra behind, is a landmark all along the coast from Cipiona to Cape Trafalgar.

We soon attained a great elevation, crossing a pass between the *Peñon de Sancho* and the main sierra on our left. The view, looking back towards Cadiz, is magnificent, and the scenery for the next four miles continues to be of the most splendid kind, the road being conducted along the side of the great sierra *Monteron*, and by the pass of *La Brocha* to the sierra *Cantarera*.

The road is by no means so bad as, from the name it bears, we were prepared to expect; in fact, there are many others in the Serranía of a far more infernal character. After riding about four hours—a distance of twelve miles—we reached a verdant little vale, enclosed on all sides by rude mountains, wherein the Celemin takes its rise, and whence it wends its way through a deep and thickly wooded ravine to the south. This gullet is called the *Garganta de los Estudientes*, from the circumstance, as our guide informed us, of some scholars having ventured down it who never afterwards were heard of—to which story Damien listened with great dismay.

We halted at this delightful spot for half an hour, as well to breathe our horses as to examine the contents of Damien's *alforjas*, who took his meal, pistol in hand, for fear of a surprise. Continuing our journey, we had to traverse some more very difficult country, the views from which were now towards Ximena, Casares, Gibraltar, and the Mediterranean; including an occasional peep of Castellar, as we advanced to the eastward.

At four miles and a half from our resting-place, the road branches into two, the left proceeding to Ximena (five miles and a half), the other leading toward Estepona, and the towns bordering the Mediterranean. Taking the latter path, in about two hours we reached the river Sogarganta, along the right bank of which is conducted the main road from Ximena to Gibraltar.

Damien's countenance brightened on his once more finding himself in *"un pays reconnu,"* and, turning joyfully into the well-known track, he struck up one of his most *scherzosa* arias; the heretofore dreaded *Boca de Leones* and Almoraima forest (which we had yet to pass), being robbed of their terrors by the superior dangers we had safely surmounted; and, in the words of the favourite poet of his country,

"Dopo sorte si funesta
Sarà placida quest alma
E godrà—tornata in calma—
I perigli rammentar."

CHAPTER XI

THE next and last excursion of which I purpose extracting some account from my notebook, was commenced with the intention of proceeding from Gibraltar to Madrid, late in the autumn of the year 1833; at which time, the cholera having broken out in various parts of the kingdom of Seville, it was necessary to "shape a course" that should not subject my companion and self to the purifying process of a lazaret; a rigid quarantine system having been adopted by the other kingdoms bordering the infected territory.

We hired three horses for the journey; that is to say, for any portion of it we might choose to perform on horseback: two for ourselves, and one to carry our portmanteaus, as well as the *mozo* charged with their care and our guidance.

We found, on enquiry, that by avoiding two or three towns lying upon the road, we could reach Cordoba without deviating much from the direct route to that city, whence we purposed continuing our journey to the capital by the diligence. We proceeded accordingly to Ronda, which place being in the kingdom of Granada, was open to us; and thither I will at once transport my readers, the road to it having already been fully described. After sojourning a couple of days at the little capital of the Serranía, comforting my numerous old and kind friends with the opinion (which the event, I was happy to find, confirmed), that the new enemy against which their country had to contend—the dreaded cholera—would not cross the mountain barrier that defended their city; we proceeded on our journey, taking the road to Puente Don Gonzalo, on the Genil, thereby avoiding Osuna, which lay upon the direct road to Cordoba, but in the infected district.

In an hour from the time of our leaving Ronda, we crossed the rocky gulley which has been noticed as traversing the fertile basin in which the city stands, laterally, bearing the little river Arriate to irrigate its western half, and in the course of another hour reached the northern extremity of this fruitful district. The hills here offer an easy egress from the rock-bound basin; but, though nature has left this one level passage through the mountains, art has taken no advantage of it to improve the state of the road, for a viler *trocha* is not to be met with, even in the rudest part of the Serranía.

The view of the rich plain and dark battlements of Ronda is remarkably fine.

After winding amongst some round-topped hills, the road at length reaches a narrow rocky pass, which closes the view of the vale of Ronda, and a long deep valley opens to the north, the mouth of which appears closed by a barren mountain, crowned by the old castle of *Teba*.

The path now undergoes a slight improvement, and, after passing some singular table-rocks, and leaving the little village of *La Cueva del Becerro* on the left, reaches the *venta de Virlan*. We, however, had inadvertently taken a track that, inclining slightly to the right, led us into the bottom of the valley, and in about four miles (from the pass) brought us to the miserable little village of *Serrato*. The proper road, from which we had strayed, keeps along the side of the hills, about half a mile off, on the left; and upon it, and three miles from the first venta, is another, called *del Ciego*. Yet a little further on, but situated on an elevated ridge overlooking the valley, is the little town of *Cañete la Real*.

From Serrato our road led us to the old castle of Ortoyecar, ere rejoining the direct route; which it eventually does, about a mile before reaching the foot of the mountain of Teba.

This singular feature is connected by a very low pass with the chain of sierra on the left, and, stretching from west to east about three-quarters of a mile, terminates precipitously along the river *Guadaljorce*. The road, crossing over the pass, and leaving on the right a steep paved road, that zig-zags up the mountain, winds round to the west, keeping under the precipitous sides of the ridge, and avoiding the town of Teba, which, perched on the very summit, but having a northern aspect, can only be seen when arrived at the north side of the rude mound; and there another winding road offers the means of access to the place.

The base of the mountain is, on this side, bathed by a little rivulet that flows eastward to the Guadaljorce, called the *Sua de Teba*. It is erroneously marked on the Spanish maps as running on the south side of the ridge, but the only stream which is there to be met with, is a little rivulet that takes its rise near Becerro and waters the valley by which we had descended; and it does not approach within a mile of Teba, but sweeps round to the eastward a little beyond the old castle of Ortoyecar, and discharges itself into the river Ardales.

The deep-sunk banks and muddy bottom of the *Suda de Teba*, render it impassable excepting at the bridge. This rickety structure is apparently the same which existed in the time of Rocca, who, in his "Memoirs of the War in Spain," gives a very spirited account of the military operations of the French and *serranos* in this neighbourhood.

The locality of Teba is most faithfully described by that author; indeed I know no one who has given so graphic an account of this part of Spain generally.

The ascent to the town on this (the northern) side, is yet more difficult than that in the opposite direction; but the place will amply repay the labour of a visit, for the view from it is extremely fine, and the extensive ruins of its ancient defences, evidently of Roman workmanship, are well worthy of observation.

The position of Teba, with reference to other places in the neighbourhood, and to the circumjacent country, is so inaccurately given in all maps which I have seen, that the antiquaries seem quite to have overlooked it as the probable site of *Ategua*, so celebrated for its obstinate defence against Julius Cæsar.

Morales—without the slightest grounds, as far as the description of the country accords with the assumption—imagined *Ategua* to have stood where he maintains some ruins, "called by the country-people *Teba la Vieja*," are to be seen between Castrò el Rio and Codoba; but, as I pointed out in the case of Ronda, and Ronda *la Vieja*, it is absurd to suppose that an *old Teba* could ever have existed, since Teba itself is a Roman town, and its present name a mere corruption of that which it bore in times past.

Other Spanish authors place *Ategua* at Castro el Rio, some at Baena, some elsewhere; but almost all appear anxious to fix its site near the river Guadajoz, which they have determined, in their own minds, must be the *Salsus* mentioned by Hirtius.

La Martinière, with his usual *inaccuracy*, says, that the Guadajoz falls into the *Salado*: he should rather have said, that it is *formed* from the confluence of *various salados*; for, as I have elsewhere observed, salado is a general term for all water-courses, and not the name of a river. [122]

It seems, however, probable, that the Romans gave the name *Salsus* to some river impregnated with salt, which many streams in this part of Spain are; and since there is an extensive salt-lake still existing near Alcaudete, on the very margin of the Guadajoz, that river has hastily been concluded to be that of the Roman historian. But, it appears strange, if the Guadajoz be the Salsus of Hirtius, that Pliny, when describing the course of the Bœtis, and the principal streams which fell into it, should have omitted to mention that river, as being one of its affluents; for the Salsus, from the recentness of the war between Cæsar and the sons of Pompey, must have been much spoken of in Pliny's time.

But what, to me, proves most satisfactorily that the *Guadajoz* is *not* the Salsus, is, that it so ill agrees with the minute description given of the river by Hirtius himself;—for, in speaking of the Salsus he says, [123] "It runs through the plains, and *divides* them from the mountains, which all lie upon the side of Ategua, at about two miles' distance from the river;" and again, "But what proved principally favourable to Pompey's design of drawing out the war, was the nature of the country, (i. e. about Ategua) full of mountains, and extremely well adapted to encampments;" [124] and, from what again follows, it is evident that Ategua stood upon the summit of a mountain.

Now the Guadajoz nowhere runs so as to *divide* the plains from the mountains. It *issues from* the mountains of Alcalà Real, many miles before reaching Castrò el Rio, and between that last-named town and Cordoba, there is no ground that can be called mountainous.

The country bordering the Guadajoz, in the lower part of its course, differs as decidedly with the statement that the neighbourhood of Ategua was "full of mountains," if we suppose the town to have stood anywhere *below* Castrò el Rio.

It is again improbable that Ategua could have stood on the site of the supposed *Teba la Vieja*, or any place in that neighbourhood, since it is mentioned [125] as being a great provision dépôt of the Pompeians; which would scarcely have been the case had it been within twenty miles of the city of Cordoba. And again, it is not likely that Cæsar would have commenced the campaign by laying siege to a place within such a short distance of Cordoba, since the invested town might so readily have received succour from that city, and his adversary would, by such a step, have had the advantage of combining all his forces to attack him during the progress of the siege.

Again, another objection presents itself, namely, that Ategua is represented as a particularly strong place, [126] which, from the nature of the ground in that part of the country—that is, between Castrò el Rio and Cordoba—no town could well have been; situation, rather than art, constituting the strength of towns in those days.

We will now return to Teba, the locality of which agrees infinitely better with the account of Ategua given by Hirtius, whilst the River *Guadaljorce*, which flows in its vicinity, answers perfectly his description of the Salsus; for, along its right bank a plain extends all the way to the Genil; on its left, "at two miles' distance," rises a wall of Sierra; and the whole country, beyond, is "full of mountains, all lying on the side of" Teba. That is to say, the mountain range continues in the same direction, and possesses the same marked character, although the Guadaljorce breaks through it ere reaching so far west as Teba; for, by a vagary of nature, this stream quits the wide plain of the Genil to throw itself into a rocky gorge, and after describing a very tortuous course, gains, at length, the vale of Malaga.

Now this very circumstance strikes me, on attentive consideration, as tending rather to strengthen than otherwise the supposition that Teba is Ategua; for Cæsar's army is not stated to have *crossed* the Salsus on its march from Cordoba to Ategua; from which we must conclude that Ategua was on the *right* bank of the river; whilst other circumstances prove that the town was some distance from the river, and encompassed by mountains.

Pompey, however, following Cæsar from Cordoba, and proceeding to the relief of Ategua, *crosses the Salsus*, and fixes his camp "on these mountains (i. e. the mountains 'which all lie on the side of Ategua') between Ategua and Ucubis, but within sight of both places," being, as is distinctly said afterwards, separated from his adversary by the Salsus.

Thus, therefore, though his camp was on the same range of mountains as Ategua, yet he was separated from that town by a river: a peculiarity, in the formation of the ground, which suits the locality of Teba, but would be difficult to make agree with any other place.

The only very apparent objection to this hypothesis is, that Cæsar's cavalry is mentioned as having, on one occasion, pursued the foraging parties of his adversary "almost to the very walls of Codoba." But this was when Pompey (after his first failure to relieve Ategua) had drawn off his army towards Cordoba. It does not follow, therefore, that Cæsar's troops pursued his adversary's parties from Ategua, though he was still besieging that place, but it may rather be supposed that his cavalry was sent after the enemy to harass them on their march, and watch their future movements.

One might, indeed, on equally good grounds, maintain that Ategua was *within a day's march of Seville*; since, on Pompey's finally abandoning the field, Hirtius says, [127] "the same day he decamped, (from Ucubis, which was within sight of Ategua) and posted himself in an olive wood over against Hispalis."

With respect to this knotty point of distance it is further to be observed, that on Cæsar's breaking up his camp from before Cordoba, his march is spoken of as being *towards* Ategua, implying that the two places did not lie within a day's march of each other; and the supposition that they were more than a few leagues apart is strengthened by the place, and order in which Ategua is mentioned by the methodical Pliny; viz., amongst the cities lying between the Bœtis and the Mediterranean Sea, and next in succession to *Singili*, [128] which, doubtless, was on the southern bank of the Genil, towards Antequera.

The Guadaljorce has as good claims to the name of *Salsus*, as any other river in the country, since the mountains about Antequera, amongst which it takes its rise, were in former days noted for the quantity of salt they produced; and though the river Guadaljorce now carries its name to the sea, yet, in the time of the Romans, such was not the case; for, in those days, by whatever name that river may have been distinguished, it was dropt on forming its junction with the Sigila, (now the Rio Grande) in the *vega* of Malaga, although, of the two, the latter is the inferior stream.

The fort of Ucubis, stated by Hirtius to have been destroyed by Cæsar, we may suppose stood on the side of the mountains overlooking the Salsus or Guadaljorce, towards Antequera; and it does not seem improbable that that city is the *Soricaria* mentioned by the same historian; for *Anticaria*, though noticed in the Itinerary of Antoninus, is not amongst the cities of Bœtica enumerated by Pliny.

Teba was taken from the Moors by Alphonso XI., A.D. 1340. The inhabitants are a savage-looking tribe, and boast of having kept the French at bay during the whole period of the "war of independence." [129]

There is a tolerable venta at the foot of the hill, near the bridge, at which we baited our horses. The distance from Ronda to Teba is 21 miles; from hence to Campillos is about six; the country is undulated, and road good, crossing several brooks, some flowing eastward to the Guadaljorce, others in the opposite direction to the Genil.

Campillos is situated at the commencement of a vast track of perfectly level country, that extends all the way to the river Genil. By some strange mistake it is laid down in the Spanish maps due east of Teba, whereas it is nearly north. It is four leagues (or about seventeen miles) from Antequera, and five leagues from Osuna. It is a neat town, clean, and well-paved, and contains 1000 *vecinos escasos*; [130] which may be reckoned at 5000 souls, six being the number usually calculated per *vecino*.

Campillos lies just within the border of the kingdom of Seville, and was, therefore, on forbidden ground; since, had we entered it, our clean bills of health would have been thereby tainted. We were consequently obliged to skirt round the town at a tether of several hundred yards. I regretted this much, for the place contains an excellent *posada*, bearing the—to Protestant ears—somewhat profane sign of "*Jesus Nazarino*," and its keepers were old cronies of mine, our friendship having commenced some years before under rather peculiar circumstances, viz., in travelling from Antequera to Ronda, my horse met with an accident which obliged me to halt for the night at Campillos. Leaving to my servant the task of ordering dinner at the inn, I proceeded on foot to examine the town, and gain, if possible, some elevated spot in its vicinity whence I could obtain a good view of the country, being desirous to correct the mistake before alluded to, in the relative positions of Teba and Campillos on the maps.

Having found a point suited to this purpose, from whence I could see both Teba and the *Peñon de los Enamorados*, (a remarkable conical mountain near Antequera,) I drew forth a pocket surveying compass, and took the bearings of those two points, as well as of several other conspicuous objects in the neighbourhood.

These ill-understood proceedings caused the utmost astonishment to a group of idlers, who, at a respectful distance, but with significant nods and mysterious whisperings, were narrowly watching my operations. These concluded, and the result of my observations committed to my pocket-book, I took a slight outline sketch of the bold range of mountains that stretches towards Granada, and returned to the inn.

On my first arrival there, I had merely addressed the usual compliment of the country to the innkeeper and his wife, and now, repeating my salutation to the lady—who only was present—I seated myself at the fire-place of the common apartment, and began writing in my pocket-book, replying very laconically to her various attempts at conversation; and at length obtaining no immediate answer to another endeavour to *draw me out*, she said, addressing herself, "*no entiende,*" [131] and offered no further interruptions to my scribbling.

I confess to the practice of a little deceit in the matter, as my answers certainly must have led her to believe that I was a very *tyro* at the Spanish vocabulary—a fancy in which I used often to indulge the natives when I wished to shirk conversation.

Soon afterwards the *Posadero* came in, and a whispered communication took place between him and his spouse, which gradually acquiring *tone*, I at length was able to catch distinctly, and heard the following conversation.

"You are quite certain he does not understand Spanish?" said mine host.

"Not a syllable," replied his helpmate.

"He is about no good here, wife, that I can tell you."

"There does not appear to be much mischief in him."

"We must not trust to looks; I was at the chapel of the Rosario just now, and he walked up there, took an instrument from his pocket, marked down all the principal points of the country, and then drew them in that little book he is now writing in ... are you quite sure he does not understand Spanish?—I observed him smile just now."

"*No tienes cuidado,*" [132] replied the wife; "I have tried him on all points."

"Depend upon it he is *mapeando el pais,*" [133] resumed the husband.

"I think you ought forthwith to give notice of his doings to the *Justicia,*" answered the lady.

"Ay, and lose a good customer by having him taken to prison!" rejoined the patriotic innkeeper; "time enough to do that in the morning after he has paid his bill; but as to the propriety of giving information wife, I agree with you perfectly."

"He must be one of the rascally *gavachos* from Cadiz," (a French garrison at this time occupied that fortress,) "but what right has he to take his notes of our *pueblo*? [134] I thought of questioning the servant, who does speak a few words of Spanish, before he took the horses to the smithy, but Don Guillelmo came in and put it out of my head. Suppose I make another attempt to find out from himself what brings him here?"

"Do so," said her lord and master; and, with this permission, she advanced towards me with a very gracious smile, and *articulating* every syllable most distinctly, in the hope of making her interrogation perfectly intelligible, "begged to know if my worship was a Frenchman."

"*Yo,*" said I, pointing to myself, as if I did not clearly understand her; "*nix.*"

"*Ingles?*" demanded she, returning to the charge.

"*Si,*" replied I, with a nod affirmative.

"*Valga mi Dios!*" exclaimed she, turning to her husband; "he is English! how delighted I am! what a time it is since I saw an Englishman! how can we make him comfortable?"

"*Poco a poco,*" [135] observed the inn-keeper—"English or French he has no business to be *mapeando* our country, and the Alcalde ought to know of it."

"*Disparate!*" [136] exclaimed the wife; "what does his *mapeando* signify if he is an Englishman? are they not our best friends? [137] Is it not the same as if a Spaniard were doing it, only that it will be better done?"

"Very true," admitted mine host; "they have, indeed, been our friends, and will soon again, I trust, give us a proof of their friendship, by assisting to drive these French scoundrels across the Pyrenees, and allowing us to settle our own differences."

Pocketing my memorandum book, I now rose from my seat and addressing the landlady, "*con gentil donayre y talante,*" [138] as Don Quijote says, asked, in the best Castillian I could put together, when it was probable I should have dinner, as from having been the greater part of the morning on horseback, I was not only very hungry, but should be glad to retire early to my bed.

Never were two people more astonished than mine host and his spouse at this address. Had I detected them in the act of pilfering my saddlebags, they could not have looked more guilty. They offered a thousand apologies, but seemed to think the greatest affront they had put upon me was that of mistaking me for a Frenchman.

"I ought at once to have known you were no braggart *gavacho,*" said the landlord, "by your not making a noise on entering the house—calling for every thing and abusing every body—How do you think one of these gentry, who came into Spain as *friends,* to tranquillize the country, behaved to our *Alcalde*? The Frenchman wanted a billet, and finding the office shut, went to the *Alcalde's* house for it. The *Alcalde* was at dinner with a couple of friends; he begged the officer to be seated, saying he would send for the *Escribano* and have a billet made out for him—'And am I to be kept waiting for your clerk?' said the Frenchman; 'a pretty joke, indeed.' 'He will be here in an instant,' said the *Alcalde*; 'pray have a little patience, and be seated.' 'Patience, indeed!' exclaimed the other; 'make the billet out directly yourself, or I'll pull the house about your ears.' '*Juicio!* señor,' replied the Mayor; 'do you not see that I am at dinner?' 'What are you at *now*?' said the Frenchman; and, laying hold of one corner of the tablecloth, he drew it, plates, dishes, glasses, and every thing, off the table. This is the way our French *friends* behave to us!"

I now satisfied the worthy couple that their fears of mischief arising from my "*mapeando el pais,*" were quite groundless; and mine host showed great intelligence in comprehending what I wished to correct in the Spanish map; the error in which he saw at once, when I pointed to the setting sun; his wife standing by and exclaiming "*que gente tan fina los Ingleses!*" [139]

No advantage was taken of the knowledge of *my* country in making out *the bill,* and I departed next morning with their prayers that I might travel in company with all the saints in the calendar.

The direct road from Campillos to Cordoba is by way of La Rodd; but, in the present instance, it was necessary to avoid that town, and proceed to *La Fuente de Piedra*, which is situated a few miles to the eastward, and without the sanitary circle drawn round the cholera.

The distance from Campillos to this place is two long leagues, which may be reckoned nine miles.

La Fuente de Piedra is a small village, of about sixty houses, surrounded with olive-grounds, and abounding in crystal springs. The medicinal virtues of one of these sources (which rises in the middle of the place) led to the building of the village; and the painful disease for which in especial this fountain is considered a sovereign cure, has given its name to the place. We arrived very late in the evening, and found the *posada* most miserable.

On leaving *La Fuente de Piedra* we took the road to *Puente Don Gonzalo*, and at about three miles from the village crossed the great road from Granada to Seville, which is practicable for carriages the greater part, but *not all* the way; a little beyond this the *Sierra de Estepa* rises on the left of the route, to the height of several hundred feet above the plain. The town of Estepa is not seen, being on the western side of the hill; it is supposed to be the Astapa of the Romans, the horrible destruction of which is related by Livy.

The inhabitants, on the approach of Scipio, aware of the exasperated feelings of the Romans towards them, piled all their valuables in the centre of the forum, placed their wives and children upon the top, and leaving a few of their young men to set fire to the pile in the event of their defeat, rushed out upon the Roman army. They were all killed, the pile was lighted, and a heap of ashes was the only trophy of their conquerors.

The Roman historian says, the people of Astapa "delighted in robberies." I wonder if he thought his countrymen exempt from similar propensities!

In three hours we reached Cazariche. The road merely skirts the village, being separated from it by an abundant stream, which, serving to irrigate numerous gardens and orchards, renders the last league of the ride very agreeable, which otherwise, from the flatness of the country to the eastward, would be uninteresting. This rivulet is called *La Salada*; but its volume is far too small to make one suppose for a moment that it is the *Salsus*.

At five miles from Cazariche, keeping along the left bank of the Salada the whole distance, but not crossing it, as marked on the maps, the road reaches Miragenil. This is a small village, situated on the southern bank of the Genil, and communicating, by means of a bridge, with *Puente Don Gonzalo*.

The river here forms the division between the kingdoms of Seville and Cordoba; and the two governments not having agreed as to the superior merits of wood or stone, one-half the bridge is built of the former, the other half of the latter material.

Puente Don Gonzalo stands on a steep acclivity, commanding the bridge and river. It is a town of some consideration, containing several manufactories of household furniture, numerous mills, and a population of 6000 souls.

Florez, on the authority of a *stone* found *near* Cazariche (which he calls Casaliche), whereon the word VENTIPO was inscribed, supposed *Ventisponte*, [140] to have been situated somewhere in the vicinity of Puente Don Gonzalo. But if this stone had been *carried* to Cazariche, it may have been taken there from any other point of the compass as well as from that in which Puente Don Gonzalo is situated.

Other authorities suppose this town to be on the site of Singilis; but that place, as already stated, has been pretty clearly proved to have been nearer Antequera.

The *"provechasos aguas del divino Genil,"* [141] after cleansing the town of Puente Don Gonzalo, are turned to the best possible account, in irrigating gardens and turning mill-wheels; and the road to Cordoba, after proceeding for about a mile along the verdant valley that stretches to the westward, ascends the somewhat steep bank which pens in the stream to the north, and for four hours wanders over a flat uninteresting country to Rambla; passing, in the whole distance of fifteen miles, but two running streams, three farm-houses, and the miserable village of Montalban. This latter is distant about a mile and a half from Rambla.

We saw but little of this town, having arrived late at night, and departed from it at an early hour on the following morning; but it is of considerable size, and situated on the north side of a steep hill. We found the inn excessively dirty and exorbitantly dear; indeed it may be laid down as a general rule with Spanish as well as Swiss inns, that the charges are high in proportion to the *badness* of the fare and accommodation.

The ground in the vicinity of Rambla is planted chiefly with vines, and but two short leagues to the eastward is situated Montilla, where, in the estimation of Spaniards, the best wine of the province is grown. It is extremely dry; and, as I have mentioned before, gives its name to the Sherry called *Amontillado*.

Rambla is just midway between Puente Don Gonzalo and Cordoba, viz. sixteen miles from each. The country is hilly, and mostly under tillage, but where its cultivators reside puzzles one to guess, as there is not a house on the road in the whole distance, and but two towns visible from it, viz. Montemayor and Fernan Nuñez, both within six miles of Rambla.

The first-named of these places disputes with Montilla the honour of being the Roman city of *Ulía*, the only inland town of Bœtica that held out for Cæsar against the sons of Pompey, previous to his arrival in the country. [142] It appears doubtful [143] whether *Ulía* is mentioned by Pliny, but it is noticed in the Roman Itinerary (*Gadibus Cordubam*) as eighteen miles from Cordoba, a distance that agrees better with Montilla than Montemayor; indeed the former almost declares itself in the very name it yet bears, *Montilla*; the double *l* in Spanish having the liquid sound of *li*, making it a corruption of *Mont Ulía*.

At about four miles from Cordoba the Guadajoz, or river of Castro, is crossed by fording, and between it and the Guadalquivír the ground is broken by steep hills. The road falls into the *Arrecife* from Seville, on reaching the suburb on the left bank of the river.

We took up our abode at the *Posada de la Mesangería*; a particularly comfortable house, as Spanish inns go, that had been opened for the accommodation of the diligence travellers since my former visit to the city. The *patio*, ornamented with a bubbling fountain of icy-cold water, and shaded with a profusion of all sorts of rare creepers and flowering shrubs, afforded a cool retreat at all hours of the day; which, though we were in the month of October, was very acceptable.

Whilst seated at breakfast, under the colonnade that encompasses the court, the morning after our arrival, the master of the inn waited upon us to know if we required a *valet de place* during our sojourn at Cordoba, as a very intelligent old man, who spoke French like a native, and was in the habit of attending upon *caballeros forasteros* [144] in the above-named capacity, was then in the house, and begged to place his services at our disposition.

I replied, that having before visited his city, I considered myself sufficiently acquainted with its *sights* to be able to dispense with this, otherwise useful, personage's attendance; but our host seemed so desirous that we should employ the old man, "We might have little errands to send him upon—some purchases to make; in fact, we should find the Tio Blas so useful in any capacity, and it would be such an act of charity to employ him,"—that we finally acceded to his proposal, and the *Tio* was accordingly ushered in.

He was a tall, and, though emaciated, still erect old man, whose tottering gait, and white and scanty hairs, would have led to the belief that his years had already exceeded the number usually allotted to the life of man, but that his deep-sunk eyes were shaded by dark and beatling brows, and yet sparkled occasionally with the fire of youth; proving that hardships and misfortunes had brought him somewhat prematurely to the brink of the grave.

It struck me at the first glance that I had seen him before, but when, and under what circumstances, I could not recall to my recollection. After some conversation, as to what had been his former occupation, &c., he remarked, addressing himself to me, "I think, *Caballero*, that this is not the first time we have met—many years have elapsed since—many (to me) most eventful years, and they have wrought great changes in my appearance. And, indeed, some little difference is perceptible also in yours, for you were a mere boy then; but, still, time has not laid so heavy a hand on you as on the worn-out person of him who stands before you, and in whom you will, doubtless, have difficulty in recognizing the reckless *Blas Maldonado!*"

Time had, indeed, effected great changes in him, morally as well as physically; for not only had the powerful, well-built man, dwindled into a tottering, emaciated driveller, but the daring, impious bandit, had become a weak and superstitious dotard.

My curiosity strongly piqued to learn how changes so wonderful had been brought about, we immediately engaged the *Tio* to attend upon us; and, during the few days circumstances compelled us to remain at Cordoba, I elicited from him the following account of the events which had chequered his extraordinary career since we had before met.

CHAPTER XII
HISTORY OF BLAS EL
GUERRILLERO—continued.

"La rueda de la fortuna anda mas lista que una rueda de molino,
y que los que ayer estaban en pinganitos, hoy estan por el suelo."
[145] —

Don Quijote.

IT was at Castrò el Rio that we last met Don Carlos; it is now eleven years since,—rather more, but still I have a perfect recollection of it. My memory, indeed, is the only thing that has served me well through life. Friends have abandoned—riches corrupted—success has hardened—ambition disappointed me; and now, as you see, my very limbs are failing me, but memory—excepting for one short period, when my brain was affected—has never abandoned me. I cannot flee from it—it pursues me incessantly: it is as impossible to get rid of, as of one's shadow in the sun's rays, and seems indeed, like it, to become more perfect, as I too proceed downward in my rapidly revolving course.

Alas! it often brings to mind the words of my good father, addressed, whilst I was yet a child, to my too-indulgent mother:—"If we consult the happiness of our son, we must not bring him up above the condition to which it has pleased Providence to call him." It was my unhappy lot, however, to become an *educated pauper*. I grew up discontented, and became a profligate: I coveted riches, to feed my unnatural cravings, and became criminal: I scoffed at religion, and came to ridicule the idea of a future state of rewards and punishments. And as I thus brought myself to believe that I was not an accountable creature, nothing thenceforth restrained me from committing any act which gratified my passions. What is man, I argued, that I should not despoil him, if he possess that which I covet? What should deter me from taking his life, if he stand between me and that which I desire? *Crime* is a mere word,—a term for any act which certain *men*, for their mutual advantage, have agreed shall meet with punishment. But what right have those men to say, this is just, and that is unlawful?

Such were my feelings at the time I met and related to you the adventures of my early life; adventures of which I was then not a little proud, though, nevertheless, I slurred over some little matters that I thought would not raise me in your opinion. Well was it for me that I was not cut off in the midst of my iniquitous career, but have, on the contrary, been allowed time, by penance and prayer, to make what atonement is in my power for my former sinful life.

My journey to Castrò had been undertaken at the desire of the political chief of — —, for the purpose of watching the proceedings of the Royal Regiment of Carbineers, which, as you may remember, was at that time quartered there.

I soon, under pretence of being a stanch royalist, wormed myself into the confidence of the officers, and learnt that they were in communication with the King's Guards at Madrid, and were plotting a counter-revolution, to reestablish Ferdinand on a despotic throne. The advice I gave them, and the information I furnished the government, led to the unconnected and premature developement of their treason, and to the vigorous steps which were taken by the executive to meet and put it down.

These, however, are matters of history, on which it is unnecessary to dwell; suffice it, therefore, to say, that my good services on the occasion were rewarded by promotion to a more lucrative *corregimiento*. I did not long enjoy this new post, for, on the French columns crossing the Pyrenees the following spring, I threw up my civil employment, and, collecting a small band of *guerrillas*, flew to the defence of my country; joining the traitor Ballasteros, then entrusted with the command of the army of the south.

The deplorable events which followed deprived me of a home; but, leaving my wife and infant son (the only child, of three, whom it had pleased Providence to spare us) at the secluded little town of Cañete la Real, perched high up in the Sierra de Terril, I wandered about the country with a few adherents, seeking opportunities of harassing the French during their operations before Cadiz.

They afforded us no opportunities, however, of attacking their convoys with any chance of success, and my followers could not be brought to engage in any daring enterprise without the prospect of booty. The feeling of patriotism appeared, indeed, to be extinct in the breasts of Spaniards, and after a few weeks my band, which was nowhere well received, having been induced to commit excesses in some of the villages situated in the open country about Arcos, several parties of royalist volunteers were formed to proceed in quest of us; and so disheartened were my followers, that I shortly found my band reduced to a dozen desperadoes, who, like myself, had no hopes of obtaining pardon.

We betook ourselves, therefore, to the innermost recesses of the Ronda mountains, moving constantly from place to place, as well to harass our pursuers, as to avoid being surrounded by them; and such is the intricacy of the country, and so numerous are the rocky fastnesses of the smugglers (from whom we were always sure of a good reception), that we readily baffled all pursuit, and exhausted the patience of our enemies; and, at length, seizing a favourable opportunity of inflicting a severe loss upon one of their parties, the patriotic zeal of these gentry so completely evaporated, that we were left in the undisturbed command of the Serranía.

All hope of being serviceable to our country at an end, we were compelled, as a last resource, to adopt the only calling to which we were suited, viz., that of highway robbers; and for several months every road between Gibraltar and Malaga, and the inland towns, was, in turn, subject to our predaceous visits.

On one occasion a dignitary of the church, whose name and particular station it would not be prudent of me to mention, fell into our hands. His attendants, who were of a militant order, defended their master with great obstinacy. They were eventually overpowered, however, but several of my men having been badly wounded in the scuffle, were so exasperated, that they determined to shoot all those who had fallen into our hands, as well as the — — himself; who, though he had not taken an active part in the combat, had made no attempt to restrain his pugnacious adherents.

As soon as our prisoners had been secured, therefore, the portly ecclesiastic was directed to descend from his sleek mule, deliver up his money, and prepare for death. He inveighed in eloquent terms at our barbarity, pointed out to us the iniquity of our proceedings, the probability of a speedy punishment overtaking us in this life, and the certainty of having to endure everlasting torments in that which is to come. But it was to no purpose; indeed, it only tempted my miscreants to prolong his misery; and, having tied him to a tree, they insisted upon his blessing them all round, ere they proceeded to shoot him.

"My children," said the worthy — —, "my blessing, from the tone in which you ask it, would serve you little. My life is in the hands of my Maker, not in your's; and if it be His pleasure to make you the instruments of his divine will, so be it. I am prepared; death has no terrors for me; and may you obtain *His* forgiveness for the sin you are about to commit, as readily as I grant you *mine*. Now, I am ready;" and, looking upwards to the seat of all power and grace, he paid no further attention to their scoffing.

"Now Señor Bias," said one of my men, "since he will give us no more sport, give the word, and let us finish his business."

"Hold!" exclaimed one of the — —'s suite, addressing me, "Is your name Blas Maldonado?"

"It is: wherefore?"

"Because, if such be the case, in his Excellency's *portefuille* you will find a letter addressed to you."

I forthwith proceeded to examine its contents, and, true enough, found a letter bearing my address. It was from my old friend *Jacobo*, requesting, should the — — fall into my hands, that I would suffer him to pass without molestation, in return for services conferred on him, which would be explained at our next meeting. [146]

Jacobo, though we had not met for many months, I knew was in that part of the country, following the honest calling of a *Contrabandista*, and I felt, in honour, bound to grant this request of my old friend and ever faithful lieutenant. My followers, however, objected strongly to spare either the — —, or his attendants, and a violent altercation ensued; for, I declared that my life must be taken ere that of any one of our prisoners.

Four only of the band sided with me, and we had already assumed a hostile attitude, when the — — called earnestly upon me to desist.

"Peril not your sinful souls!" he exclaimed, "by hurrying each other, unrepented of your manifold sins, into the presence of an offended Maker.— Take our gold—take every thing we possess; and if those misguided men cannot be satisfied without blood, let mine flow to save the lives of these, my followers, who have stronger ties than I to bind them to this world."

My hot temper, little used to contradiction, would listen, however, to no terms; my word was pledged that the — — and his attendants should go free, and my word was never given in vain. I persisted, therefore, in declaring that those must pass over my body who would touch a hair of the — —'s head, or take a m*aravedi* from his purse.... If he chose to make them a present after he had been released, he was his own master to do so.

This delicate hint was eagerly seized by the worthy dignitary's attendants, and a large sum of money was distributed amongst the gang, in which I declined sharing. The — —, meanwhile, remounted his mule, and, calling me to his side, placed a valuable ring upon my finger. "I am indebted to you for my life, Blas Maldonado," he said, with the most lively emotion; "but that is little; I owe to you—what I value infinitely more— the safety of these faithful attendants, whose attachment had led them, like

Simon Peter, to defend their Pastor. Such debts cannot be cancelled by any gift I can bestow, and it is not with that view I offer you this bauble, but a day may come when you may need an intercessor—if so, return this ring to me by some faithful member of our holy church, and let me know how I can serve you: or—which is probable, considering my age and infirmities—should I, ere that comes to pass, have been called from this world to give an account of my stewardship; then, fear not to lay it at the foot of Fernando's throne, and, in the name of its donor, beg for mercy. I trust you may not have occasion to require its services, for my prayers shall not be wanting for your conversion from your present evil ways—my blessing be upon you—farewell."

How powerful is the influence of religion! Whilst listening to the worthy — —'s words, my head, which since the days of my childhood no act of devotion had ever led me to uncover, was bared as if by instinct; and, to receive the blessing he had called down upon me, I humbled myself to the earth!

Although those of the band who had so vehemently opposed sparing the — —'s life had finally been satisfied with the *donation* bestowed upon them, yet their disobedience made me determine on ejecting them from my band, and accordingly, accompanied only by my four supporters in the late dispute, I proceeded to my old rendezvous, Montejaque, hoping to pick up some recruits. I purposed, also, availing myself of the first favourable opportunity to remove my wife and child to that place, it being more conveniently situated, and offering greater security than even Cañete la Real.

We had been there but a few days, when I received a letter without a signature, but in the well-known characters of my bosom friend, Miguel Clavijo, under whose protection I had placed my wife and child, giving warning of impending danger to them. There was yet time to avert it, my correspondent concluded, but in twenty-four hours from the date of this communication, their fate would probably be sealed.

It was within two hours of sunset when I received this letter, and eight hours had already elapsed since it had been written. Not a moment, therefore, was to be lost. I procured a pillion, and, placing it on an active horse, set off with all possible haste for Cañete, keeping along the course of the river Ariate to avoid the town of Ronda, and traversing at full speed the village bearing the name of the stream, in order to escape recognition.

I reached the rounded summit of the chain of hills which forms the northern boundary of the cultivated valley of Ronda, just as the sun was sinking behind the western mountains; and, checking my horse to give him a few moments' breath ere commencing the rugged descent on the opposite side, I turned round to see if all were quiet in the wide-spread plain I had just traversed, and that no one was following my traces. At this moment the last ray of the glorious luminary lit upon the distant town of Grazalema. The remarkable coincidence of the warning of treason I had received there on this very day, twelve years before, came vividly to mind, and with it the recollection of my extraordinary escape from the snare laid for me—the debt of gratitude due to her who had risked her life, and sacrificed her honour to save me—the cruelty with which my preserver had been treated. Poor abandoned Paca! From the moment of our angry separation, never had I once taken the trouble of enquiring what had been her fate. Scarcely, indeed, had I ever bestowed a thought upon her.

I resumed my way down the rough descent, pondering, for the first time in my life, on the ingratitude I had been guilty of, and had reached some high cliffs that border the road beneath the village of La Cuera del Becerro, when a pistol was discharged within a few yards of me, and, looking up, I saw a witchlike figure standing on the edge of the precipice overhanging the path—It was Paca!

Had my eyes wished to deceive me, she would not have allowed them, for, with a wild, demoniacal laugh, she screamed out "*Adelante, Adelante, embustero desalmado!* [147] —You will yet be in time to dig the grave for your child, though too late to snatch your *wife* from the arms of her paramour. Forward, forward; recollect the old saying, '*no hay boda, sin tornabóda;*' [148] you may have forgotten Paca of *Benaocaz*, but I shall never forget Blas Maldonado. The creditor has ever a better memory than the debtor. I have paid myself now, however—ride on, and see the receipt I have left for you at Cañete—ha, ha, ha!"

There was something perfectly fiendish in her laughter. A horrible presentiment possessed me.—With a hand tremulous with passion, I drew forth a pistol and fired. Paca staggered, and fell backwards; but, not waiting to see if she were killed, I put spurs to my horse, and hurried forward to Cañete.

I rode straight to the house where I had left my wife, but it was uninhabited. I turned from it with a shudder, and proceeded to the abode of my faithful friend Clavijo, who was confined to his bed with ague. He received me with a face foreboding evil.

"Where is my wife?" I hastily demanded—"my child, where is he?"

"Alas!" he replied, "why came you not earlier?"

"Earlier! how could that be? It is but twelve hours since your summons was penned! Tell me, I implore you — what horrible misfortune has befallen?"

"But twelve hours, say you?" exclaimed Clavijo; "It is now *three days* since I intrusted my letter to Paca to convey to you! she it was who informed me of the plot to carry off your wife, (which has been but too truly effected,) and offered to be herself the bearer of my letter to you at Montejaque, where she assured me you were. I have not seen her since, and fancied she had not succeeded in finding you."

I stood stupified whilst listening to this explanation — for such it was to me; the truth, the horrible truth, at once flashing upon me — and then, without waiting to obtain further information from the bed-ridden Miguel, hastened to the late residence of my wife, which one of his domestics pointed out to me. In few words, I explained to its owner the object of my visit, begging for information concerning my child. "This will explain all, Señor Blas," she replied, taking a letter from a cupboard, and placing it in my hands; "would to God it had been in my power to prevent what has happened."

The letter was in my wife's hand-writing, I tore it open, and to my astonishment read as follows.

"Monster of iniquity! The veil that has but too long concealed thy unequalled crimes from the eyes of a confiding woman, has been rudely torn aside. Murderer of my brother! Apostate! Traitor! Adulterer! receive at my hands the first stroke of the Almighty's anger. The illegitimate offspring of our intercourse lies a mangled corpse upon our adulterous bed! Yes, unparalleled villain; my hand, like thine own, is stained with the blood of my child — *our* child. But on thy head rests the sin. In a moment of delirium, produced by the sight of my husband, and the knowledge of thy atrocious crimes, the horrid deed was committed. I leave thee to the pangs of remorse. I cannot curse thee. Even with the bleached corpse of my poor boy before me, I cannot bring myself to call down a heavy punishment upon thee. We shall never meet again; but fly instantly and save thyself if possible; and may the Almighty Being, whose every command thou hast violated, extend the term of thy life for repentance; and may a blessed Saviour and the holy saints, whose mediation thou hast ever derided, intercede for the salvation of thy sinful soul."

My first feeling on reading this epistle was incredulity! I, who had stopped at no crime to gratify any evil passion; even I could not persuade myself that it was not a forgery, nor believe that one so gentle, so affectionate, as Engracia, could be guilty of so diabolical an act. I took up a lamp and walked composedly to the adjoining chamber, to satisfy my doubts. With a steady hand I drew aside the curtain of the bed—nothing was visible. A thrill of delight ran through my veins. I tore off the counterpane, and—horrible revulsion of feeling!—discovered my boy, my darling boy, with anguish depicted in every feature, and every muscle contracted with excessive suffering; a cold—black—fetid—putrid corpse!

Until that moment I had not known the full extent to which the chords of the human heart are capable of being stretched. All my love of life had centred in that child. Each of his infantile endearments came fresh upon my memory. The pangs of jealousy and hate, too, had never before been so acutely felt; and, lastly, I thought of my Fernando's dying malediction! It seemed as if a poisoned dart had pierced to the very innermost recess of the heart, and that my envenomed blood waited but its extraction, to gush forth in one irrepressible flood.

I stood speechless—awe-struck—motionless; but not yet humbled. I thought of Paca, and a curse rose to my throat; but ere I had time to give it utterance, a noise, as of many persons assembled at the door of the house, attracted my attention, and I heard an unknown voice say, "This, *Tio*, you are sure is the house? Then in with you, comrades, without ceremony, and bring out every soul you may find there, dead or alive."

In another moment the door was broken open and a party of armed men rushed in. My precaution of extinguishing the lamp was vain, as several of them bore blazing torches. I rushed to a back window of the inner apartment, and drew forth a pistol to keep them at bay whilst I effected my escape by it. It had the desired effect. Not one of the dastard crew would approach to lay his hand upon me. The shutter was already thrown open; the strength of desperation had enabled me to tear down one of the iron bars of the *reja*; and one foot rested on the window-sill; when, rushing past the soldiers, a ghost-like female figure, whose face was bound up in a cloth clotted with gore, seized me in her convulsive grasp, and in a half-articulate scream cried, "Wretch! you shall not so escape me!"—It was Paca! I tried in vain to shake her off; she clung to me with the pertinacity of a vampire, I placed the muzzle of my pistol to her temple, and pulled the trigger; but, in my hurry, I had drawn that which I had already fired at her. I attempted to snatch another from my belt, but the soldiers taking courage rushed forward and overpowered me, just as Paca, from whose mouth I now perceived blood was rapidly issuing, fell exhausted upon the floor.

The commander of the party was now called in, who gave directions for a priest and a surgeon to be instantly sent for, and that I should be bound hand and foot with cords. They took the bedding from under the corpse of my son to form a rest for Paca, whose life seemed ebbing rapidly.

In a few minutes the surgeon arrived, and shortly after a tinkling bell announced the approach of the Host. The doctor having examined Paca's wounds, pronounced them to have been inflicted by the discharge of some weapon loaded with slugs, one of which had fractured her jaw-bone, whilst another had inflicted a wound that occasioned an inward flow of blood which threatened immediate dissolution, and consequently the services of the church were more likely to be beneficial than his own. The priest then approached, and offered the last and cheering consolation that our holy religion offers to a dying penitent.

Paca opened her now lustreless eyes, and with a motion of impatience, putting aside the proffered cup, pointed to me. "There is my murderer," she muttered in broken accents; "Villain! monster! my vengeance is at length complete. I leave you in the hands of justice, and die ... happy." An agonized writhe belied her assertion. She never spoke after, but continued groaning whilst the worthy priest attempted to call her attention to her approaching end.

I have not much more to add to my history. It appeared, by what I learnt afterwards, that Beltran had most miraculously escaped death, when thrown from the rock of Montejaque, and having been discovered by some French soldiers who made an attack upon the place a few days afterwards, was conveyed to Ronda, when the loss of his ears led to his being recognised by the French governor, who had, in the meanwhile, received my *present*, and discovered the trick I had played him.

Beltran's tale thus proved to have been the true one, he was well-treated, and sent with a party of prisoners to France, where he remained until the conclusion of the war. He was then on his way back to his native country, in company with several other Spaniards, when he was arrested as being an accomplice, "*sans préméditation*," in a robbery, attended with loss of life, and was sentenced to ten years' imprisonment; but, before this term was fully completed, he obtained his release, returned to Spain, and proceeding immediately to his native province, there first learnt that Engracia had become my wife.

I think, by the way, that in the former part of my narrative I omitted to mention—for fully persuaded as I *then* was of Beltran's death, it was a matter of no moment—that previous to Engracia's becoming my wife, she informed me of her having, at the urgent instances of her brother Melchor, consented to a private marriage with my rival; and from this circumstance she had expressed the greatest anxiety to ascertain his fate with certainty, and had delayed for so long a period bestowing her hand upon me.

This marriage with Beltran had taken place at Gaucin within an hour of my departure from that town, after making the arrangements for our combined attack on Ronda; and had been strongly advocated by Melchor, from an apprehension that, should any thing happen to him in the approaching conflict, his elder brother, Alonzo, who was kept in perfect ignorance of this proceeding, would abandon his friend Beltran, and insist on their sister's marrying me, whom he (Melchor) detested.

I, however, as you are aware, had every reason to believe that Beltran had been killed by his fall from the rock of Montejaque; and therefore, on eventually eliciting from Engracia the reason of her reluctance to marry me, I had no scruple in declaring that Beltran's dead body had been seen rolling down the shallow pebbly bed of the Guadiaro, after our action with the French. The crime I had led her to commit was consequently unintentional. Would I could as easily acquit myself of another her letter accused me of, namely, that of being the murderer of her brother: for, through my machinations was his death brought about.

Whilst the crop-eared traitor, Beltran, (the *Tio's* revengeful feelings were not so entirely allayed as to prevent his bestowing an occasional term of reproach on those who had thwarted his prosperous career of iniquity) was skulking about the mountains, endeavouring to obtain tidings of his re-married wife, chance threw him in the way of Paca, engaged in a similar pursuit, but with a very different purpose.

This wretched woman had, for many years after our separation, been the inmate of a mad-house; but, at length, her keepers finding that, excepting on the subject of her supposed wrongs, she was perfectly tractable, became careless of watching her, and she effected her escape.

The sole object of this vindictive creature's life appears now to have been to wreak vengeance upon me. But not satisfied with the mere death of her victim, she sought first to torture him with worldly pangs; and informed that Engracia lived, and had given birth to a son, whom I loved with a more fervent affection than even the mother, she determined *they* should first be sacrificed to her revenge.

On discovering Beltran alive, however, a scheme yet more hellishly devised entered her imagination; in the execution of which he became a willing agent, though in some degree her dupe.

Well acquainted with all my haunts, she soon got upon my track; and that discovered, had little difficulty in finding out the hiding-place of Engracia. Making a shrewd guess at the person under whose protection I had placed my wife and child, she forthwith presented herself to Don Miguel, and informed him that a plot was laid, and on the eve of execution, to carry them both off; adding, that it might yet be frustrated if I could but arrive at Cañete within twenty-four hours—that she knew where I then was, and would undertake to have any warning conveyed to me which his prudence might suggest—that her messenger was sure, but still the utmost caution, as well as despatch, was necessary.

Miguel, quite taken by surprise, and unable from illness to leave his bed, wrote the short note which has already been given; and this point gained, Paca proceeded to the nearest town to give information to the authorities that the bandit Blas, whom they were seeking in every direction, was to be at Cañete la Real on a certain night; and proposed, if a detachment of troops was sent quietly to the neighbouring village of El Becerro, that she would repair thither at the proper time, and conduct the soldiers to the traitor's very lair.

This proposal was readily acceded to, and Paca then repaired to Cañete, to tell Miguel not to be uneasy as to the result of his message to me, as, since sending it, she had ascertained on good authority that something had occurred to postpone the elopement of Engracia for a day or two.

Bending her steps thence to where Beltran was anxiously awaiting her return, she told him that after much difficulty she had discovered Engracia was at Cañete; he had therefore but to proceed there after dark, provided with the means of carrying her off. But this, she informed him, must be done with the utmost celerity and circumspection, as the inhabitants of the place were so desperate a set, and so attached to me, that, if they got the slightest inkling of what was going forward, they certainly would handle him very roughly; and the authorities, unless backed by a body of troops, would be afraid to interfere in his behalf.

If, however, she pursued, he preferred waiting until an escort could be procured, that he might avoid all personal risk—but delays were dangerous, for frequently

"*De la mano a la boca
se cae la sopa.*" [149]

The law, too, was uncertain.—He thought so also, and they proceeded together to Cañete.

Beltran, imagining that Paca had informed Engracia of his being alive, conceived that no intimation of his coming was requisite; but such was not the case, and the shock given by his unexpected visit caused the aberration of mind which led the hapless Engracia to commit the horrid crime of infanticide; and, in the state of inanition that followed, she was carried out of the town.

The letter to me was written afterwards, and delivered to the old woman of the house by Paca, the last act of whose fiendish plot now commenced.

Altering the date of Miguel's letter, so as to make it correspond with the time arranged for the arrival of the troops at *La Cueva del Becerro*, she forwarded it to me at Montejaque—what followed has already been stated.

These details became known on my trial, which took place shortly afterwards. I was condemned to suffer death by the *garrote*. The day was fixed; I sent for a priest, and entrusting to him the ring given me by the — —, begged he would forward it without delay to Madrid.

This was done, but day after day passed without bringing any answer to my appeal. At first I had been so sanguine as to the result, that I was affected but little at my position, for I knew how easily a pardon is obtained in Spain, when application is made in the proper quarter; but, as the fatal time approached, the darkest despair took possession of my soul.

I cannot indeed convey to you, Don Carlos, an adequate idea of the horrible torments I endured during the last few days preceding that fixed for my execution. The pious father Ignacio—he has since (sainted soul!) been taken from this earth, and is now, I trust, my intercessor in heaven—was unremitting in his endeavours to bring me to repentance; but Satan was yet strong within me, and my heart remained hardened. The pardon came not, and I exclaimed against the justness of the Most High: I, whom no considerations of justice had influenced in any one action of my life—who had recklessly transgressed each of His commandments!

"We must not ask for *justice* at the hands of the Almighty," urged Ignacio; "We are all born in sin, in sin we all live; *mercy* is what we must pray for."

"Mercy!" I exclaimed; "*Why* was I born in sin? Why led to commit crime? Why...."

"Your unbridled passions led you to transgress the laws of your Creator," replied Ignacio; "be thankful that you were not cut short in your mad career, and that time has been allowed you for repentance."

"Repent!—I cannot—I have ever denied, I cannot now believe in the existence of a Maker."

"Unhappy man!" ejaculated the worthy priest; "unhappy, impious, inconsistent man! You deny the existence of the Being against whose justice your voice was raised e'en now in reproaches! Do you not look forward to behold again to-morrow the bright luminary round which this atom of a world revolves? Look on that pale moon, which perhaps you now see rising for the last time—Observe that fiery meteor which has this moment dashed through the wondrous, boundless firmament; and ask yourself if this admirable system can be the effect of accident? Do the trees yearly yield us their fruits by chance? Is the punctual return of the seasons a mere casualty? If so, how is it that this accidental atom—this globe we inhabit, has so long held together *without* accident? Has any work of man, however cunningly devised, in like manner withstood the effects of time? Is not the protecting hand of the Deity clearly perceptible in the unvarying continuance of these phenomena?

"My son, had you studied the Holy Scriptures more, and the philosophy of Voltaire and other infidels less, you would not have been brought to this strait; neither would you have shocked my ears with a confession, which, a few years since, would have consigned you to the dungeons of the Inquisition. Repent! unhappy man, repent! and save your soul—there is still time. Nay, an omnipotent Maker may even yet think fit to prolong your life here below, for the perfection of this good work, if you will but pray to him in all sincerity."

The pious father saw that I was touched, and, pouring in promises of future happiness, brought me to reflect. I begged him to be with me early on the following morning. He came; I had passed the night in prayer; and now unburdened my mind, by making to him a full confession of my sins.

Ignacio remained comforting me, until the hour of the arrival of the post, when he repaired, as usual, to the *Corregidor*, to ascertain whether any pardon had reached him. He returned not, however. Eleven o'clock was the hour fixed for my execution; it came, but still Ignacio did not appear. Hours passed away, and not a soul visited me; the sun again sank below the horizon, and I yet lived.

It was evident—so, at least, I thought—that a pardon had arrived, and my spirits rose accordingly. At length, towards nightfall, Ignacio entered my cell. "Blas," he said, "though it would appear there is no longer a chance of your receiving a pardon, yet your life has been miraculously spared this day, to give you time for repentance. I trust you have turned it to good account."

"How!" I exclaimed, "have I not been pardoned? What, then, has occasioned this delay?"

"You owe your life," he replied, "to a rumour, that a band of robbers had appeared in the vicinity—some of your old friends, it was thought—which caused all the troops to be sent out in pursuit. They have but now returned, and to-morrow you will be executed."

A pang of withering disappointment ran through me, for I had confidently imagined that the delay had been the consequence of the arrival of a pardon, and Satan once more obtained dominion over me.

Ignacio read in my overcast countenance the change his information had wrought in my feelings. "Your repentance is not sincere, my son," he observed. "Alas! when death is in sight, how fondly do we cling to this earth. And yet you have braved death in the field a thousand times!"

"Father," I replied, "it is not death I fear—it is the disgrace of a public execution."

"What absurd sophistry is this?" said he. "Can one, who but yesterday denied the existence of a future state, care for one moment *how* he quits this world, or regard the opinion of those he leaves behind in it?—as well might he be fearful of losing the good opinion of a herd of swine. Away with such fine-spun subtilties—it is the prospect of meeting your Maker face to face that makes you quail. You are yet but ill prepared, I see. Oh! may He yet mercifully extend your life, if but a short span."

The morrow came, but the pious Ignacio's prayer remained apparently unheard. He repaired to my call soon after the arrival of the post, to exhort and prepare me. Alas! I was as much in want of his assistance as ever, for I had all along clung to the hope of obtaining a pardon through the influence of the ——, and was more inclined to rail than to pray.

A party of soldiers at length arrived, and I was led off in chains to the place of execution. A vast crowd was assembled from all the neighbouring towns to witness my punishment. Ignacio addressed the multitude on our way, saying, I was a repentant sinner, and implored the prayers of all good Christians. For myself I said not a word, and the crowd gave no signs of either gratification or commiseration. I mounted the scaffold, the fatal instrument was placed round my throat, a curse was yet on my lips, when a distant shout attracted the Father's attention. Laying a hand upon the arm of the executioner to stay his proceedings, he watched with eager eyes the signs of some one who was approaching at a rapid pace, holding a paper high in the air. The paper was handed to Ignacio by the breathless messenger. "It is a pardon," he exclaimed; "your life is miraculously spared—it has been sent express from the Escurial! Return your thanks, to Him, who has been pleased thus to extend his mercy towards you."

I had already sunk on my knees—I prayed earnestly for the first time in my life.

Marvellously, indeed, had my life been preserved. But for the rumoured appearance of the band of robbers, I should have suffered death the day before; again, this day, but for Ignacio's presence, the pardon would have arrived too late.

I was immediately released, but a fever, caused, probably, by my previously excited feelings, confined me to my bed for many weeks. I became delirious, and my life was despaired of. Ignacio tended me like a brother. A second time he saved my life; but, alas! he himself contracted the contagious disorder, and fell a victim to his warm and disinterested friendship.

I expended all I was worth in masses for his soul, and was once more thrown upon the world to seek a livelihood.

I thought of applying to the — — to procure me some employment, but learnt that he too had closed his mortal career. The fever had given such a shock to my constitution, that old age, I may say, came suddenly upon me, and to gain a livelihood by hard labour was out of the question. I had no relations; my friends were all new; so that I had no claims on any one: my present occupation presented itself, as the only one I was fit for; and, thank God, it enables me to earn my bread without begging, and even to lay by a little store for pious purposes:—for much of my time is devoted to the performance of penances and austerities, to expiate the sins of my past life. Thrice, on my knees, have I ascended to the *Ermita* you see there peeping through the clouds gathered round the peaks of the Sierra Morena. Once, too, have I walked barefoot to prostrate myself before the *Santa faz* [150] of Jaen; and this winter (God willing!) I purpose visiting the most holy shrine of *Sant' Iago de Compostela.*

It is a long journey, and will, probably, be my last pilgrimage, for I feel myself sinking fast.

You have now had the history of my whole life, Don Carlos—I wish it could be published. It might, probably, warn my fellow-creatures to rest contented with the lot to which it has pleased God to call them; and, if so, I may have lived to some purpose.

CHAPTER XIII

I FOUND Cordoba the same dull, sultry, loyal city as at the period of my former visit; after devoting a day, therefore, to the incomparable *Mezquita*, we repaired to the police office to redeem our passports, and have them *visé* for Madrid, purposing to proceed to the capital by *Diligence*. We there learnt, however, that our route from Gibraltar, having passed *near* the district wherein the cholera had appeared, the public safety demanded that our journey should be continued on horseback, and, moreover, that each day's ride should not exceed eight leagues!

The prospect of a fortnight's baking on the parched plains of La Mancha and Castile, which this preposterous precaution held out, was, of itself, enough to make any one *crusty*; but the additional vexation of finding that all our precautions had been unavailing, all our information erroneous, made us return to the *posada*, thoroughly out of humour with *Las Cosas de España*. Our landlord comforted us, however, by engaging—if we would but wait patiently for a few days, and leave the business entirely in his hands—to get matters arranged so that we might yet proceed on to Madrid by the diligence; and, knowing the wheels within wheels by which Spanish affairs of state are put in motion, we willingly came to this compromise, and remained quietly paying him for our breakfasts and dinners during the best part of a week, receiving each day renewed assurances that every thing was proceeding *"corriente."*

The second day after our arrival at Cordoba, the inhabitants were moved to an unusual degree of excitement, in consequence of an *estafette* having passed through the city during the night, bearing despatches from Madrid to the Captain General of the Province, and rumours were afloat that the king was so seriously ill as to occasion great fears for his life; and, on the following day, public anxiety was yet further excited by a report that the Captain General had passed through Cordoba on his way to the capital; leading to the general belief that Ferdinand was actually dead.

In the evening our host came to us with a very long face, and informed us, confidentially, that such was the case, though, for political reasons, it had been deemed prudent not to make the melancholy news public; adding, that, in consequence of this unforeseen and unfortunate event, he regretted to say the authorities had been seized with such a panic, that he had altogether failed in his endeavour to have the stain effaced from our bill of health. Nevertheless, he said, he hoped yet to be able to arrange matters so as to ensure our being received into the diligence, *without any questions being asked* at Andujar, if we would but remain quietly where we were for a few days longer, and then proceed to that place on horseback.

The news received from Madrid had, however, decided us to give up the plan of continuing our journey thither. I knew enough of Spain to foresee what would be the result of all the intrigues which had been carried on behind the curtains of the imbecile Ferdinand's death-bed.

"You are quite right, Señor," said Blas, to whom I made known our change of plans, "we shall now have a disputed succession, for, be assured, Don Carlos is not the man to forego his just rights without a struggle.— Alas! this only was wanting to fill my unhappy country's cup of misery to overflowing."

Although thus unwillingly forced to abandon the project of crossing the Sierra Morena, we determined, whilst the country yet remained quiet, to extend our tour further to the eastward, and, by proceeding along the *arrecife* to Madrid as far as Andujar, gain the road which leads from thence to Jaen; a city, which the want of practicable roads leading from it to the south has, until late years (during which that deficiency has been remedied), been very rarely visited by travellers.

Recommending Señor Blas to postpone his projected barefoot pilgrimage into Gallicia, until the rainy season had set in, and made the roads soft, we departed from Cordoba by the great post route to the capital, which, as far as Alcolea, is conducted along the right bank of the Guadalquivír, and is a fine, broad, and well-kept gravel road.

Alcolea is seven miles from Cordoba. It is a small village of but twenty or thirty houses, and, in the opinion of Florez, occupies the site of the ancient town of Arva. The *arrecife* here crosses to the left bank of the river by a handsome marble bridge, of eighteen arches, built in 1788-92. The passage of this bridge was obstinately contested by the Spaniards, in the campaign of 1808, but a party of the French, which had crossed the river at Montoro, falling upon its defenders in flank, forced them to retreat.

From hence to Carpio is ten miles. The country is undulated, and the road—along which there is not a single village, and scarcely half a dozen houses—keeps within sight of the Guadalquivír the whole way, affording many pleasing views of the winding stream and its overhanging woods and olive groves.

The town of Carpio is left about a quarter of a mile off, on the right. It is situated on a hill, and by some is supposed to be the ancient city of Corbulo. Pliny, however, distinctly says that place was *below* Cordoba, and Florez fixes it in the vicinity of Palma.

From Carpio to Aldea del Rio is twelve miles, the country continuing much the same as heretofore. At three miles, the road reaches the small town of Pedro Abad (or Perabad) in the vicinity of which is a *despoblado*, [151] where various medals and vestiges have been found that determine it to be the site of Sacili, mentioned by Pliny.

Proceeding onwards, the town of Bujalance may occasionally be seen on the right, distant about a league and a half from the Guadalquivír; and at seven miles from Carpio, we passed Montoro, a large town situated on the margin of the river, and about three quarters of a mile to the left of the *arrecife*. This town has been determined by antiquaries to be Ripepora.

The country about Aldea del Rio is rather pretty, and the place has a thriving look compared with the miserable towns we had lately seen; its population is about 1,800 souls. We halted here for the night, and found the *posada* most wretched.

At a distance of nine (geographic) miles from Aldea del Rio, in a south-east direction, is the town of Porcuna; its situation, Florez justly observes, agreeing so well with that of Obulco, as given both by Strabo [152] and Pliny, [153] as to leave no doubt of their identity. Inscriptions, monuments, coins, &c., which have been found there, quite confirm this opinion, and an important point is thus gained in tracing the operations of Cæsar in his last campaign against the sons of Pompey; since Obulco, which he is mentioned as having reached in twenty-seven days from Rome, may be considered the advanced post of the country that was favourable to his cause.

The present ignoble name of the town—Porcuna,—appears to have been bestowed upon it from the extraordinary fecundity of a *sow*; an inscription, commemorative of the birth of thirty young pigs at one litter, being preserved to this day in the church of the Benedictine friars, and is thus worded:—

C. CORNELIVS. C. F.

CN. GAL. CÆSO.

AED. FLAMEN. II. VIR

MVNICIPII. PONTIF

C. CORN. CÆSO. F.

SACERDOS. GENT. MVNICIPII
SCROFAM CVM PORCIS XXX
IMPENSA IPSORVM.
D. D.

From Aldea del Rio to Andujar is fourteen miles, making the whole distance from Cordoba to that place forty-three miles. The country is very gently undulated, and principally under tillage; the ride, however, is dreary, there being but one house on the road.

Andujar stands altogether on the right bank of the Guadalquivír, which is crossed by a bridge of nine arches. The town is reputed to contain a population of 12,000 souls, but that number is a manifest exaggeration. It is encompassed by old Roman walls, and defended by an ancient castle, and is celebrated for its manufacture of pottery. It is, nevertheless, a dilapidated, impoverished looking place.

By some Andujar is supposed to be the Illiturgi, [154] or, as it is otherwise written, Illurtigis of the ancient historians; but Florez fixes the site of that city two leagues higher up, but on the same bank of the Guadalquivír, and imagines Andujar to be Ipasturgi. The locality of the existing town certainly but ill agrees with the description of Illurtigis given by Livy, for no part of Andujar is "covered by a high rock." [155]

The *arrecife* to Madrid leaves the banks of the Guadalquivír at Andujar, striking inland to Baylen, and thence across the Sierra Morena by the pass of *Despeña Perros*. After devoting a few hours to exploring the old walls of the town, we recrossed the river, and bent our steps towards Granada, taking the road to Jaen.

We proceeded that afternoon to Torre Ximena, twenty miles from Andujar. The country is undulated, and mostly under cultivation. The road is—or, more properly, I should say, perhaps, the places upon the road are—very incorrectly laid down on the Spanish maps; for, instead of being scattered east and west over the face of the country, they are so nearly in line, as to make the general direction of the road nearly straight. Though but a cross-country track, it is tolerably good throughout. The first town it visits is Arjona, said to be the ancient Urgao, or Virgao. [156] It is a poor place, of some twelve or fifteen hundred inhabitants, and distant seven miles from the Guadalquivír.

Five miles beyond Arjona, but lying half pistol shot off the road to the right, is the miserable little village of Escañuela; and three miles further on, the equally wretched town of Villa Don Pardo. From hence to Torre Ximeno (five miles) the road traverses a vast plain, but, ere we had proceeded half way, night overtook us, and on reaching the town we found all the entrances most carefully closed.

After making various attempts to gain admission—groping our way from one barricade to another, until we had nearly completed the circuit of the town—we perceived a light glimmering at some little distance in the country, and hoping it proceeded from some *rancha*, where we might obtain shelter from an approaching storm, if not accommodation for the night, we spurred our jaded animals towards it as fast as the ruggedness of the ground would admit. It proved, however, to be only the remains of a fire made for the purpose of destroying weeds; but a peasant lad, who was warming his evening meal over the expiring embers, pointed out a path leading to one of the town gates, at which, he said, we might, perhaps, gain admission.

Following his directions, we found the gate without much trouble; but a difficulty now arose that promised to be of a more insuperable nature, namely, that of *awaking the guard*, for the combined efforts of our voices proved quite inadequate to the purpose.

It was very vexatious, but irresistibly ludicrous; and, prompted by this mixed feeling of wrath and merriment, we determined to try what effect would be produced by a general discharge of our pistols, and, accordingly riding close up to the gate, fired a volley in the air.

A tremendous discharge of *carajos!* responded to our *salvo,* and soldiers, policemen, custom-house officers, and health-officers, sallied forth, helter skelter, from the guard-house and adjacent dwellings, making off "with the very extremest inch of possibility," under the impression that the place was attacked.

One *aduanero,* however, more enterprising and valiant than the rest, ventured to peep through the bars of the stockade and demand our business; on learning which he encouragingly invited the *urbanos* to return to their *military duty,* whilst he despatched a messenger to the *Alcalde* to request instructions for their further proceedings.

We were subjected meanwhile to a most vexatious detention, occasioned by various causes. Firstly, because the village dictator was nowhere to be found. He had—so it eventually turned out—started from his comfortable seat at the fire of the *posada* (where, surrounded by a knot of politicians, he was discussing the justice of abrogating the Salique law), at the first report of our fire-arms, and, wrapping his cloak around him, had rushed into the street, declaring his intention of meeting death like the last of the Palæologi, rather than be recognised and spared, to grace the triumph of a victorious enemy. Then we had to wait for the key of the gate, which had been carried off in the pocket of one of the runaway soldiers; and, lastly, for a light, the guard-lamp having been overturned in the general confusion, and all the oil spilt.

During the half hour's delay occasioned by these various untoward circumstances, we were subjected to a long verbal examination, touching the part of the country whence we had come; for having wandered round the town in our attempts to gain admission, until we had reached a gate at the very opposite point of the compass to that which points to Andujar, the account we gave seemed to awaken great doubts of our veracity in the minds of these vigilant functionaries; and, even after a lantern had been brought, and our passports delivered up, we underwent a minute personal examination, ere being permitted to repair to the posada.

The Spaniards say, that we English are *"victimas de la etiqueta;"* and, certes, we may compliment them, in return, on being the most complete *slaves to form.* Instances in proof thereof,—which, though on a smaller scale, were scarcely less laughable than the foregoing,—occurred daily in the course of our journey. *Par example,* on leaving the *venta* at Fuente de Piedra, where our sleeping apartment was little better than the stable into which it opened, the hostess insisted on serving our morning cup of chocolate on a table partially covered with a dirty towel, saying, it would not be *"decente"* to allow us to take it standing at the kitchen fire.

Here again, at Torre Ximeno, the landlord was conducting us into what he conceived to be a befitting apartment, when his better half cried out, *"à la sala! à la sala!"* [157] We pricked up our ears, fancying we were to be in clover. The *sala,* however, proved to be a room about ten feet longer than that into which we were first shown, but in every other respect its *fac simile;* that is to say, it had bare white-washed walls and a plastered floor, was furnished with half a dozen low rush-bottomed chairs, and ventilated by two apertures, which at some distant period had been closed by shutters.

The floor presented so uneven a surface, and was marked with so many rents, that, until encouraged by the landlord's *"no tiene usted cuidado,"* [158] I was particularly careful where I placed my feet, taking it to be a highly finished model of the circumjacent sierras and water-courses.

After more than the usual difficulties about bills of health and passports, we received a very civil message from the *Alcalde,* to say, that his house, &c. &c., were at our disposal; but our host and his helpmate seemed so well inclined to do what was in their power to make us *comfortable,* that we declined his polite offer.

Our landlady was still remarkably pretty, though the mother of four children—a rare occurrence in Spain, where mothers, however young they may be, usually look like old women. We had some little difficulty in persuading her that we did not like garlic, and that we should be satisfied with a very moderate quantity of oil in the *guisado* [159] she undertook to prepare for our supper, and on which, with bread and fruit, and some excellent wine, we made a hearty meal.

Contrasts in Spain are most absurd. We slept on thin woollen mattresses, spread upon the before-mentioned mountainous floor—the serrated ridges of which we had some little difficulty in fitting to our ribs—and in the morning were furnished with towels bordered with a kind of thread lace and fringe to the depth of at least eighteen inches; very ornamental, but by no means useful, since the serviceable part of the towel was hardly get-at-able.

On asking our hostess for the bill, we were referred to her husband, which, as the Easterns say, led us to regard her with the eyes of astonishment; for this reference from the lady and mistress to her helpmate, is the exception to the rule, and it was to save trouble we had applied to her, experience having taught us that the landlady was generally the oracle on these occasions; *invariably*, indeed, when there is any intention to cheat.

This, without explanation, may be deemed a most ungallant accusation; I do not mean by it, however, to screen my own sex at the expense of the fairer, for the truth is, the man adds duplicity to his other sins, by retiring from the impending altercation. This he does either from thinking that imposition will come with a better grace from his better half, or, that she will be more ingenious in finding out reasons for the exorbitance of the demand, or, at all events, words in defending it; for any attempt at expostulation is drowned in such a torrent of whys and wherefores, that one is glad, *coute qui coute*, to escape from the encounter. And thus, whilst the lady's volubility is extracting the money from their lodger's pocket, mine host stands aloof, looking as like a hen-pecked mortal as he possibly can, and shrugging his shoulders from time to time, as much as to say, "It is none of my doing! I would help you if I dare, but you see what a devil she is!"

On the present occasion, however, we had no reason to remonstrate, for, to a very moderate charge, were added numerous excuses for any thing that might have been amiss in our accommodation, in consequence of their ignorance of our wants.

Torre Ximeno is situated in a narrow valley, watered by a fine stream; its walls, however, reach to the crest of the hills on both sides, and apparently rest on a Roman foundation. It contains a population of 1,800 souls. From hence a road proceeds, by way of Martos and Alcalà la Real, to Granada, but it is more circuitous than that by Jaen.

From Torre Ximeno to that city is two long leagues, or about nine miles. The road now takes a more easterly direction than heretofore, and, at the distance of three miles, reaches the village of Torre Campo. The rest of the way lies over an undulated country, which slants gradually towards the mountains, that rise to the eastward.

Jaen is situated on the outskirts of the great Sierra de Susana, which, dividing the waters of the Guadalquivír and Genil, spreads as far south as the vale of Granada. The city is built on the eastern slope of a rough and very inaccessible ridge, whose summit is occupied by an old castle, enclosed by extensive outworks.

The ancient name of the place was Aurinx, and it appears to have stood just without the limits of ancient Bœtica. It is now the capital of one of the kingdoms composing the province of Andalusia, and the see of a bishop in the archbishoprick of Toledo. Its population amounts to at least 20,000 souls.

Jaen is in every respect a most interesting city. It is frequently mentioned by the Roman historians, was equally noted in the time of the Moors, from whom it was wrested by San Fernando, A.D. 1246, and of late years has held a distinguished place in the pages of military history. Its situation is picturesque in the extreme, the bright city being on the edge of a rich and fertile basin, encased by wild and lofty mountains. The asperity of the country to the south is such indeed, that, until within the last few years no road practicable for carriages penetrated it, and Jaen has consequently been but very-little visited by travellers; for Granada and Cordoba, being the great objects of attraction, the most direct road between those two places was that which was generally preferred.

A direct and excellent road has now, however, been completed, between Granada and the capital, passing through Jaen. This route crosses the Guadalquivír at Menjiber, and, directed thence on Baylen, falls into the *arrecife* from Cordoba to Madrid, ere it enters the défilés of the Sierra Morena.

The castle of Jaen stands 800 feet above the city, and is still a fine specimen of a Moslem fortress, though the picturesque has been sacrificed to the defensive by various French additions and demolitions. It crowns the crest of a narrow ridge much in the style of the castle of Ximena, to which, in other respects, it also bears a strong resemblance. Its tanks and subterraneous magazines are in tolerable preservation, but the exterior walls of the fortress were partially destroyed by the French, in their hurried evacuation of it in 1812.

The view it commands is strikingly fine. An extensive plain spreads northward, reaching seemingly to the very foot of the distant Sierra Morena, and on every other side rugged mountains rise in the immediate vicinity of the city, which, clad with vines wherever their roots can find holding ground, present a strange union of fruitfulness and aridity.

The city contains fifteen convents, and numerous manufactories of silk, linen and woollen cloths, and mats, and has a thriving appearance. The streets are, for the most part, so narrow, that, with outstretched arms, I could touch the houses on both sides of them.

The cathedral is a very handsome edifice of Corinthian architecture, 300 feet long, and built in a very pure style; indeed every thing about it is in good keeping for Spanish taste. The pavement is laid in chequered slabs of black and white marble; the walls are hung with good paintings, but not encumbered with them; the various altars, though enriched with fine specimens of marbles and jaspers, are not gaudily ornamented; the organ is splendid in appearance and rich in tone.

Some paintings by Moya, particularly a Holy Family, and the visit of Elizabeth to the Virgin Mary, are remarkably good; and the *Capilla sagrada* contains several others by the same master, which are equally worthy of notice: their frames of polished red marble have a good effect.

The only specimens of sculpture of which the cathedral can boast, are some weeping cherubim, done to the very life. The greatest curiosity it contains is the figure of Our Saviour on the cross, dressed in a kilt; but the treasure of treasures of the holy edifice, the proud boast of the favoured city itself, in fact, is the *Santa faz*—the Holy face.

The *Santa faz*—so our conductor explained to us—is the impression of Our Saviour's face, left in stains of blood on the white napkin which bound up his head when deposited in the sepulchre. This cloth was thrice folded over the face, so that three of these "*pinturas*," as the priest called them, were taken. That of Jaen, he said, was the second or middle one, the others are in Italy—where, I know not, but I have some recollection of having heard of them when in that country.

This miraculous picture is only to be viewed on very particular occasions, or by paying a very considerable fee; but we were perfectly satisfied with our cicerone's assurance of its "striking resemblance" to Our Saviour, without requiring the ocular demonstration he was most solicitous to afford.

Attached to the cathedral is a kitchen for preparing the morning chocolate of the priests, and which serves also as a snuggery, where-unto they retire to smoke their *legitimos* during the breaks in their tedious lental services.

The *Parador de los Caballeros*, in the Plaza *del Mercado* is remarkably good, and the view from the front windows, looking towards the castle is very fine.

The distance from Jaen to Granada, by the newly made *arrecife*, is fifty-one miles. It descends gradually into the valley of the Campillos, arriving at, and crossing the river about two miles from Jaen.

The valley is wide, flat, and covered with a rich alluvial deposit; and extends for several leagues in both directions along the course of the stream, encircling the city with an ever-verdant belt of cultivation.

For the succeeding three leagues, the road proceeds along this valley, at first bordered with gardens, orchards, and vineyards, amongst which numerous cottages and water-mills are scattered, but, after advancing about five miles, overhung by rocky ridges, and occasionally shaded with forest-trees.

On a steep mound, on the right hand, forming the first mountain gorge that the road enters, is situated the *Castillo de la Guarda*, and, at the distance of three leagues from Jaen, is the *Torre de la Cabeza*, similarly situated on the left of the road. Beyond this, another verdant belt of cultivation gladdens the eye, extending about a mile and a half along the course of the Campillos. In the midst of this, is the *Venta del Puerto Suelo*, on arriving at which our *mozo*, who for several days had been suffering from indisposition, came to inform us "*que no podía mas*," [160] requested we would leave him there to rest for a couple of days; when he hoped to be able to rejoin us at Granada by means of a *Galera* that travelled the road periodically.

We could not but accede to his request, and as we purposed reaching Granada on the following day, the loss of his attendance for so short a period was of little importance; the only difficulty was, who should lead the baggage animal.—Fortune befriended us.

On our arrival at the inn we had been accosted by a smart-looking young fellow, in the undress uniform of a Spanish infantry soldier, who, seeing the disabled state of our Esquire, volunteered his services to lead our horses to the stable, and minister to their wants; and now, learning from our *mozo* how matters stood, he again came forward, and offered to be our attendant during the remainder of the journey to Granada, to which place he himself was proceeding.

We gladly accepted his proffered services, and, after a short rest, remounted our horses, and pursued our way; the young soldier—like an old campaigner—seating himself between our portmanteaus on the back of the baggage animal. Whilst jogging on before us, I observed, for the first time, that he carried a bright tin case suspended from his shoulder by a silken cord, and curious to know the purpose to which it was applied, asked what it contained.

Without uttering a word in reply, he took off the case, produced therefrom a roll of parchment, and, spreading before us a long document concluding with the words *Io el Rey*, [161] offered it for my perusal. If my surprise was great at the length of the scroll, it was not diminished on finding, after wading through the usual verbose and bombastic preamble, that it dubbed our new acquaintance a knight of the first class of *San Fernando*, and decorated him with the ribbon and silver clasp of the same distinguished order.

On first addressing him at the Venta, I had noticed a bit of ribbon on his breast, but, aware that the very smell of powder, even though it should be but that of his own musket, often *entitles* a Spanish soldier to a decoration; and, indeed, that it is more frequently an acknowledgment of so many months' pay due, than of so much good service done, [162] I had abstained from questioning him concerning it; but that the first class decoration of a military order should have been bestowed on one so low in rank as a corporal, I confess, surprised me; and I concluded that its possessor was either the brother of the mistress of some great man, or that he was passing off some other person's *honors* as his own.

Being a very young man, it was evident he could not have seen much service; my suspicions were, therefore, excusable, and I took the liberty of cross-questioning him concerning the fields wherein his laurels had been gathered. The result gave me such satisfaction that I feel in justice bound to make the *amende honorable* to the gallant fellow for the foul suspicions I had entertained, by giving my readers his history. As, however, it is somewhat long, I will postpone it for the present—as, indeed, not having arrived at its conclusion for several days, it is but methodically correct I should do—merely premising in this place, that, besides the *Diploma*, the tin case contained a statement of the particular services for which he obtained his knighthood, drawn up and attested by the officers of his regiment.

About a mile beyond the Venta where we had fallen in with our new attendant, the country again becomes very wild and broken, and the hills are covered with pine woods. The valley of the Campillos gets more and more confined as the road proceeds, and is bounded by precipitous rocks; and, at length, on reaching the *Puerta de Arenas*, the passage, for the road and river together, does not exceed sixty feet, the cliffs rising perpendicularly on both sides to a considerable height.

This is a very defensible pass, looking towards Granada, but not so in the opposite direction, as it is commanded by higher ground. It is about eighteen miles from Jaen.

On emerging from the pass, an open, cultivated valley presents itself; towards the head of which, distant about four miles, is Campillos Arenas, a wretched village, containing some fifty or sixty *vecinos*. We were stopt at the entrance by an old beggarman, who was officiating as *health* officer, and demanded our passports, which, on receiving, he ceremoniously forwarded to Head Quarters by a ragged, barefoot urchin, with the promise of an *ochavo* [163] if he used despatch in bringing them back to us.

Our passports had now become a serious nuisance, from being completely covered with *visés* both inside and out; for, of course, the curiosity of the natives was proportioned to the number of signatures they contained, and their astonishment was boundless that we should be travelling south at such a moment. At length, our papers were returned to us, and the boy gained his promised reward by running with all his might, to prove that the tedious delay we experienced was not attributable to him.

Proceeding onwards, in three quarters of an hour, we reached the *Parador de San Rafael*, a newly built house of call for the diligence, recently established on this road. It is about twenty-four miles from Jaen, and twenty-seven from Granada, though, as the crow flies, the distance is rather shorter, perhaps, to the latter city than to the first named. It is a place of much resort, and we were happy to find that San Rafael presided over comfortable beds, and good dinners, though rather careless of the state of the wine-cellar.

We started at an early hour next morning, our knightly attendant, with his red epaulettes, and janty foraging cap, together with a *de haut en bas* manner assumed towards the passing peasantry and arrieros, causing us to be regarded with no inconsiderable degree of respect.

The road, for the first eight miles, is one continuation of zig zags over a very mountainous country, and must be kept up at an immense expense to the government, for there is but very little traffic upon it. The hills are principally covered with forests of ilex, but patches of land have recently been taken into cultivation in the valleys, and houses are thinly scattered along the road. At ten miles and a half, we passed the first village we had seen since leaving Campillos Arenas. It is about a mile from the road on the left. The country now becomes less rugged than heretofore, though it continues equally devoid of cultivation and inhabitants.

We were much disappointed at not finding a good *posada* on the road, as we had been led to expect. We passed two in process of building on a magnificent scale, but nothing could be had at either. At last, after riding four long leagues—at a foot's pace, on account of our baggage animal—a farmer took compassion upon us, and, leading the way to his *Cortijo*, supplied our famished horses with a feed of barley, and set before ourselves all the good things his house afforded—melons, grapes, fresh eggs, and delicious bread.

We arrived at the farmer's dinner hour, and a wide circle, comprising his wife, children, cowherds, ploughboys, and dairymaids, was already formed round the huge family bowl of *gazpacho fresco*, of which we received a general invitation to partake. It was far too light a meal, however, to satisfy the cravings of our appetites, and politely declining to dip our spoons in their common mess, we commenced making the usual preparations for an English breakfast, by unpacking our travelling canteen and placing a skillet of water upon the fire.

The curiosity of the peasantry on these occasions amused us exceedingly. In this instance the spectators, who probably had never before come in such close contact with Englishmen, watched each of our movements with the greatest interest. The beating up an egg as a substitute for milk, excited universal astonishment; and the production of knives, forks, and spoons, took their breath away; but when our travelling teapot was placed on the table, their wonderment defies description; many started from their seats to obtain a near view of the extraordinary machine, and our host, after a minute examination, venturing, at last, to expose his ignorance by asking to what use it was applied, exclaimed in raptures, as if it was a thing he had heard of, "*y esa es una tepà!*" [164] "*Una tepà!*" was repeated in all the graduated intonations of the three generations of spectators present; "*una tepà! caramba! que gente tan fina los Ingleses!*"

We now carried on the joke by inflating an air cushion, but the use to which it was applied alone surprised them; for our host with a nod signifying "I understand," took down a huge pig-skin of wine, and made preparations to transfer a portion of its contents to our portable *caoutchouc* pillow. On explaining the purpose to which it was applied, "*Jesus! una almohada!*" [165] exclaimed all the women with one accord—"*Que gente tan deleytosa!*" [166]

Our percussion pistols next excited their astonishment, and by ocular demonstration only could we convince them that they were fired without "*una piedra;*" [167] but when I assured our host that, in England, *diligences* were propelled by steam at the rate of ten leagues an hour, his amazement was evidently stretched beyond the bounds of credulity. "*Como! sin caballos, sin mulas, sin nada, sino el vapor!*" [168] he ejaculated; and his shoulders gradually rising above his ears, as I repeated the astounding assertion, he turned with a look, half horror, half amazement, to his assembled countrymen, saying as plainly as eyes could speak—either these English deal largely with the devil, or are most extraordinary romancers.

If our equipment surprised them, we were not less astonished at the number of cats, without tails, that were prowling about the house; and asking the reason for mutilating the unfortunate creatures in this unnatural way, our host replied, "These animals, to be useful, must have free access to every part of the premises; but, when their tails are long, they do incredible mischief amongst the plates, dishes, and other friable articles, arranged upon the dresser, or left upon the table; whereas, docked as you now see them, they move about without ceremony, and, even in the midst of a labyrinth of crockery, do not the slightest damage. All the mischief of this animal is in his tail."

We had great difficulty in persuading our hospitable entertainer to accept of any remuneration for what he had furnished us, and only succeeded by requesting he would distribute our gift amongst his children.

From his farm, which is called the *Cortijo de los Arenales*, to Granada, is nine miles. The country, during the whole distance, is undulated, and mostly covered with vines and olives. On the right, some leagues distant, we saw the town and *tajo* of Moclin; and at three miles from the *Cortijo* crossed the river Cubillas, which, flowing westward to the plain of Granada, empties itself into the Genil. A little way beyond this the Sierra de Elvira rises abruptly on the right, and thenceforth the ground falls very gradually all the way to Granada.

Our sojourn at Granada was prolonged much beyond the period we had originally intended, by the difficulty of ascertaining the truth of a report that the cholera had appeared at Malaga; but, at length, it was officially notified by a proclamation of the captain-general, that in answer to a despatch sent to the governor of Malaga, he had been assured that city was perfectly free from the disease; and a caravan, composed of numberless *galeras*, *coches*, and *arrieros*, that had been detained at Granada for a fortnight in consequence of this rumour, forthwith proceeded to the sea-port.

Sending our baggage animal forward, directing the mozo—whose indisposition had abated so as to allow of his rejoining us, and resuming his duty—to proceed along the high road to Loja until we overtook him, we set off ourselves at mid-day to visit the *Soto de Roma*. [169]

The road thither strikes off from the *arrecife* to Loja, soon after passing the city of Santa Fé, [170] and traversing Chauchina, after much twisting and turning, reaches Fuente Vaquero, a village belonging to the Duke of Wellington, where his agent, General O'Lawler, has a house.

From thence a long avenue leads to the *Casa Real*, which is situated on the right bank of the Genil. The avenue, both trees and road, is in a very bad state. On the left hand there is a wood of some extent; the forest-trees it contains are chiefly elms and white poplars, but there are also a few oaks. The ground is extremely rich, and was covered with fine crops of maize and hemp; and, on the whole, it struck me the estate was in better order than the properties adjoining it.

The house, however, which at the period of my former visit to Granada was in a tolerable state of repair, I now found in a wretched plight. The court-yard was made the general receptacle for manure; the coach-house and stables were turned into barns and cattle-sheds; the garden was overgrown with weeds; and, basking in the sun, lay young pigs amongst the roses.

From having been the favourite retreat of the Minister Wall, it has degenerated, in fact, into a very second-rate description of farmhouse. This change, however, was inevitable; for, besides that the taste for country-houses is very rare amongst Spaniards, and that the difficulty of procuring a tenant who would keep it in order would, consequently, be very great, the situation of the house is not such as a lover of fine scenery would choose in the vicinity of Granada.

The estate of the Soto de Roma has suffered great damage within the last few years, from the Genil having burst its banks, laid waste the country, and formed itself a new bed; and the stream not being now properly banked in, keeps continually *"comiendo"* [171] the ground on both sides. This evil should be corrected immediately, or, in the event of another extraordinary rise in the river, it may lead to incalculable mischief. The best and cheapest plan of doing this, would be to force the stream back into its old channel. The elm woods on the estate would furnish excellent piles for this purpose, and, by being cut down, would clear some valuable ground which at present lies almost profitless.

After recrossing the Genil we arrived at another village, inhabited by the peasantry of the Soto de Roma, and soon after at a wretched place called Cijuela. The country in its vicinity was flooded for a considerable extent, and we had great difficulty in following the road, and avoiding the ditches that bound it. At length we got once more upon the *arrecife*, and reached Lachar; a vile place, reckoned four leagues from Granada.

From thence to the Venta de Cacin is called two leagues, but they are of Brobdignag measurement. The road is heavy, and the country becomes hilly soon after leaving Lachar. A league beyond the Venta de Cacin is the Venta del Pulgar, situated in the midst of gardens and olive plantations.

It was 11 P.M. when we arrived, for, having missed our way in fording the wide bed of the river Cacin (which crosses the road just beyond the Venta of that name), we had wandered for two hours in the dark; and might have done so until morning, but that our progress was cut short by the river Genil. We thought the wisest plan would be to return to the venta, and endeavour to procure a guide, which we fortunately succeeded in doing. The *ventero* had previously informed us that he had seen our *mozo* pass on with the baggage animal towards Loja, which made us rather anxious for its safety, otherwise we should have rested at his house for the night.

On arriving at the Venta del Pulgar, we found our attendant established there, and in some little alarm at our prolonged absence. Indeed the faithful fellow was so uneasy, that he was about proceeding on a fresh horse in search of us. The night was excessively cold, and we duly appreciated the fire and hot supper his providence had caused to be prepared.

This venta is but a short league from Loja, the ride to which place is very delightful, the rich valley of the Genil (here contracted to the width of a mile) being on the right, a fine range of mountains on the left, whilst the river frequently approaches close to the road, adding by its snakelike windings to the beauty of the scenery.

The town of Loja stands on the south side of a rocky gorge, by which the Genil escapes from the fertile *Vega* of Granada. The mountains on both sides the river are lofty, and of an inaccessible nature, so that the old Moorish fortress, though occupying the widest part of the défilé, completely commands this important outlet from the territory of Granada, as well as the bridge over the Genil.

It was a place of great strength in times past, and Ferdinand and Isabella were repulsed with great loss on their first attempt to gain possession of it. The second attack of the "Catholic kings," made some years afterwards (i. e. in 1487), was more successful, and the English auxiliaries, under the Earl of Rivers, particularly distinguished themselves on the occasion.

Loja is proverbially noted for the fertility of its gardens and orchards, the abundance and purity of its springs, and the loose morals and hard features of its inhabitants. Its situation is peculiarly picturesque, the town being built upon a steep acclivity, unbosomed in groves of fruit trees and overlooked by a toppling mountain. The view of the distant *Sierra Nevada* gives additional interest to the scenery. It contains a population of 9000 souls.

From Loja to Malaga is forty-three miles. The country throughout is extremely mountainous, but the road, nevertheless, is so good as to be traversed by a diligence. Soon after leaving Loja, a road strikes off to the right to Antequera, four leagues; and this, in fact, is the great road from Granada to Seville, and the only portion of it that is interrupted by mountains.

The *arrecife* to Malaga, leaving the village of Alfarnate to the left, at sixteen miles, reaches the solitary venta of the same name; and two miles beyond, the equally lonely venta of Dornejo, considered the half-way house from Loja. The view from hence is remarkably fine, and we enjoyed the scenery to perfection, having remained the night at the venta, and witnessed the splendid effects of both the setting and rising sun.

This is the highest point the road reaches, and is, I should think, about 4000 feet above the level of the Mediterranean.

From the Venta de Dornejo the road proceeds to El Colmenar, eight miles. The mountains that encompass this little town are clad to their very summits with vines, and from the luscious grapes grown in its neighbourhood is made the sweet wine, well known in England under the name of Mountain.

From El Colmenar the road is conducted nine miles along the spine of a narrow tortuous ridge, that divides the Gualmedina, or river of Malaga, from various streams flowing to the eastward, reaching, at last, a point where a splendid view is obtained of the rich vale of Malaga, encircled by the boldly outlined mountains of Mijas, Monda, and Casarabonela. The *coup d'œil* is truly magnificent; the bright city lies basking in the sun, on the margin of the Mediterranean, seemingly at the spectator's feet; but eight miles of a continual descent have yet to be accomplished ere reaching it.

The engineer's pertinacious adherence to his plan of keeping the road on one unvarying inclined plane, tries the patience to an extraordinary degree, but the work is admirably executed. In the whole of these last eight miles there is not one house on the road side, though several neat villas are scattered amongst the ravines below it, on drawing near Malaga.

This difficult passage through the Serranía has been effected only at an enormous cost of money and labour; but, as a work of art, it ranks with any of the splendid roads lately made across the Alps. The scenery along it, especially after gaining the southern side of the principal mountain-chain, when the Mediterranean is brought to view, surpasses any thing that is to be met with in those more celebrated, because more frequented, cloud-capped regions.

Another very fine road has been opened through the mountains between Malaga and Antequera. The scenery along this is very grand, though inferior to that just described. The distance between the two places is about twenty-eight miles, reckoned eight leagues. The road is conducted along the valley of Rio Gordo, or Campanillos; and, it is alleged, through some private influence was made unnecessarily circuitous, to visit the Venta de Galvez. This, and two other ventas, are almost the only habitations on the road. About four miles from Antequera, the road reaches the summit of the great mountain-ridge that pens in the Guadaljorce, which falls very rapidly on its northern side.

Antequera is situated near the foot of the mountain, but in a hollow formed by a swelling hill, which, detached from the chain of sierra, shelters it to the north. It is a large, well-built, and populous city, contains twenty religious houses, numerous manufactories of linen and woollen cloths, silks, serges, &c., and 40,000 souls.

An old castle, situated on a conical knoll, overlooks the city to the east. It formerly contained a valuable collection of ancient armour, but the greater part has been removed.

The city of *Anticaria* is mentioned in the Itinerary of Antoninus; but, as no notice is taken of it by Pliny, it probably was known in his day by some other name. Some antiquaries have imagined Antequera to be Singilia; but this is very improbable, as it is nearly four leagues distant from the Singilis (Genil).

Even the Guadaljorce does not approach within a mile of the city, which depends upon its fountains for water; for though a fine rivulet flows down from the mountains at the back of the city, washing the eastern base of the castle hill, and sweeping round to the westward, where it unites with the Guadaljorce, yet it merely serves to render the valley fruitful, and to turn the wheels of the mills which supply the city with flour and oil.

At a league north-east from Antequera a lofty conical mountain, distinguished by the romantic name of *El Peñon de los Enamorados* (Rock of the Lovers), rises from the plain; and a league beyond it is the town of Archidona, on the great road from Granada to Seville.

CHAPTER XIV

WE found Malaga a deserted city, for the dread of cholera had carried off half its inhabitants; not, however, to their last home, but to Alhaurin, Coin, Churriara, and other towns in the vicinity, in the hope of postponing their visit to a final resting-place by a temporary change to a more salubrious atmosphere than that of the fetid seaport.

Our zealous and indefatigable consul, Mr. Mark, still, however, remained at his post, and his hospitality and kindness rendered our short stay as agreeable as, under existing circumstances, it well could be.

Understanding that a vessel was about to proceed to Ceuta in the course of a few days, we resolved to take advantage of this favourable opportunity of visiting that fortress—the Port Jackson of Spain; and having already seen every thing worthy of observation in Malaga (of which due notice has been taken in a former chapter), we agreed to devote the intervening days to a short excursion to Marbella, Monda, and other interesting towns in the vicinity.

Leaving, therefore, the still hot, but no longer bustling city, late in the afternoon, we took the road to the ferry near the mouth of the Guadaljorce, and leaving the road to *El Retiro* to the right on gaining the southern bank of the river, proceeded to Churriana.

We were disappointed both in the town and in the accommodation afforded at the inn, for the place being much resorted to by the merchants of Malaga, we naturally looked forward to something above the common run of Spanish towns and Spanish posadas, whereas we found both the one and the other rather below par. The town is quite as dirty as Malaga, but, perhaps, somewhat more wholesome; for the filth with which the streets are strewed *not* being watered by a trickling stream, to keep it in a state of fermentation throughout the summer, is soon burnt up, and becomes innoxious.

The town stands at a slight elevation above the vale of Malaga, and commands a fine view to the eastward.

We left the wretched venta betimes on the following morning, and proceeded towards Marbella, leaving on our left the little village of Torre

Molinos, situated on the Mediterranean shore (distant one league from Churriana), and reaching Benalmaina in two hours and a half. The road keeps the whole way within half a mile of the sea, and about the same distance from a range of barren sierras on the right. No part of it is good but the ascent to Benalmaina (or, as it is sometimes, and perhaps more correctly written, Benalmedina), is execrable.

This village is surrounded with vineyards, and groves of orange and fig trees; is watered by a fine clear stream, which serves to irrigate some patches of garden-ground, as well as to turn numerous mill-wheels; and, from the general sterility of the country around, has obtained a reputation for amenity of situation that it scarcely deserves.

In something less than an hour, descending the whole time, we reached the Mediterranean shore, and continuing along it for a mile, arrived at the Torre Blanca—a high white tower, situated on a rugged cliff that borders the coast, and in the vicinity of which are numerous ruins. Some little distance beyond this the cliffs terminate, and a fine plain, covered with gardens and orchards, stretches inland for several miles.

Nature has been peculiarly bountiful to this sunny valley, for the river of Mijas winds through, and fertilizes the whole of its eastern side; whilst the western portion is watered by the river Gomenarro, or—word offensive to British ears—Fuengirola.

The plain is about two miles across, and near its western extremity; and a little removed from the seashore is the fishing village of Fuengirola. It is a small and particularly dirty place, but contains a population of 1000 souls. The distance from Malaga is reckoned by the natives five leagues, "three long and two short," according to their curious mode of computation; but, I think, in reducing them to English miles, the usual average of four per league may be taken. The last league of the road is very good. The town of Mijas, rich in wine and oil, is perched high up on the side of a rugged mountain, about four miles north of Fuengirola. A *trocha* leads from thence, over the mountains, into the valley of the Guadaljorce, debouching upon Alhaurinejo; and to those in whose travelling scales the picturesque outweighs the breakneck, I would strongly recommend this route from Malaga in preference to the tamer, somewhat better, and, perhaps, rather shorter road, that borders the coast.

The old and, alas! too celebrated castle of Fuengirola, or Frangirola, occupies the point of a rocky tongue that juts some way into the sea, about half a mile beyond the fishing village of the same name. It is a work of the Moors, built, as some say, on an ancient foundation, imagined to be that of

Suel; whilst others maintain, that the vestigia of antiquity built into its walls, were brought there from some place in the neighbourhood.

That *Suel* did not stand here appears to me very evident; for though the actual distance from Malaga to Fuengirola exceeds but little that given in the Itinerary of Antoninus from Malaca to Suel, viz., twenty-one miles—calculating seventy-five Roman miles to a degree of the meridian;—yet, as the Itinerary makes the whole distance from Malaca to Calpe Carteia eighty-nine miles, [172] whereas, even following all the sinuosities of the coast, it can be eked out only to eighty (of the above standard), it seems clear that the length of the mile has been somewhat overrated.

That I may not incur the reproach of "extreme confidence," in venturing to publish an opinion differing from that of various learned antiquaries who have written on the subject, I will endeavour to show that my doubt has, at all events, some reasonable foundation to rest upon.

Supposing that the distances given in the Itinerary between Malaca and Calpe Carteia were respectively correct, but that the error—which, in consequence, was evident—had been made by over-estimating the length of the Roman mile in use at the period the Itinerary was compiled, I found, by dividing the *actual* distance into eighty-nine parts (following such an irregular line as a road, considering the ruggedness of the country, might be supposed to take), that it gave a scale of eighty-three and a third of such divisions to a degree of the meridian; a scale which, as I have observed in a former chapter, is mentioned by Strabo, on the authority of Eratosthenes, as one in use amongst the Romans.

Now, by measuring off twenty-one such parts along the indented line of coast from Malaga westward, to fix the situation of Suel, I find that, according to this scale, it would be placed about a mile beyond the Torre Blanca; that is, at the commencement of the fertile valley, which has been mentioned as stretching some way inland, and at the bottom of the bay, of which the rocky ledge occupied by the castle of Fuengirola forms the western boundary; certainly a much more suitable site, either for a commercial city, or for a fortress, than the low, rocky headland of Fuengirola, which neither affords enough space for a town to stand upon, nor is sufficiently elevated above the adjacent country, to have the command that was usually sought for in building fortresses previous to the invention of artillery.

Proceeding onwards, and measuring twenty-four divisions (of this same scale) from the point where I suppose Suel to have stood, along the yet rugged coast to the westward of Fuengirola, the site of Cilniana, the next station of the Itinerary, is fixed a little beyond where the town of Marbella now stands; another most probable spot for the Phœnicians or Romans to have selected for a station; as, in the first place, the proximity of the high, impracticable, Sierra de Juanel, would have enabled a fortress there situated to intercept most completely the communication along the coast; and, in the second, the vicinity of a fertile plain, and the valuable mines of Istan (from whence a fine stream flows), would have rendered it a desirable site for a port.

The next distance, thirty-four miles to Barbariana, brings me to the *mouth* of the Guadiaro, (which *can be* no other than the Barbesula of the Romans, if we suppose that the road continued, as heretofore, along the seashore); or, carries me across that river, and also the Sogarganta, which falls into it, if, striking inland, *as soon as the nature of the country permitted*, we imagine the road to have been directed by the straightest line to its point of destination.

Now, in the first case, the discovery of numerous vestigia, and inscriptions at a spot two miles up from the mouth, on the eastern bank of the Barbesula, (i. e. Guadiaro) have clearly proved that to be the position of the city [173] bearing the same name as the river. We must not, therefore, look in its neighbourhood for Barbariana; especially as the vestiges of this ancient town are twelve *English* miles from Carteia, whereas the distance from Barbariana to Carteia is stated in the Itinerary to be but ten *Roman* miles.

In the second case, having crossed the Sogarganta about a mile above its confluence with the Guadiaro, we arrive, at the end of the prescribed thirty-four miles from Cilniana, at the mouth of a steep ravine by which the existing road from Gaucin and Casares to San Roque ascends the chain of hills forming the southern boundary of the valley, and this spot is not only well calculated for a military station, but exceeds by very little the distance of ten miles to Carteia, specified in the Itinerary.

I suppose, therefore, that Barbariana stood here, where it would have been on the most direct line that a road *could take* between Estepona and Carteia, as well as on that which presented the fewest difficulties to be surmounted in the nature of the country.

I will now follow the Roman Itinerary as laid down by Mr. Carter, in his "Journey from Gibraltar to Malaga." [174]

The first station, Suel, he fixes at the Castle of Fuengirola; the second, Cilniana, at the ruins of what he calls Old Estepona. These he describes as lying *three leagues* to the eastward of the modern town of that name, and upwards of a league to the westward of the Torre de las Bovedas, in the vicinity of which he assumes Salduba stood; but this very site of Salduba (i. e. the Torre de las Bovedas) is little more than *two leagues* from modern

Estepona, being just half way between that place and Marbella—the distance from the one town to the other scarcely exceeding four leagues, or sixteen English miles—so that, in point of fact, he fixes Cilniana at *four miles* to the eastward of Estepona, instead of three leagues.

Passing over this error, however, and allowing that his site of Cilniana was where *he wished it to be*, Mr. Carter, nevertheless, still found himself in a difficulty; for he had already far exceeded the greater portion of the *actual* distance between Malaga and Carteia, although but half the number of miles specified in the Itinerary were disposed of; so that twenty-five miles measured along the coast now brought him within the prescribed distance of Barbariana from Carteia (ten miles), instead of thirty-four, as stated in the Itinerary!

To extricate himself, therefore, from this dilemma, he carries the road, first to the town of Barbesula, situated near the mouth of the river of the same name, and then *eight miles up the stream* to Barbariana.

The objections to this most eccentric route are, however, manifold and obvious. In the first place, had the road visited Barbesula, that town would assuredly have been noticed in the Itinerary of Antoninus, because it would have made so much more convenient a break in the distance between Cilniana and Carteia, than Barbariana.

In the next,—had the road been taken to the mouth of the Guadiaro, it would *there* have been as near Carteia as from any other point along the course of that river, with nothing in the nature of the intervening country to prevent its being carried straight across it: every step, therefore, that the road was taken up the stream would have unnecessarily increased the distance to be travelled.

Thirdly,—had Barbariana been situated *eight miles* [175] up the river, the road from Barbesula must not only have been carried that distance out of the way to visit it, but, for the greater part of the way, must actually have been led back again towards the point of the compass whence it had been brought; and the town of Barbariana would thereby have been situated nearly eighteen miles from Calpe Carteia, instead of ten.

Mr. Carter probably fell into this error, through ignorance of the direction whence the Guadiaro flows, for though the last four miles of its course is easterly, yet its previous direction is due south, or straight upon Gibraltar; and, consequently, taking the road up the stream beyond the distance of *four miles*, would have been leading it away from its destination. And if, on the other hand, we suppose that Mr. Carter's mistake be simply in the name of the river, and that, by two leagues up the Guadiaro, he meant up its tributary, the Sogarganta; [176] still, so long as the road continued following the course of that stream, it would get no nearer to Carteia, and was, therefore, but uselessly increasing the distance.

It is quite unreasonable, however, to suppose that the Romans, who were in the habit of making their roads as straight as possible, should have so unnecessarily departed from their rule in this instance, and not only have increased the distance by so doing, but also the difficulties to be encountered; for, in point of fact, a road would be more readily carried to the Guadiaro by leaving the seashore on approaching Manilba, and directing it straight upon Carteia, than by continuing it along the rugged and indented coast that presents itself from thence to the mouth of the river.

Objections may be taken to the sites I have fixed upon for the different towns mentioned in the Roman Itinerary, from the absence of all vestiges at those particular spots; but when the ease with which all traces of ancient places are lost is considered, particularly those situated on the seashore, I think such objections must fall to the ground: and, indeed, Carter himself, who found fault with Florez for supposing the town of Salduba [177] *could* have entirely disappeared, furnishes a glaring instance of the futility of such objections, when he states that not the least remains of Barbesula were to be traced, whereas, *now*, they are quite visible.

The castle of Fuengirola—to which it is time to return from this long digression—has lately undergone a thorough repair; the whole of the western front, indeed, has been rebuilt, and the rest of the walls have been modernised, though they still continue to be badly flanked by small projecting square towers, and are exposed to their very foundations, so that the fortress *ought not* to withstand even a couple of hours' battering.

From hence to Marbella is four leagues. During the first, the road is bad enough, and, for the remaining three, but indifferently good. The last eight miles of the stony track may, however, be avoided by riding along the sandy beach, which, when the sun is on the decline, the breeze light and westerly, and, above all, when the *tide is out*, is pleasant enough. I may as well observe here, that the Mediterranean Sea really does ebb and flow, notwithstanding anything others may have stated to the contrary.

The whole line of coast bristles with towers, built originally to give intelligence by signal of the appearance of an enemy. They are of all shapes and ages; some circular, having a Roman look; others angular, and either Moorish, or built after Saracenic models; many are of comparatively recent construction, though all seem equally to be going to decay.

These towers can be entered only by means of ladders, and such as are in a habitable state are occupied by Custom-house guards, or, more correctly, Custom-house defrauders. Here and there a *Casa fuerta* has been erected along the line, which, furnished with artillery and a small garrison of regular troops, serves as a *point d'appui* to a certain portion of the *peculative* cordon, enabling the soldiers to render assistance to the revenue officers in bringing the smugglers to *terms*.

Marbella has ever been a bone of contention amongst the antiquaries; some asserting that it does not occupy the site of any ancient city; others, that it is on the ruins of *Salduba*. Of this latter opinion is La Martinière, who certainly has better reason for maintaining than Carter for disputing it. For if that city "stood on a steep headland, between which and the hill" (behind) "not a beast could pass," it could not possibly have been on the site where our countryman places it, viz., at the ruins near the *Torre de las Bovedas* (seven miles to the westward), where a wide plain stretches inland upwards of two miles.

In fact, there are but two headlands between the river Guadiaro and Marbella, where a town could be built at all answering the foregoing description; namely, at the *Torre de la Chullera* and the *Torre del Arroyo Vaquero*, the former only three, the latter ten miles from the Guadiaro: and a far more likely spot than either of these is the knoll occupied by the *Torre del Rio Real*, about two miles to the *eastward* of Marbella. [178]

Marbella stands slightly elevated above the sea, and its turreted walls and narrow streets declare it to be thoroughly Moorish. Its sea-wall is not actually washed by the waves of the Mediterranean, so that the town may be avoided by such as do not wish to be delayed by or subjected to the nuisance of a passport scrutiny; and the Spanish saying, "*Marbella es bella, pero no entras en ella,*" [179] significantly, though mysteriously, suggests the prudence of staying outside its walls; but this poetical scrap of advice was perhaps the only thing some luckless *contrabandista* had left to bestow upon his countrymen, and we, being in search of a dinner and night's lodging, submitted patiently to the forms and ceremonies prescribed on such occasions at the gates of a fortress.

To do the Spaniards justice, they are not usually very long in their operations, the first offer being in most instances accepted without haggling; and accordingly, the *peseta* pocketed, and every thing pronounced *corriente*, we proceeded without further obstruction to the *Posada de la Corona*, which, situated in a fine airy square, we were agreeably surprised to find a remarkably good inn.

Marbella, though invested with the pomp and circumstance of war, is but a contemptible fortress. An old Moorish castle, standing in the very heart of the town, constitutes its chief strength; for, though its circumvallation is complete and tolerably erect, considering its great age, yet, from the inconsiderable height of the walls, and the inefficient flanking fire that protects them, they could offer but slight resistance to an enemy.

A detached fort, that formerly covered the place from attack on the sea side, and flanked the eastern front of the enceinte of the town, has been razed to the ground, so that ships may now attack it almost with impunity.

The town is particularly clean and well inhabited, the fishing portion of the population being located more conveniently for their occupation in a large suburb on its eastern side. The fortress encloses several large churches and religious houses, besides the citadel or Moorish castle, so that within the walls the space left for streets is but small; the inhabitants of the town itself cannot therefore be estimated at more than five thousand, whilst those of the suburb may probably amount to fifteen hundred.

The trade of Marbella is but trifling; the fruit and vegetables grown in its neighbourhood are, it is true, particularly fine, but the proximity of the precipitous Sierra de Juanal limits cultivation to a very narrow circuit round the walls of the town; and, on the other hand, the valuable mines in the vicinity, which formerly secured Marbella a prosperous trade, have for many years been totally abandoned: so that, in fact, there is little else than fish to export.

There is no harbour, but vessels find excellent holding ground and in deep water, close to the shore; the landing also is good, being on a fine hard sand, and I found a small pier in progress of construction.

It seems probable that in remote times numerous commercial towns were situated along the coast, between Malaca and Calpe, whence a thriving trade was carried on with the East, for the whole chain of mountains bordering the Mediterranean abounds in metallic ores, especially along that part of the coast between Marbella and Estepona; and it is evident that mining operations on an extensive scale were formerly carried on here, since the tumuli formed by the earth excavated in searching for the precious metals are yet to be seen, as well as the bleached channels by which the water that penetrated into the mines was led down the sides of the mountains.

The metals contained in this range of mountains are, principally, silver, copper, lead, and iron; of the two former I have seen some very fine specimens.

The richness and comparative proximity of these mines led the Phœnicians and Romans, by whom there is no doubt they were worked, to neglect the copper mines of Cornwall; for, whilst necessity obliged them to come to England for tin, it is observable that in many places, where, in working for that metal, they came also upon lodes of copper, they carried away the tin only; a circumstance that has rendered some of the recently worked Cornish copper mines singularly profitable, and leads naturally to the supposition that the ancients procured copper at a less expense from some other country.

In the same way that the old Roman mines in England, from our knowledge of the vast power of steam, and of the means of applying that power to hydraulical purposes, have been reopened with great advantage, so also might those of Spain be again worked with a certainty of success. Capital and security—the two great wants of Spain—are required however to enable adventurers to embark in the undertaking.

Marbella is four leagues from Estepona, and ten from Gibraltar; but though the first four may be reckoned at the usual rate of four miles each, yet the remaining six cannot be calculated under four and a half each, making the whole distance to Gibraltar forty-three miles, and from Malaga to Gibraltar seventy-nine miles. [180]

CHAPTER XV

"M AS vale paxaro en mano, que buytre volando" — *Anglicè*, a bird in the hand is worth more than a vulture flying — is a proverb that cannot be too strongly impressed upon the minds of travellers in Spain; and, acting up to the spirit of this wise saw, we did not leave our comfortable quarters at the *Posada de la Corona* until after having made sure of a breakfast. For, deeming even a cup of milk at Marbella worth more than a herd of goats up the sierra, there appeared yet more reason to think that no venta on the unfrequented mountain track by which we purposed returning to Malaga could furnish anything half so estimable as the *café au lait* promised overnight, and placed before us soon after daybreak.

We commenced ascending the steep side of the *Sierra de Juanal* immediately on leaving Marbella, and, in something under an hour, reached a pass, on the summit of a ridge, whence a lovely view opens to the north. The little town of Ojen lies far down below, embosomed in a thicket of walnut, chestnut, and orange trees; whilst all around rise lofty sierras, clothed, like the valley, with impervious woods, though with foliage of a darker hue, their forest covering consisting principally of cork and ilex. Numerous torrents, (whose foaming streams can only occasionally be seen dashing from rock to rock amidst the dense foliage) furrow the sides of the impending ridges, directing their course towards the little village, threatening, seemingly, to overwhelm it by their united strength; but, wasting their force against the cragged knoll on which it stands, they collect in one body at its foot, and, as if exhausted by the struggle, flow thenceforth tranquilly towards the Mediterranean, meandering through rich vineyards, and under verdant groves of arbutus, orange, and oleander.

Excepting by this outlet, along the precipitous edge of which our road was practised, there seemed to be no possibility of leaving the sylvan valley, so completely is it hemmed in by wood and mountain. The descent from the pass occupied nearly as much time as had been employed in clambering up to it from the sea-coast, but the road is better.

The situation of the little town, on the summit of a scarped rock, clustered over with ivy and wild vines, and moistened by the spray of the torrents that rush down on either side, is most romantic; the place, however, is miserable in the extreme, containing some two hundred wretched hovels, mostly mud-built, and huddled together as if for mutual support.

An ill-conditioned *pavé* zigzags up to it, and proceeds onwards along the edge of a deep ravine towards Monda. The woods, rocks, and water afford ever-varying and enchanting vistas, but, from the vile state of the road, it is somewhat dangerous to pay much attention to the beauties of nature.

In something more than an hour from Ojen, we reached a pass in the northern part of the mountain-belt that girts it in, whence we took a last lingering look at the lovely valley, compared to which the country now lying before us appeared tame and arid.

The fall of the mountain on the western side is much more gradual than towards the Mediterranean, and the road—which does not however improve in due proportion—descends by an easy slope towards the little river Seco. The valley, at first, is wide, open, and uncultivated; but, at the end of about a mile, it contracts to an inconsiderable breadth, and the steep hills that border it give signs of the husbandman's toils, being every where planted with vines and olive trees.

Arriving now at the margin of the *Seco*, the road crosses and recrosses the rivulet repeatedly, in consequence of the rugged nature of its banks, and, at length, quitting the pebbly bed of the stream, and crossing over a lofty mountain ridge that overlooks it to the east, the stony track brings us to Monda, which is nestled in a deep ravine on the opposite side of the mountain, and commanded by an old castle situated on a rocky knoll to the north-west.

The view from the summit of this mountain is very extensive, embracing the greater portion of the *Hoya* de Malaga, the distant sea-bound city, and yet more remote sierras of Antequera, Alhama, and Granada. The descent to Monda is extremely bad, though by no means rapid. The distance of this place from Marbella is stated in the Spanish Itineraries to be three leagues, but the incessant windings of the road make it fourteen miles, at least. The houses of Monda are mostly poor, though some of the streets are wide and good. The population is estimated at 2,000 souls.

It is to this day a mooted question amongst Spanish antiquaries whether Monda, or Ronda *la Vieja*, (as some of them call the ruins of Acinippo), or any other of several supposed places, be the Roman *Munda*, where Cneius Scipio gave battle to the Carthaginian generals, Mago and Asdrubal, B.C. 211, and near whose walls Julius Cæsar concluded his wonderful career of victory by the defeat of Cneius Pompey the younger, B.C. 42.

From this discrepancy of opinion, and the inaccuracy of the Spanish maps, I am induced to offer the following observations (the result of a careful examination of the country), touching the site of this once celebrated spot. And, first, with respect to Ronda and Ronda *la Vieja*, I may repeat what I have already stated in a former chapter, that neither the situation of those places, nor the nature of the ground in their vicinity, agrees in any one respect with the description of Munda and its battle-field, as given by Hirtius; [181] nor, from discoveries that have recently been made, does there appear to be any ground left for doubting that those places occupy the sites of Arunda and Acinippo.

Of the other positions which have been assigned to *Munda*, that most insisted upon is a spot "three leagues to the *west* of the present town of Monda," [182] and here Carter, adopting the opinion of Don Diego Mendoza, confidently places it, stating that bones of men and horses had, in former days, been dug up there; that the peasants called the spot *Monda la Vieja*, and averred they sometimes saw squadrons of apparitions fighting in the air with cries and shouts!

Such a host of circumstantial and phantasmagorical evidence our countryman considered irresistible, and concluded, accordingly, that this spot could be no other than that whereon the two mighty Roman armies contended for empire. He admits, however, that, even in the days of his precursor, Don Diego, "scarcely any ruins were to be found, the *whole* having by degrees been transplanted to modern Monda and other places." Why they should have been carried three leagues across some of the loftiest mountains in the country, to be used merely as building stones, he does not attempt to explain, but, believing such to be the case, one wonders it never struck him as being somewhat extraordinary that these pugnacious ghosts should continue fighting for a town of which not a stone remains.

But, leaving Mr. Carter for the present, I will retrace my steps to modern Monda, where it must be acknowledged some little difficulty is experienced in fitting the Roman city to the spot allotted to it on the maps, as well as in placing the contending armies upon the ground in its neighbourhood, so as to agree with the order in which they were arrayed on the authority of Hirtius. Still, with certain admissions, which admissions I do not consider it by any means unreasonable to beg, all apparent discrepancies may be reconciled and difficulties overcome; and, on the other hand, unless these points be granted, Ronda, Gaucin, or Gibraltar agree just as well with the Munda of the Roman historian as the little town of Monda I am about to describe.

It will be necessary, however, for the perfect understanding of the subject,—and, I trust, my endeavour to establish the site of Cæsar's last battle-field will be considered one of sufficient interest to warrant a little prolixity,—to take a glance at the country in the vicinity of Monda, ere proceeding to describe the actual ground whereon, according to my idea, the contending armies were drawn up; as it is only from a knowledge of the country, and of the communications that intersected it, that the reasons can be gathered for such a spot having been selected for a field of battle.

The old castle of Monda, under the walls of which we must suppose— for this is one of the premised admissions—the town to have been clustered, instead of being, as at present, sunk in a ravine, stands on the eastern side of a rocky ridge, projected in a northerly direction from the lofty and wide-spreading mountain-range, that borders the Mediterranean between Malaga and Estepona. This range is itself a ramification of the great mountain-chain that encircles the basin of Ronda, from which it branches off in a southerly direction, and under the names of Sierras of Tolox, Blanca, Arboto, and Juanal, presents an almost impassable barrier between the valley of the Rio Verde (which falls into the Mediterranean, three miles west of Marbella), and the fertile plains bordering the Guadaljorce.

This steep and difficult ridge terminates precipitously about Marbella; but another branch of the range, sweeping round the little town of Ojen, turns back for some miles to the north, rises in two lofty peaks above Monda, and then, taking an easterly direction, juts into the Mediterranean at Torre Molinos. The towns of Coin and Alhaurin are situated, like Monda, on rocky projections from the north side of this range, overhanging the vale of Malaga; and the solitary town of Mijas stands upon its southern acclivity, looking towards the sea.

The rugged ramification on which Monda is situated stretches north about two miles from the double-peaked sierra above mentioned; and though completely overlooked by that mountain, yet, in every other direction, it commands all the ground in its immediate neighbourhood, and, without being very elevated, is every where steep, and difficult of access. The summit of the ridge is indented by various rounded eminences, and, consequently, is of very unequal breadth, as well as height. The castle of Monda stands on one of these knolls, but quite on the eastern side of the hill, the breadth of which, in this place, scarcely exceeds 400 yards. At its furthest extremity, however, the ridge, which extends northward, *nearly a mile*, beyond the town, sends out a spur to the east, following the course of, and falling abruptly to the Rio Seco; and the breadth of the hill may here be said to be increased to nearly two miles.

Between the river Seco and the Rio Grande (a more considerable stream, which runs nearly parallel to, and about seven miles from the Seco), the country, though rudely moulded, is by no means lofty; but round the sources of the latter river, and along its left bank, rise the huge sierras of Junquera, Alozaina, and Casarabonela, closing the view from Monda to the north.

From the description here given it will be apparent, that the communications across so mountainous a country must not only be few, but very bad. Such, indeed, is the asperity of the sierras west of Monda, that no road whatever leads through them; and, to the south, but one tolerable road presents itself to cross the lateral ridge, bordering the Mediterranean, between Marbella and Torre Molinos, viz., that by which we had traversed it.

Even on the other half circle round Monda, where the country is of a more practicable nature, only two roads afford the means of access to that town, viz., one from Guaro, where the different routes from Ronda (by Junquera), El Burgo, Alozaina, and Casarabonela, unite; the other from Coin, upon which place, from an equal necessity, those from Alora, Antequera, and Malaga, are first directed.

Monda thus becomes the point of concentration of all the roads proceeding from the inland towns to Marbella; the pass of Ojen, in its rear, offering the only passage through the mountains to reach that city.

The road from this pass, as has already been described, approaches Monda by the valley watered by the river Seco; which stream, directed in the early part of its course by the Sierra de Monda on its right, flows nearly due north for about a mile and a half beyond where the road to Monda leaves its bank, receiving in its progress several tributary streams that rise in the mountains on its left. On gaining the northern extremity of the ridge of Monda, the rivulet winds round to the eastward, still washing the base of that mountain, but leaving the hilly country on its left bank, along which a plain thenceforth stretches for several miles. The stream again, however, becomes entangled in some broken and intricate country, ere reaching the wide plain of the Guadaljorce, into which river it finally empties itself.

The situation of Monda, with reference to the surrounding country, having now been fully described, it is necessary, ere proceeding to shew that the ground in its neighbourhood answers perfectly the account given of it by Hirtius, to offer some remarks on the causes that may be supposed to have led to a collision between the hostile Roman armies on such a spot, since the present unimportant position of Monda seems to render such an event very improbable.

Cæsar, it would appear, after the fall of Ategua, proceeded to lay siege to Ventisponte and Carruca—two places, whose positions have baffled the researches of the most learned antiquaries to determine—his object, evidently, having been to induce Pompey to come to their relief. His adversary, however, was neither to be forced nor tempted to depart from his politic plan of "drawing the war out into length;" but, retiring into the mountains, compelled Cæsar, whose interest it was, on the other hand, to bring the contest to as speedy an issue as possible, to follow him into a more defensible country.

With this view, leaving the wide plain watered by the Genil and Guadaljorce on the northern side of the mountains, Pompey, we may imagine, retired towards the Mediterranean, and stationed himself at Monda; a post that not only afforded him a formidable defensive position, but that gave him the means of resuming hostilities at pleasure, since it commanded the roads from Cartama to Hispalis (Seville), by way of Ronda, and from Malaca, along the Mediterranean shore, to Carteía, [183] where his fleet lay; and, should his adversary not follow him, the situation thus fixed upon was admirably adapted for carrying the war into the country in arms against him, the two opulent cities of Cartama and Malaca (which there is every reason to conclude were attached to the cause of Cæsar), being within a day's march of Monda.

Here, therefore, Pompey occupied a strategical point of great importance; and Cæsar, fully aware of the advantage its possession gave his opponent, determined to attack him at all risks.

The hostile armies were separated from each other by a plain five miles in extent. [184] That of Cæsar was drawn up in this plain, his cavalry posted on the left; whilst the army of Pompey, whose cavalry was stationed on *both* wings, occupied a strong position on a range of mountains, protected on one side by the town of Munda, "*situated on an eminence;*" on the other, by the nature of the ground, "*for across this valley*" (i.e. that divided the two armies), "*ran a rivulet, which rendered the approach to the mountain extremely difficult, because it formed a morass on the right.*"

Now although the town of Munda is here described as protecting Pompey's army on one side, yet from what follows it must be inferred that it was some distance in the rear of his position, since, not only is it stated that "*Pompey's army was at length obliged to give ground and retire towards the town,*" but it may be taken for granted that, had either flank rested upon the town, the cavalry would *not* have been posted on "*both wings.*"

Moreover, it is stated that "*Cæsar made no doubt but that the enemy would descend to the plain and come to battle,*" the superiority of cavalry being greatly on Pompey's side—*"but,"* Hirtius proceeds to say, *"they durst not advance a mile from the town,"* and, in spite of the advantageous opportunity offered them, *"still kept their post on the mountain in the neighbourhood of the town."*

It may therefore be fairly concluded, that Pompey's position was on the edge of a range of hills, some little distance in advance of the town of Munda, having a stream running in a deep valley along its front, and a morass on one flank. Now the question is, Can the ground about Monda be made to agree with these various premises? Certainly not, if, as is generally assumed, the battle was fought on the eastern side of the town; for Pompey's position must, in that case, have extended along the ridge, so as to have the peaked Sierra, above Monda, on its right, and the river Seco on its left, whilst Monda itself would have been an advanced post of the line; and so far from there being a plain *"five miles"* in extent in front, the country to the east of Monda—though for some way but slightly marked—is, at the distance of *two* miles, so abruptly broken as to render the drawing up of a Roman army impossible.

In addition to these objections it will be obvious that the half of Pompey's cavalry on the right, would have been posted on a high mountain, where it could not possibly act, whilst the whole of Cæsar's (on his left), would have been paralyzed by having to manœuvre on the acclivity of a steep mountain and against a fortified town, instead of being kept in the valley of the river Seco, ready to fall upon the weak part of the enemy's line as soon as it should be broken.

What, however, seems to me to be fatal to the supposition that this was the side of the town on which the battle was fought is, that Cæsar's army would have occupied the road by which alone the small portion of Pompey's army, that escaped, could have retired upon Cordoba.

Against the supposition that the battle took place on the *western* side of the ridge on which Monda is situated, the objections, though not so numerous, are equally insurmountable; since there is nothing like a plain whereon Cæsar's army could have been drawn up; the valley of the river Seco being so circumscribed that, for Pompey's army to have *"advanced a mile from Monda,"* it must not only have crossed the stream, but mounted the rough hills that there border its left bank; whereas Cæsar's army is stated to have been posted in a plain that extended five miles from Monda. The half of Pompey's cavalry on the *left* would, in this case also, have been uselessly posted on an eminence. In other respects the supposition is admissible enough, since Monda would have been in the rear of the left of Pompey's position, but still a support to the line, and the whole front would have been *"difficult of approach,"* and along the course of a rivulet.

We will now examine the ground to the north of the town, to which it strikes me no insuperable objections can be raised.

We may suppose that Pompey took post with his army fronting Toloz and Guaro, the only direction in which his enemy could be looked for, and where the ground is so little broken, as certainly to allow of its being called *a plain*, as compared with the rugged country that encompasses it on all sides; and his position would naturally have been taken up along the edge of the last ramification of the ridge of Monda, which extends about two miles from west to east along the right bank of the river Seco.

The town would then have been half a mile or so *in rear* of the left centre of Pompey's position; *a rivulet, "rendering the approach of the mountain difficult,"* would have run along its front. His cavalry would naturally have been disposed on *both flanks*, where, the hills terminating, it would be most at hand either to act offensively, or for the security of the position; and the cavalry of Cæsar, on the contrary, would *all* have been posted on *his* left, where the access to Pompey's position was easiest, and where, in case of his enemy's defeat, its presence would have produced the most important results.

We may readily conceive, also, that in times past *a morass* bordered the Seco where it first enters the plain, since several mountain streams there join it, whose previously rapid currents must have experienced a check on reaching this more level country. The industrious Moslems, probably, by bringing this fertile plain into cultivation, drained the morass so that no traces of it are now perceptible, but twenty years hence there may possibly be another.

Every condition required, therefore, to make the ground agree with the description given of it by Hirtius, is here fulfilled; and, occupying such a position, the army of Pompey seemed likely to obtain the ends which we cannot but suppose its general had in view.

The objections of Mr. Carter to modern Monda being the site of the Roman city are, first, the want of space in its vicinity for two such vast hosts to be drawn up in battle array; and, secondly, the little distance of the existing town from the river Sigila and city of Cártama, which, according to an ancient inscription, referring to the repairs of a road from Munda to Cártama, he states was twenty miles.

In consequence of these imaginary discrepancies, he suffered himself to be persuaded that the spot where the apparitions are fighting "three leagues to the westward of the modern town," is the site of the Roman *Munda*. In which case it must have been situated in a *narrow valley*, bounded on all sides by lofty mountains, and *twenty-eight* Roman miles, at least, from the city of Cártama!

With respect to his first objections, however, it may be observed, that the *want of space* can only apply to the army posted on the mountain, for, on the level country between its base and the village of Guaro, an army of any amount might be drawn up. And as regards the mountain, as I have already stated, its north front offers a strong position, nearly two miles in extent, and one in depth. Now, considering the compact order in which Roman armies were formed; the number of lines in which they were in the habit of being drawn up; and making due allowance for exaggeration [185] in the number of the contending hosts; such a space, I should say, was more than sufficient for Pompey's army.

In reply to the second objection urged by Mr. Carter, I may, in the first place, observe, that the inscription whereon it is grounded —

A MVNDA ET FLVVIO SIGILA

AD CERTIMAM VSQVE XX M.P.P.S. RESTITVIT. [186] —

seems to have no reference to the actual distance between Munda and Cártama, since, by attaching any such meaning to it—coupled as Munda is with the river Sigila—the inscription, to one acquainted with the country, becomes quite unintelligible.

Thus, if translated: "From Munda and the river Sigila, he (i. e. the Emperor Hadrian) restored the twenty miles of road to Cártama," any one would naturally conclude that Munda was upon the Sigila, and Cártama at a distance of twenty miles from it; whereas, whatever may have been the situation of Munda, Cártama certainly stood upon the very bank of the river.

It must, therefore, either have been intended to imply that the Emperor restored twenty miles of a road which from Munda and the sources, [187] or upper part of the course of the Sigila, led to Cártama, and various traces of such a Roman road exist to this day on the road to Ronda by Junquera; or, that the road from Munda was conducted along part of the course of the Sigila ere it reached Cártama: and such, from the nature of the ground, undoubtedly was the case, since Cártama stood at the eastern foot of a steep mountain, the northern extremity of which must (in military parlance) have been turned, to reach it from Monda, and the road, in making this détour, would first reach the river Guadaljorce, or Sigila.

In this case it must be admitted that the *twenty miles* refer to the actual distance between the two towns, and this tends only more firmly to establish modern Monda on the site of the Roman town, since the distance from thence to Cártama, measured with *a pair of compasses* on a *correct* map, [188] is fourteen English miles, which are equal to fifteen Roman of seventy-five to a degree, or seventeen of eighty-three and one third to a degree; and considering the hilly nature of the country which the road must unavoidably have traversed, the distance would have been fully increased to twenty miles, either by the ascents and descents if carried in a straight line from place to place, or by describing a very circuitous course if taken along the valley of the Rio Seco.

Carter further remarked upon the foregoing inscription that "it seems to place" Munda to the *west* of the river Sigila, which ran *between* that town and Cártama; but this, he said, does not agree with the situation of modern Monda, which is on the same side the river as Cártama.

I suppose for *west* he meant to say *east*, but, in either case, his assumed site for Munda, "three leagues to the west of the present town," is open to this very same objection, and to the yet graver one, of being—even allowing that he meant English leagues—*twenty-three English miles* in a *direct* line from the town of Cártama, and in a contracted and secluded valley, to the possession of which, no military importance could possibly have been attached.

On the whole, therefore, I see no reason to doubt what, for so many years was looked upon as certain, viz., that the modern town of Monda is on the site of the ancient city. I must nevertheless own that in following strictly the text of Hirtius, an objection presents itself to this spot with reference to the relative position of Ursao; that is, if Osuna be Ursao; since, in allusion to Pompey's resolve to receive battle at Munda, he says that Ursao "served as a sure resource *behind* him." [189]

This objection holds equally good with the position Carter assigns to Munda; but that there is some error respecting Ursao is evident, for, if Osuna be Ursao, then Hirtius described it most incorrectly by saying it was exceedingly strong by nature, and eight miles distant from any rivulet. [190] And, on the other hand, it is clear that Ursao did *not* serve as a *sure* resource to Pompey, since no part of his defeated army found refuge there.

We must read this passage, therefore, as implying rather that Pompey *calculated* on Orsao as a place of refuge, but that, by the able manœuvres of his adversary, he was cut off from it. Now a town placed high up in the mountains like Alozaina, or Junquera, and like them distant from any stream but that which rises within their walls, answers the description of Orsao, much better than Osuna; [191] and, supposing one of these, or any other town in the vicinity, similarly situated, to have been Orsao, Pompey might have flattered himself that he could fall back upon it in the event of being defeated at Monda. Cæsar, however, by moving along the valley of the Seco, and, taking post in the plain to the north of Pompey's position, effectually deprived him of this resource.

The modern town of Monda contains numerous fragments of monuments, inscriptions, &c., which, though none of them actually prove it to be on the site of the ancient place of the same name, satisfactorily shew that it stands near some old Roman town, and that, therefore, to call it *new* Monda, in contradistinction to *Monda la vieja*, is absurd.

The road to Coin traverses a succession of tongues, which, protruding from the side of the steep Sierra de Monda on the right, fall gradually towards the Rio Seco, which flows about a mile off on the left. For the first three miles the undulations are very gentle, and the face of the country is covered with corn, but, on arriving at the Peyrela, a rapid stream that rushes down from the mountains in a deep rocky gully, the ground becomes much more broken, and the hills on both sides are thickly wooded. The road, nevertheless, continues very good, and in about two miles more reaches Coin.

The approach to this town is very beautiful. It is situated some way up the northern acclivity of a high wooded hill, and commands a splendid view of the valley of the Guadaljorce.

Coin is supposed to be of Moorish origin, and, from the amenity of its situation, abundance of crystal springs and fruitfulness of its orchards, was, no doubt, a favourite place of retreat with the turbaned conquerors of Spain. Nor are its merits altogether lost upon the present less contemplative race of inhabitants, for they flee to its pure atmosphere whenever any endemic disease frightens them from the close and crowded streets of filthy Malaga.

During the last few years that the divided Moslems yet endeavoured to struggle against the fate that too clearly awaited them, the fields of Coin were doomed to repeated devastations, though the city itself still set the Christian hosts at defiance; but at length the artillery of Ferdinand and Isabella reduced it to submission, A.D. 1485.

The population of Coin is estimated by the Spanish authorities at 9000 souls, but I should say it is considerably less. The houses are good, streets well paved, and the place altogether is clean and wholesome.

The posada, except in outward appearance, is not in keeping with the town. It is a large white-washed building, with great pretensions and small comfort. We left it at daybreak without the least regret, carrying our breakfast with us to enjoy *al fresco*.

At the foot of the hill two roads to Malaga offer themselves, one by way of Cártama (distant ten miles), which turns the Sierra Gibalgalía to the north, the other by Alhaurin, which crosses the neck of land connecting that mountain with the more lofty sierras to the south. The distance is pretty nearly the same by both, and is reckoned five leagues, but the *leguas* are any thing but *regulares*, and may be taken at an average of four miles and a half each. The first named is a carriage road, and the country flat nearly all the way; we therefore chose the latter, as likely to be more picturesque.

In about an hour from Coin, we reached a clear stream, which, confined in a deep gulley, singularly scooped out of the solid rock, winds round at the back of Alhaurin, and tumbles over a precipice on the side of the impending mountain. The crystal clearness of the water and beauty of the spot, tempted us to halt and spread the contents of our alforjas on the green bank of the rivulet, though the white houses of Alhaurin, situated immediately above, peeped out from amidst trellissed vines and perfumed orange groves, seeming to beckon us on. But appearances are proverbially deceitful all over the world, and more especially in Spanish towns, as we had recently experienced at Coin.

Our repast finished, we remounted our horses, and ascended the steep acclivity, on the lap of which the town stands. The environs are beautifully wooded, and the place contains many tasteful houses and gardens, wide, clean, and well-paved streets, abundance of refreshing fountains, and groves of orange and other fruit trees, and, in fact, is a most delightful place of abode. The view from it is yet finer than from Coin, embracing, besides the fine chain of wooded sierras above Alozaina and Casarabonela, the lower portion of the vale of Malaga, and the splendid mountains that stretch into the Mediterranean beyond that city. Nevertheless, in spite of these advantages, the scared *Malagueños* consider Coin a more secure retreat from the dreaded yellow fever than Alhaurin, perhaps because from the former even the view of their abandoned city is intercepted.

Alhaurin contains, probably, 5000 inhabitants. The road from thence to Malaga is *carriageable* throughout. It winds along the side of the mountain, continuing nearly on a dead level from the town to the summit of the pass that connects the Sierra Gibalgalía with the mountains of Mijas; thence it descends gradually, by a long and rather confined ravine, into the vale of Malaga.

Arrived in the plain, it leaves the little village of Alhaurinejo about half a mile off on the right, and at thirteen miles from Alhaurin reaches a bridge over the Guadaljorce. This bridge, commenced on a magnificent scale by one of the bishops of Malaga, was to have been built entirely of stone; but, before the work was half completed, either the worthy dignitary of the church came to the last of his days, or to the bottom of his purse, and it is left to be completed, "*con el tiempo*" —a very celebrated Spanish bridge-maker.

Forty-four solid stone piers remain, however, to bear witness to the good and liberal intentions of the bishop; and the weight of a rotten wooden platform, which has since been laid down, to afford a passage across the stream when swollen by the winter torrents, for at most other times it is fordable.

A road to the Retiro and Churriana continues down the right bank of the river; but that to Malaga crosses the bridge, and on gaining the left bank of the river is joined by the roads from Casarabonda and Cártama. From hence to Malaga is about five miles.

On arriving at Malaga we found the dread of cholera had attained such a height during our short absence, that the *Xebeque*, for Ceuta, had sailed, whilst clean bills of health were yet issued. We also thought it advisable to save our passports from being tainted, and, without further loss of time, departed for Gibraltar by land. Our haste, however, booted us but little; for, amongst the absurdities of quarantine be it recorded, on reaching the British fortress, on the morning of the third day from Malaga, admittance was refused, until we had undergone a three days' purification at San Roque. Thither we repaired, therefore; and there we remained during the prescribed period, shaking hands daily with our friends from the garrison, until the dreaded *virus* was supposed to have parted with all its infectious properties. Our *decorated* attendant had left us on reaching Malaga, promising to take the earliest opportunity of acquainting us with the result of an ordeal, to which the little blind God, in one of his most capricious moods, had been pleased to subject two of his votaries.

The circumstances attending this trial of *true love*, will be found related in the following chapter, which contains also a sketch of the previous history of the hero of the tale, the knight of San Fernando.

CHAPTER XVI
THE KNIGHT OF SAN FERNANDO

D ON Fernando Septimo, por la gracia de Dios, rey de Castilla, de Leon, de Aragon, de las dos Sicilias, de Jerusalem, de Navarra, de Granada, de Toledo, de Valencia, de Galicia, de Mallorca, de Sevilla, de Cerdeña, de Cordoba, de Corcega, de Murcia, de Jaen, de los Algarbes, de Algeciras, de Gibraltar, de las islas de Canaria, de las Indias Orientales y Occidentales, islas y tierra ferme del Mar Oceano; archiduque de Austria; duque de Borgoña, de Brabante y de Milan; conde de Absparg, Flandes, Tirol y Barcelona; señor de Viscaya y de Molina, [192] *&c.*

Such was the heading of the document which conferred the honour of knighthood (silver cross of the first class of the royal and military order of St. Ferdinand), upon *Don* Antonio Condé, a soldier of the light company (cazadores) of the Queen's, or second regiment of the line, in acknowledgment of his distinguished services against the *revolutionarios* of the *isla de Leon*, who surrendered at Bejer on the 8th March, 1831.

The bearer of this *certificate* of gallant conduct—for the gratification that its possession afforded his vanity was the only sense in which it could be considered a *reward*—was in person rather below the usual stature of the Andalusian peasantry; but his square shoulders, open chest, and muscular limbs, bespoke him to be possessed of more than their wonted strength and activity.

In other respects too he differed somewhat from his countrymen, his hair being light, even lighter than what they call *castaños*, or chestnut, his chin beardless, and his eyes hazel. His manners were those of a frank young soldier, rather, perhaps, of the French school, with a dash of the *beau garçon* about him, but, on the whole, very prepossessing. In his carriage to us, though rather inquisitive, he was at all times respectful; but towards his fellow countrymen, not of *the cloth*, a certain hauteur was observable in his deportment, which clearly showed that he prided himself on the "*Don.*"

The document, encased with the brevet of knighthood, of which mention has before been made, briefly, but in very honourable terms, described the gallant conduct of the young soldier, and forms the groundwork of the following *memoir*; a circumstance I feel called upon to mention, lest my hero should be wrongfully accused of vain-gloriously boasting of his achievements; and this also will explain why his story is not, throughout, told in the first person.

The secluded little village of Guarda, which has been noticed in the course of my peregrinations, as lying to the right of the high road from Jaen to Granada (about five miles from the former city), was the birth-place of Antonio Condé. His parents, though in a humble station of life, were of *sangre limpio*; [193] and never having heard of Malthus, had married early, and most unphilosophically added a family of seven human beings to the already overstocked population of this wisdom-getting world.

Five of these unfortunate mortals were daughters, and our hero was the younger of the two masculine lumps of animated clay. His brother, who was many years his senior, had joined the army at an early age, and at the conclusion of the war had proceeded with his regiment to the Habana, where he still remained; their parents, therefore, now declining in years, were anxious to keep their remaining son at home, to assist in supporting the family. Such, however, was not to be the case, for, on the *quintos* being called out in 1830, it fell to Antonio's lot to be one of the quota furnished by the district that included his native village.

To purchase a substitute was out of the question—the price was quite beyond his parents' means; and though his brother had, at various times, transmitted money home, which, with praiseworthy foresight, had been hoarded up to make some little provision for his sisters, but was now urgently offered to buy him off, yet Antonio would not listen to its being so applied. To confess the truth, indeed, he secretly rejoiced at his lot, having always wished to be a soldier, though he could never bring himself voluntarily to quit his aged parents. Now, he maintained, there was no alternative; and accordingly, with the brilliant prospect of making a fortune, which the military life opened to him, he marched from his native village, and joined the Queen's regiment, then quartered at Seville, to the cazador company of which he was shortly afterwards posted.

Antonio's zeal, and assiduous attention to his duties, as well as his general good conduct and intelligence, made him a great favourite with his officers; whilst his youth, good humour, and gay disposition, endeared him equally to his comrades, in whose amusements he generally took the lead. In fact, he soon became the pattern man of the pattern company, and attained the rank of corporal.

Early in the month of March, 1831, the Queen's regiment received orders to proceed by forced marches to Cadiz, where the *soi-disant* "liberals," having again raised the standard of revolt, commenced the work of regeneration by murdering the governor of the city in the streets at noon day. The cold-blooded, calculating miscreants, who committed this act, excused themselves for the premeditated murder of a man *universally* beloved and respected, by saying it was necessary for the success of their plans to commence with a blow that should strike terror into the hearts of their opponents. They killed, therefore, the most virtuous man they could select, to show that no one would be spared who thenceforth ventured to entertain a doubt, that the constitution they upheld was the *beau idéal* of liberal government; and, I regret to say, Englishmen were found who applauded this atrocious doctrine, and considered the subsequent punishment inflicted on Torrijos, and the other abettors and instigators of this barbarity, as an act of unprecedented cruelty on the part of the "tyrant Ferdinand" and his "*servile*" ministers.

Antonio's regiment proceeded to the scene of revolt by way of Utrera and Xeres, and on reaching Puerto Santa Maria received orders to continue its march round the head of the bay of Cadiz, and occupy, without delay, the Puente Zuazo, with the view of confining the rebels to the isla de Leon, their attempt to gain possession of Cadiz having failed, through the loyalty and firmness of the troops composing its garrison.

The rebels, however, effected their escape, ere the Queen's regiment reached its destined position, and had marched to Chiclana, in the hope of being there joined by another band of "*facciosos*," under an ex-officer, named Torrijos; which, long collected in the bay, and protected by the guns of Gibraltar, was to have effected a landing on the coast to the westward of Tarifa, and marched thence to support the ruffians of the isla.

The royal troops were instantly sent in pursuit of the rebels, who, abandoning Chiclana, fell back successively upon Conil and Vejer. The strength of the position of this latter town induced them to make a stand, and await the momentarily expected reinforcement under Torrijos; and the King's troops having assembled in considerable force at the foot of the mountain, determined on attempting to dislodge them from the formidable post, ere they received this accession of strength; a sharp conflict was the consequence, which terminated in the royalists being repulsed with severe loss.

Antonio, who was well acquainted with the ground, now respectfully hinted to the captain of his company, that the retreat of the rebels might be effectually cut off by taking possession of the bridge over the Barbate, which—all the boats on the river having been destroyed—alone offered the rebels the means of reaching Tarifa, or Torrijos that of coming to the assistance of the blockaded town.

The captain communicated our hero's plans to the commander of the expedition, who immediately adopted it, wisely abstaining from wasting further blood to obtain a result by force, which starvation, sooner or later, would be sure to bring about.

In pursuance, therefore, of Antonio's project, the Queen's regiment received orders to take possession of the bridge, and the *cazador* company was pushed on with all speed, to facilitate the execution of this rather difficult operation.

The bridge, as I have described in a former chapter, is situated immediately under the lofty precipitous cliff whereon the town of Vejer is perched, and the road to it is conducted, for nearly half a mile, along a narrow strip of level ground, between the bank of the Barbate and the foot of the precipice.

In their advance, therefore, the *cazadores* were exposed to a most destructive shower of bullets, stones, &c. from above, and, of the whole company, only Corporal Condé, and seven of his comrades, made good their way, and threw themselves into the venta; which stands on the right bank of the stream, close to the bridge. They instantly opened a fire from the windows of the inn upon the rebels in the town overhead, who, at first, returned it with interest; but after some time Antonio was beginning to flatter himself, from the slackening of their fusillade, that he was making their post too hot for them, when, looking round, he perceived the whole force of the *facciosos* descending from the town in one long column, by the road which winds down to the bridge, round the eastern face of the mountain, their intention evidently being to force a passage *à todo precio*. [194]

Antonio's comrades were daunted; they had no officer with them; there was no appearance of support being at hand; and the odds against them were fearful. Prudence suggested, therefore, that they should shut themselves up in the venta, and let the enemy pass.

Our hero, however, saw how much depended on the decision of that moment. If the rebels succeeded in crossing the bridge, nothing could prevent their forming a junction with the band of Torrijos, and in that case the country might, for many months, be subjected to their outrages and rapine, and Gibraltar would afford them a sure retreat; he determined, therefore, to make an effort to intimidate them, and knowing the weight his example would have upon his comrades, rushed out of the venta, calling upon them to follow; and taking post behind some old walls, that formed, as it were, a kind of *tête de pont*, opened a brisk fire upon the advancing column of the enemy.

The boldness of the manœuvre intimidated the rebels, who, thinking that this handful of men must be supported by a considerable force, hesitated, halted for further orders, and, finally, threw out a line of skirmishers to cover their movements, between whom and Antonio's party a sharp fire was kept up for several minutes.

In this skirmish one of Antonio's companions was killed, another fell badly wounded by his side, and he himself received a wound in his head, which, but that the ball had previously passed through the top of his chako, would, probably, have been fatal.

The rebels, discovering at length that the small force opposed to them was altogether without support, again formed in column of attack to force the bridge. The word "forward" was given, and Antonio feared that his devotion would prove of no avail, when, at the critical moment, the remainder of his company advanced from behind the venta at the *pas de charge*, rending the air with loud cries of "*Viva el Rey*," and opening a fire which took the enemy in flank.

The rebels saw that the golden opportunity had been missed, and, seized with a panic, retired hastily to their stronghold, closely pressed by the *cazadores*, who hoped to enter the town pêle mêle with them.

The commander of the king's troops, who had galloped to the spot where he heard firing, determined, however, to adhere to the plan of reducing the rebels to starvation; which now, by Antonio's gallantry, he was certain of eventually effecting; and ordered, therefore, the recall to be sounded as soon as he saw the enemy had regained the town. Unfortunately for our hero, who, attended by a single comrade, was at the extreme left of the extended line of skirmishers, and had taken advantage of one of the deep gullies that furrow the side of the mountain to advance unobserved on the enemy; he neither heard the signal to retire, nor saw his companions fall back; continuing, therefore, to advance, it was only on gaining the head of the ravine that he suddenly became aware of the extreme peril of their situation, and that a quick retreat alone could save them. It was, however, too late; his comrade—his bosom friend, Gaspar Herrera—fell, apparently dead, a dozen paces from him, and he, himself, in the act of raising up his brave companion, was brought to the ground by a ball, which splintered his ankle-bone. He managed, with great difficulty, to crawl to some palmeta bushes, having first sheltered the body of his friend behind the stem of a stunted olive tree, which would not afford cover for both; and, lying flat on the ground, waited for some time in the hope that his company had merely moved round to the left to gain a more accessible part of the mountain, and would speedily renew the attack.

At length, his patience becoming exhausted, he thought it would be well to let his comrades know where he was, and once more levelling his musket, resumed the offensive by attacking a pig, which, unconscious of danger, came grunting with carniverous purpose towards that part of the gory field where the body of his friend Gaspar lay extended. This drew a heavy fire upon Antonio, but, as he was much below the rebels, who had all retired into the town, and was tolerably well sheltered by the friendly palmetas, he escaped further damage.

In the meanwhile, Antonio and Gaspar had had been reported as killed to the captain of the *cazadores*, who, whilst deploring with the other officers the loss of the two most promising young men of his company, heard the renewed firing in the direction of the late skirmish. "*Corajo!*" he exclaimed, "that must be Condé and Herrera still at it." "No, Señor," replied the serjeant, "they were both seen to fall as we retreated from the hill; that firing must be an attack upon our friends posted on the other side of the town; the rebels are probably attempting to force a passage in that direction." "Well then, I cannot do wrong in advancing," said the captain, "so let us on. Nevertheless, I still think it is the fire of Condé and his comrade, and I know, my brave fellows," he continued, addressing his men, "I know that if it be possible to bring them off, you will do it."

They advanced, accordingly, in the direction of the firing, and, as the captain had conjectured, there they found Condé continuing the combat *à l'outrance*, extended full length upon the ground under cover of the palmeta bushes, with his head and ankle bandaged, and his ammunition nearly exhausted. They fortunately succeeded in bearing him off without sustaining any loss, though Condé insisted on their first removing the seemingly lifeless body of his friend Gaspar, which he pointed out to them.

The detachment at the venta had now been reinforced by some cavalry and artillery, and the remainder of the Queen's regiment, whilst the rest of the Royalist force took post on the opposite side of the town, in a position that covered the roads to Chiclana, Medina, Sidonia, and Alcalà de los Gazules, thereby depriving the beleaguered rebels of all chance of escape.

Towards dusk that same evening, one of Torrijos's troopers was brought in a prisoner. Unconscious of the state of affairs, he had mistaken a cavalry piquet of the king's troops for the advanced guard of the *facciosos*, and had not even discovered his error in time to destroy the despatches of which he was the bearer. By these it was learnt that Torrijos, apprized of the failure on Cadiz and subsequent escape of the rebel-band from the Isla de Leon, had not budged from the spot where he had effected his landing; but he now sent to acquaint his coadjutors that he had collected a sufficiency of boats to take them all off, and that the bearer would be their guide to the place of embarkation.

This information was forwarded to the rebels at Vejer, who, not giving credit to it, continued to hold out until the third day, when their provisions being exhausted and no Torrijos appearing, they agreed to capitulate, and were marched prisoners to the Isla, where, but a few days before, "*Quantam est in rebus inane!*" they had styled themselves the liberators of Spain.

The queen's regiment was now marched in all haste towards Tarifa, in the hope of surprising and capturing Torrijos and his band, ere the news of what had passed at Vejer could reach him, but he had taken the alarm at the prolonged absence of his messenger, and, re-embarking his doughty heroes, regained the anchorage of Gibraltar without having fired a shot to assist their friends. The regiment, therefore, proceeded to Algeciras, and from thence marched to San Roque, where it remained stationary for several months.

Here Antonio rejoined it, accompanied by his friend Herrera, who, thanks to the timely surgical aid his comrade had been the means of procuring him, yet lived to evince his gratitude to his preserver. Here, also, our hero received the distinction which his gallant conduct had so well earned, as well as the grant of a—to-this-day-unpaid—pension of a real per diem. Promotion, too, was offered, but he chose rather to wait for a vacancy in his own regiment than to receive immediate rank in any other.

Our hero's military career was shortly, however, doomed to be brought to a close. He had resumed his duty but a few days, when an order arrived for the queen's regiment to proceed to Seville. The wound in Antonio's ankle, though apparently quite healed, had been suffered to close over the bullet that had inflicted it, and the first day's march produced inflammation of so dangerous a character as to threaten, not only the loss of his shattered limb, but even of life itself.

In this deplorable state Antonio was left behind at Ximena, where, fortunately, an aunt of Gaspar resided. The good Dame Felipa required only to hear the young soldier's name—his noble act of friendship having long made it familiar to her ear—to receive him as her son. "Never can I forget her kindness," said Antonio; "my own mother could not have tended me with more unremitted attention, and—under the Almighty—I feel that my recovery is entirely their work." Here an "*Ay!*" drawn seemingly from the innermost recess of his heart, escaped from the young soldier's lips, which, appearing quite out of keeping with the terms in which he spoke of Dame

Felipa's *maternal* solicitude, induced me, after a moment's pause, to ask, "But who are *they*, Antonio?"

"The aunt and sister of Gaspar," he replied, with some little confusion.

"And you find the wounds of Cupid more incurable than those of Bellona?" said I, jestingly—"*Vamos*, Don Antonio! As Sancho says, '*Gusto mucho destas cosas de amores*,' [195] so let us have the sequel of your story by all means."

"I shall not be very long in relating it," continued our hero. "For three months I remained the guest of Doña Felipa. A fever, produced by my intense sufferings, rendered me for many days quite insensible to the extraordinary kindness of which I was the object; at length it was subdued, leaving me, however, so reduced, that for weeks I could not quit my couch. Indeed, the most perfect repose was ordered on account of my wound, the cure of which was rendered far more tedious and troublesome from former mismanagement. During this long period, the sister of my friend Gaspar was my constant attendant. She read to me, sang to me, or touched the guitar to break—what she imagined must be—the wearisome monotony of my confinement. I have even, when consciousness first returned, on the abatement of the fever, heard her, thinking I was sleeping, *pray* for the recovery of her brother's preserver.

"It was impossible to be thus the object of Manuela's tender solicitude, without being impressed with the most ardent love and admiration for one so pure, so engaging, and so beauteous! Had she indeed been less lovely and captivating, had she even been absolutely plain, still her assiduous and disinterested attention could not but have called forth my warmest gratitude and regard; but I trust you will one day see Manuela, and then be able to judge if I could resist becoming the captive of such *enganchamientos* [196] as she possesses.

"Vainly I endeavoured to stifle the rising passion at its birth. Alas! the greater my efforts were to eradicate it, the deeper it took root in my heart. I hoped, nevertheless, to have sufficient self-control to conceal my passion from the eyes of all, even of her who had called it into existence, for gratitude and honour equally forbade my endeavouring to engage the affections of one whose family, placed in a walk of life far above mine— that is in point of *wealth*, added the K. S. F. somewhat proudly—I had little right to hope, would consider a poor soldier of fortune a suitable match for the daughter of the rich Don Fadrique Herrara. Nor did I know, indeed, how Manuela herself would receive my addresses, for I scarcely ventured to attribute the soft glances of her love-inspiring eyes to any other feeling than that of compassion for the sufferings of her brother's friend.

"The day of separation came, however, and the veil which had so long concealed our mutual feelings was gently and unpremeditatedly drawn aside. Manuela's father and her brother Gaspar came to Ximena to pass a few days with Doña Felipa, and finding that, though still a prisoner to my room, I was now declared to be out of all danger, Don Fadrique announced his intention of taking his daughter home with him—her visit having already been prolonged far beyond the time originally fixed, in consequence of my illness, and the fatigue which, unassisted, the attendance upon me would have imposed on her aunt.

"When the dreaded hour of departure arrived, my lovely nurse came to the side of my couch, to bid her last farewell. A tear stood in her bright eye; the silvery tones of her voice faltered; her hand trembled as she placed it in mine, and a blush suffused her cheeks as I pressed it to my lips. But that soft hand was not withdrawn until her own lips had confessed her love, and had sealed the unsolicited promise, never to bestow that hand upon another!

"The difficulty now was to make known our mutual attachment to her father, who I dreaded would think but ill of me, for the return thus made for all the kindness of his family. My pride pinched me, also, lest allusion should be made to my poverty, for, though poor, the blood of the Condé's is pure as any in the Serranía.

"I had but little time for consideration, for Don Fadrique was about to mount his horse, and I thought the best channel of communication would be my friend Gaspar. He listened attentively to my tale, which was not told without much embarrassment, and then, to my confusion, burst into a loud laugh.

"'Pretty *news*, truly, *amigo* Antonio,' he at length exclaimed. '*My* eyes, however, have not been so exclusively occupied with one object for this week past—like your's and my sister's—as to render the communication of this wonderful secret at all necessary. But be of good cheer; I have seen how the matter stood, and, on the part of my sister, encouraged it; and I hope to be able to overcome all difficulties, so leave the affair in my hands:—on our way homewards I will talk the matter over with my father, and you shall hear the result shortly.'

"Nor did he disappoint me. In a few days a letter came from Gaspar: the result of his interference exceeded my expectations: Don Fadrique had received his communication very calmly, and told him that before returning any definite answer, he should take time to fathom Manuela's feelings.

"Not long after this, I received a letter, of a less satisfactory kind, however, from Don Fadrique himself. It simply stated that he could not at present give his consent to his daughter's accepting me; that he had no objections to urge on the score of my rank in life, or the way in which I had acted in the matter, but that his daughter's expectations entitled him to look for a wealthier son-in-law, and that, in fact, it had long been a favorite plan of his, to unite her to the son of an old and intimate friend, when they should be of a proper age.

"Nevertheless—his letter concluded—provided I would abstain from seeing, writing to, or holding *in any way* communication with his daughter for the space of two years, he would, at the expiration of that period, consent to our union, should we both continue to wish it.

"This chilling letter was accompanied by a hastily written billet from Manuela. It was as follows:—'I know my father's conditions—accept them, and have full confidence in the constancy of your Manuela.'

"I accordingly wrote to Don Fadrique, subscribing to the terms he proposed, and, from that day to this, have neither seen nor communicated with either Manuela or any member of her family."

"But have you not heard from time to time of the welfare of your Manuela?" I asked; "are you sure she is yet unmarried?" For it struck me that the young son of "an old and intimate friend" was a dangerous person to have paying court to one's mistress during a two years' absence; especially in Spain, where *love matches* are rather scouted. A story that one of Manuela's countrywomen related to me of herself, recurring to me at the same time.

This lady had, early in life, formed an attachment to a young officer, whom poverty alone prevented her marrying. His regiment was ordered to Ceuta, and she remained at Malaga, consoling herself with the hope that brighter days would dawn upon them. Her friends laughed at the idea of such interminable constancy, especially as a most advantageous *parti* presented itself for her acceptance. The proposer—it is true—was neither so handsome nor so youthful as the exile, but then he was also an officer, and "*in very good circumstances.*" She could not forget her first love, however—indeed, she *never* could—and long turned a deaf ear to the tender whisperings of her new admirer; but, at length, her relations became urgent, as well as her lover; the mail boat from Ceuta gradually came to be looked for with less impatience; and, "*por fin,*" she observed, "*como era Capitan por Capitan (!!),* [197] I had no great objections to urge, and we were married!"

She confessed to me, however, that this exchange was not effected "*without paying the difference,*" as the treatment she experienced from her rich husband, caused her ever after to regret having given up her poor lover.

But to return to Antonio—"I have had but few opportunities of hearing from Manuela," he replied, "for my native village is removed from any high road, and the close attendance required by my aged parents—my wound having incapacitated me from further military service—has been such, that I seldom could get as far as Jaen to make enquiries amongst the *contrabandistas* and others who visit the neighbourhood, of her place of residence; but about a month since I met an *arriero* of Arcos, who knew Don Fadrique well, and from him I learnt that Manuela is still unmarried, has lost all her beauty, is wasted to a shadow; and said to be suffering from some disease that baffles the skill of the most eminent physicians of the place.

"This intelligence has made me the more anxious to see her, and claim her promised hand, for no change in her personal appearance—even if the account be true—can alter the sentiments I entertain for her; but, at the same time, it has placed a weight upon my spirits which in vain I endeavour to throw off.

"The morning it was my good fortune to fall in with you, Caballeros, I had set out from my home to proceed to Ximena, whither I understand Manuela has been removed for change of air. For the term of my probation, though not yet expired, is fast drawing to a close, and having some business to transact with the military authorities at Granada and Malaga respecting my pension (of which not a *maravedi* has ever been paid), I have timed my movements so as to reach Ximena by the day on which I may again present myself to Manuela, and receive, I trust, the reward of my constancy."

Antonio's narrative was here brought to a conclusion, but ere he left us, I exacted the promise mentioned in the preceding chapter, that he would acquaint us with the result of Don Fadrique's essay in experimental philosophy. Circumstances, however, occurred to prevent our meeting him at the place of appointment, and I had almost given up the hope of hearing more of Antonio and his love story, when, to my surprise, he one morning presented himself at my breakfast table at San Roque.

I saw, at the first glance, that the course of true love had not run smooth—he was pale and hagged—flurried, yet dispirited. "My good Antonio," said I, unwilling to give utterance to a doubt of his fair one's constancy, "I fear Don Fadrique has not proved to be a man of his word."

"*Perdon usted*," he replied—"he has been faithful to his word"—worse and worse, thought I—"And Manuela not less constant in her affection," he continued; guessing at once the suspicion that flitted across my mind—"Alas! I could even wish it were not so, if all otherwise were well; but fate has ordered differently. A calamity has befallen Manuela; compared to which, death would be a mercy. She is in a state that is heart-rending to behold.

Her sufferings are almost beyond the power of bearing. Oh, Caballero! it is fearful—it is awful to see her. She has the best advice that money can procure, but nothing can be done to give us a hope of her recovery."

"Mad?" I exclaimed, with a shudder—"Oh, cursed love of riches...."

"Nada, nada," [198] interrupted Antonio, "she is as sensible as ever. Alas! I could even bear to see her insane, for then I might hope that time would effect a change."

"Is it Etica?" I asked, knowing that the Spaniards consider consumption both incurable and highly infectious.

A mournful shake of the head was his reply.

"What then, my good Antonio, is the nature of her malady?"

"Ojala [199] that it could be called a malady, Don Carlos," ejaculated the silver cross of San Fernando; "it might not then be beyond the reach of the physician's art. But Dios de mi vida! there is no hope for her, unless a miracle can be wrought. It is to have a consultation on that point, I am come to San Roque."

"What," said I, my patience thoroughly exhausted, "has she embraced Mohammedanism?"

"Not far from it, Don Carlos—she is possessed of a devil!"

"Friend Antonio," said I, "congratulate yourself;—such discoveries are seldom made before marriage. Let me, however, persuade you, instead of consulting with priests, to allow an heretical English doctor to meet this devil face to face; his simple nostrums may perchance be found more efficacious than the exorcisms of the most pious divines. But explain to me the signs and symptoms of the presence of this imp of darkness; and pardon my making light of so serious an affair, for, rest assured, the evil one is not now permitted to torment the human frame with bodily anguish; his toils are spread for catching souls; and worldly pleasures, not personal sufferings, are the means he employs to effect his purpose."

Antonio then entered into a detailed account of his betrothed's ailment, as well as of the mode of treatment that had been adopted; but, ignorant, superstitious, and bigoted, as I knew the campestral Spanish faculty to be, I had yet to learn how far they could practise on the credulity of their infatuated patients.

Manuela, it appeared, had, one day during the preceding Lent, been so imprudent as to taste some chicken broth that had been prepared for her sick father; and it was supposed, that the devil, assuming the appearance of the egg of some insect, had gained admission to her throat and settled in her breast, where he had ever since been nurtured and was gradually "*comiendo su vida!*" [200]

The Doctors assured her friends that the only way of appeasing the monster's appetite, was by the constant application of thick slices of raw beef to the exterior of the part affected—but this remedy was daily losing its effect.

My astonishment knew no bounds.—Was it possible such gross ignorance could exist, or such horrible imposition be practised in the nineteenth century!

After much persuasion, Antonio promised to bring his betrothed to San Roque, to have the advice of an English doctor; my proposal of taking one to see her, at Ximena, having at once been negatived on the grounds that it would cause great irritation amongst the people of that town; and, accordingly, on the day appointed for the meeting, Manuela, borne on a kind of litter, and accompanied by her aunt, came to San Roque on the pretence of its being her wish to offer a wax bust at the shrine of one of the Emigré Saints of Gibraltar "now established in the city of *San Roque de su Campo;*" which said saint, having taken a very active part in expelling the Moors from Spain, it was naturally concluded might feel an interest in driving the devil out of Manuela's breast.

Antonio's mistress had evidently been a lovely creature. Her features were beautifully outlined, but her white lips and bloodless cheeks, her sunken eyes and wasted figure, declared the ravages making by some terrible inward disease. She was suffering excessive pain from the effects of the journey, but received us with a faint smile.

"I fear, sir," she said, with some emotion, addressing herself to my friend, Dr. ——, "I fear, sir, that I have given you unnecessary trouble in coming to see me, for I am told that my disorder is beyond the reach of medical skill; but my friend here," pointing to her lover, who, with brimful eyes, stood watching alternately the pain-distorted countenance of his mistress and that of the Doctor, hoping, if possible, to discover his thoughts, "my friend here requested me so earnestly to come and meet you, that, as we shall be so short a time together on this earth, I could not, as far as concerned myself, refuse him so slight a favour, and I hope you will pardon the inconvenience to which we have put you."

Antonio and myself now withdrew, leaving Manuela and Doña Felipa with Dr. ——, who, in a short time rejoined us, and, to Antonio's inexpressible delight, informed him that the case of his betrothed was not by any means hopeless, though she would have to submit to a painful surgical operation, and then turning round to me, he added, "the poor creature is suffering from a cancerous affection, which, fortunately, is just in the state that I could most wish it to be. But no time must be lost."

The nature of the case having been fully explained to Antonio, it was left to him to persuade Manuela to submit to the necessary operation, and to inform her, that though it might be performed with safety *then*, yet death must inevitably be the consequence of delay.

The prejudices we were prepared to encounter were numerous, but they were propounded chiefly by Manuela's aunt, she herself agreeing without hesitation to every thing Antonio suggested. At length, however, the old lady said a positive answer should be given after consulting with a priest, and I forthwith accompanied Antonio to Don — — — —, and requested his attendance.

Antonio was present at the consultation, and gave us an amusing account of it. The main objection of the Doña Felipa was to the heretical hand that was to direct the knife; but the worthy *Padre*—who had good reason to know the superior skill of the English faculty over those of his own country, and was himself *spelling* for a little advice on the score of an over-strained digestion—took the case up most zealously, and eventually overcame all their scruples.

"Fear not," said he, winding up his arguments, "Fear not, good dame, to trust the maiden in his hands. Like as the Lord opened the mouth of Balaam's ass to admonish her master, so has he put wisdom into the heads of these heretical doctors for the good of us, his faithful servants. Quiet your conscience, Señora Felipa, I myself have been physicked by these semi-christian *Medicos*."

The case was not much in point, but it served the purpose. Doña Felipa was convinced; her niece submitted; the operation was successfully performed; the colour in a short time returned to the cheeks of the truly lovely and loveable Manuela; the smile of health once again lighted up her intelligent countenance. And, ere I left the country, the small share it had fallen to my lot to take in producing this happy change, was gratefully acknowledged by the expressive, though downcast glance that gleamed from Manuela's bright and joyous eyes, on my addressing her as the bride of the knight of San Fernando.

APPENDIX

Itinerary of the principal Roads of Andalusia, and of the three great Routes leading from that Province to the Cities of Madrid, Lisbon, and Valencia.

N.B. The measurements on the Post Roads are given in Spanish leagues, conformably with the Government Regulations by which Postmasters are authorized to charge for their horses. On these, therefore, the distances from stage to stage cannot be calculated with much precision; but a Spanish *Post* league may generally be reckoned 3½ [201] English miles. On the other roads the distances are more accurately specified in English miles.

No. 1.

BAYLEN TO MADRID.

(A Post Road, travelled by Diligences.)

	Leagues.
From Baylen to Guarroman	2
thence to La Carolina	2
Santa Elena	2
La Venta de Cardenas	2
Visillo	2
Sta. Cruz de Mudela	2
Val de Peñas	2
N. S. de la Consalacion	2
Manzanares	2
La Casa nueva del Rey	2½
Villaharta	2½
Vta. del Puerto Lapice	2
Madridejos	3
Caña de la higuera	2
Tembleque	2
Guardia	2
Ocaña	3½

Aranjuez	2
Espartinas	2½
Los Angeles	3
Madrid	2½
Total leagues	47½

47½ leagues = 164 English miles.

No. 2.
SEVILLE TO LISBON.
(Post road, travelled by Carriages.)

	Leagues.
From Seville to Santi Ponce	1
thence to La Venta de Guillena	3
Ronquillo	3
Santa Olalla	4
Monasterio	4
Fuente de Cantos	3
Los Santos de Maimona	4
Santa Marta	5
Albuera	3
Badajos	4
Elvas (Portugal)	3
Lisbon	30
Total leagues	67

67 leagues = 232 miles.

No. 3.
GRANADA TO VALENCIA.
(Post road, no Diligence.)

	Leagues.
From Granada to Diezma	6
thence to Guadiz	3
From Guadiz to Baza	7
thence to Lorca	18
Murcia	12
Alicante	13

San Felipe	9
Valencia	14
Total leagues	82

82 leagues=284 miles.

No. 4.
CADIZ to MADRID.
(Post road travelled by carriages.)

	Leagues.
From Cadiz to San Fernando	3
thence to Puerto Sta. Maria	3
Xeres de la Frontera	2½
de Casa Real del Cuervo	3½
Ventllo de la Torre de Orcas	3½
Utrera	3½
Alcalà de Guadaira	3
Mairena del Alcor	2
Carmona	2
da Venta de la Portugueza	2½
Luisiana	3½
Ecija	3
La Carlota	4
Cortijo de Mangonegro	3
Cordoba	3
Alcolea	2
Carpio	3
Aldea del Rio	3½
Andujar	3½
La Casa del Rey	2½
Baylen	2½
By No. 1, from Baylen to Madrid	47½
Total leagues	109½

109½ leagues=378 miles

No. 5.
CADIZ to SEVILLE.
(Post and carriage road.)

	Leagues.
From Cadiz to Alcalà de Guadaira, by Route No. 4	22
Thence to Seville	2
Total leagues	24

24 leagues=83 miles.

No. 6.
CADIZ to SEVILLE, by the Marisma.
(Direct road, passable for carriages in summer only.)

	Miles.
From Cadiz, by boat, to El Puerto de Santa Maria	5
Thence to Xeres	9
Lebrija	15
Seville	28
Total miles	57

No. 7.
CADIZ to LISBON.
(Post road.)

	Leagues.
From Cadiz to Seville, by No. 5.	24
Seville to Lisbon, by No. 2.	67
Total leagues	91

91 leagues = 315 miles.

No. 8.
GIBRALTAR to CADIZ.
(Bridle road.)

	Miles.
From Gibraltar to Los Barrios	12
Thence to La Venta de Ojen	9
La Venta de Tabilla	11

La Venta de Vejer	14
(Town of Vejer ½ a mile on left.)	
Chiclana	16
El Puente Zuazo	4½
Cadiz	9
Total miles	75½

No. 9.

GIBRALTAR to CADIZ.

(Another bridle road.)

	Miles.
From Gibraltar to Algeciras [202]	9
Thence to La Venta de Ojen	10
by No. 8	54½
Total miles	73½

No. 10.

GIBRALTAR to XERES.

(Bridle road.)

	Miles.
From Gibraltar to San Roque	6
Thence to La Venta la Gamez	4½
La Casa de Castañas	15
Alcalà de los Gazules	13
(The town left ½ a mile to the right.)	
Paterna	9
Xeres	16
Total miles	63½

No. 11.

GIBRALTAR to SEVILLE.

(Bridle road.)

	Miles.
From Gibraltar to Ximena	24

thence to Ubrique	20
El Broque	10
Villa Martin	8
Utrera	21
Dos Hermanos	8
Seville	7
Total miles	98

No 12.
GIBRALTAR to LISBON.
(Bridle road to Seville, from thence a carriage road.)

	Miles.
From Gibraltar to Seville, by Route No. 11	98
From Seville to Lisbon, by Route No. 2	232
Total miles	330

No. 13.
GIBRALTAR to MADRID.
(A post, but only bridle road to Osuna, from thence a carriage route.)

		Miles.
From Gibraltar to San Roque		6
thence to Gaucin		25
Atajate		14
Ronda		10
From Ronda to Saucejo		21
thence to Osuna		11
Ecija		20
By Route No. 4, from thence to Baylen,	27 leagues =	93
By Route No. 1, from Baylen to Madrid,	47½ leagues =	164
Total miles		364

No. 14.
GIBRALTAR to MADRID.
BY BENEMEJI.
(A bridle road only as far as Andujar.)

	Miles.
From Gibraltar to Ronda, by Route No. 13	55
From Ronda to La Venta de Teba	21
(Town of Teba ½ mile on the right)	
thence to Campillos	6
Fuente de Piedra	9
Benemeji	16
Lucena	12
Baena	18
Porcuna	24
Andujar	14
Baylen	17
By Route No. 1, to Madrid, 47½ leagues =	164
Total miles	356

No. 15.
GIBRALTAR to MALAGA.
(Bridle road.)

	Miles.
From Gibraltar to Venta Guadiaro	12
thence to Estepona	15
Marbella	16
Fuengirola	16
Benalmedina	6
Malaga	14
Total miles	79

No. 16.
GIBRALTAR to GRANADA.
(Bridle road.)

	Miles.
From Gibraltar to Malaga, by Route No. 15	79
From Malaga to Valez	18
thence to La Venta de Alcaucin	12
Alhama	12
La Venta de Huelma	15
La Mala	6
Granada	9
Total miles	151

No. 17.
GIBRALTAR to VALENCIA.
(Bridle road.)

	Miles.
From Gibraltar to Granada, by Route No. 16	151
Thence to Valencia, by Route No. 3	284
Total miles	435

No. 18.
MALAGA to SEVILLE.
(Bridle road.)

	Miles.
From Malaga to Venta de Cartama	13½
(leaves town of Cartama 1 mile on left.)	
Venta de Cartama to Casarabonela	11½
(the ascent to this town may be avoided, keeping it to the left)	
Casarabonela to El Burgo	9
thence to Ronda	11
Zahara	15
(Town half a mile off, on the left.)	
thence to Puerto Serrano	7

Coronil	10
Utrera	8
Dos Hermanos	8
Seville	7
Total miles	100

No. 19.
MALAGA to CORDOBA.
(Practicable for Carriages.)

	Miles.
From Malaga to Venta de Galvez	15¾
thence to Antequera	12¼
Puente Don Gonzalo	27
Rambla	16
Cordoba	16
Total miles	87

No. 20.
MALAGA to MADRID.
(Post road, travelled by a Diligence.)

	Miles.
From Malaga to El Colmenar	17
Thence to Venta de Alfarnate	10
Loja	16
Venta de Cacin	8
Lachar	9
Santa Fé	8
Granada	8
Venta de San Rafael	27
Jaen	24
Menjiber	14
Baylen	10
To Madrid by Route No. 1	164
Total miles	315

No. 21.
MALAGA to MADRID.
(a more direct road, but in part only practicable for carriages.)

	Miles.
From Malaga to Loja, by Route	43
Thence to Montefrio	12
Alcalà la real	14
Alcaudete	11
Martos	12
Arjona	17
Andujar	7
Baylen	17
Madrid by Route No. 1	164

No. 22.
MALAGA to VALENCIA.
(Bridle road.)

	Miles.
From Malaga to Granada, by Route No. 16	72
Thence to Valencia, by Route No. 3	284
Total miles	356

No. 23.
GRANADA to CORDOBA.
(A wheel road as far as Alcalà.)

	Miles.
From Granada to Pinos de la Puerte	12
thence to Alcalà la Real	18
Baena	24
Castro el Rio	6
Cordoba	24
Total miles	84

No. 24.

GRANADA to MADRID.
(Diligence road.)

	Miles.
From Granada to Baylen, by Route No. 20	75½
Thence to Madrid by Route No. 1	164
Total miles	239½

No. 25.

GRANADA to SEVILLE.
(Not a wheel road throughout.)

	Miles.
From Granada to Santa Fé	8
thence to Lachar	8
La Venta de Cacin	9
Loja	8
Archidona [203]	18
Alameda	11
Pedrera	12
Osuna	11
Marchena	14
Maraina del Alcor	14
Alcalà del Guadiaro	7
Seville	8
Total miles	128

No. 26.

SEVILLE to MADRID.
(Post and Diligence road.)

	Miles.
From Seville to Alcalà de Guadaira	8
Thence to Beylen, by Route No. 4	138
Baylen to Madrid, by Route No. 1	164
Total miles	310

No. 27.
SEVILLE to VALENCIA.

	Miles.
From Seville to Granada, by Route No. 25	128
From Granada to Valencia, by Route No. 3	284
Total miles	412

FOOTNOTES:

[1] See the Posting Itinerary in the Appendix.

[2] The post league has already been stated to contain 3 English miles, and 807 yards.

[3] Town-hall.

[4] Lobster-hunting—such is the name for Locust in Spanish.

[5] Or Genua urbanorum.—Pliny.

[6] Hirt. Bel. Hist. Cap. LXI.

[7] In an abundant house supper is soon cooked.

[8] Red pepper.

[9] Cabbage.

[10] A kind of sausage, resembling those made at Bologna.

[11] Bacon.—Spanish bacon is certainly the best in the world, which may be accounted for by the swine being fed principally on acorns, chesnuts, and Indian corn.

[12] No vain boast—the fact being established on the testimony of Rocca.

[13] Florez Medallas de las Colonias, &c.

[14] Mentioned in the Itinerary of Antoninus—not the Ilipa of Strabo and Pliny, situated on the river Bœtis, and in the county of Seville.

[15] The orchard.

[16] Evil doer.

[17] Alleys.

[18] The dead body.

[19] Roguish.

[20] La Martinière fell into a strange error in describing this river and the battle field on its bank; making the stream fall into the bay of Cadiz, and the scene of Alfonso's victory some fifty miles from Tarifa. This mistake has been followed by several modern authors.

[21] Not the Mellaria of Pliny, which was a city of the Turduli, within the county of Cordoba.

[22] A ruined town, no longer inhabited.

[23] By Strabo ninety-four miles, following the coast: i.e. 750 Stadia.

[24] Lib. III. Some editions enumerate two cities called *Besippo*, thus, "Bæsaro Tauilla dicte Bæsippo, Barbesula, Lacippo, Bæsippo, &c.;" but Holland and Harduin give only one, calling the first "*Belippo.*"

[25] There is no Epidemic here.

[26] There are more direct cross-roads to these places, but they are not always passable in winter.

[27] *Toll-house.*

[28] Strabo.

[29] This one amongst the various restraints laid on the trade of Gibraltar has very lately been removed on the remonstrance of our government.

[30] Shops where ice is sold.

[31] I understand this Cathedral is now being patched up in an economical way to render it serviceable.

[32] Road of Hercules. The causeway connecting Cadiz with the Isla de Leon is so called, and supposed to be a work of the Demi-god.

[33] 400 or 500 butts of Wine are shipped yearly from this place.

[34] The old mouth of the Guadalete is obstructed by a yet more impracticable bar.

[35] 10,000 butts of Wine are collected annually from the vineyards of Puerto Santa Maria. The exports amount to 12,000.

[36] Camomile.

[37] Mother.

[38] So called from the town of *Montilla*, whence the grape, that originally produced this description of dry, light-coloured wine, was brought to Xeres.

[39] Carthusian convent.

[40] Strabo and Pliny.

[41] A Fen, subject to the inundations of the sea. Such, however, is not the case here.

[42] Water-courses, which are dry in summer.

[43] Written *Vrgia* by Pliny—*Vcia* by Ptolemy.

[44] Itin. Anton.

[45] España Sagrada.

[46] This supposes the earth's circumference to have been reckoned 240,000 stadia, giving 83⅓ miles to a degree of the meridian. By the calculation of Eratosthenes, the circumference of the earth was 252,000 stadia, which gives exactly 700 stadia, or 87½ miles to a degree.

[47] Mariana (lib. 3. cap. 22) has quite mistaken the situation of this place, which he describes as two leagues from Xeres, *on the banks of the Guadalete.* It is two leagues from Xeres, certainly, but nearly three from the Guadalete, and but one and a half from the Guadalquivir.

[48] The area of the Mezquita at Cordoba, taken altogether, is larger, but not the enclosed portion of Gothic architecture, which is, properly speaking, the Episcopal church.

[49] A long time since.

[50] In England, however, it must be the taste of the nation that is suffering from disease, rather than its drama, if, with such writers as Sheridan Knowles, Talfourd, and Bulwer, the theatre does not once more become a popular place of resort.

[51] Farce; but, literally, goût, highly seasoned dish.

[52] Low and disorderly people.

[53] Florez Medallas descubiertas, &c.

[54] Old Seville.

[55] De Bell. Civ.

[56] Hollond—intending, of course, the Itipa of the Itinerary, since the city of that name, mentioned by Pliny, was on the right bank of the Guadalquivír; and from medals discovered of it, whereon a fish is borne, may be concluded to have stood on the very margin of the river.

[57] The gallant and talented author of the "History of the Peninsular War" has fallen into some slight topographical errors (caused, probably, by the extraordinary inaccuracy of the Spanish maps) in describing the movements of the contending armies. He describes, for instance, the French as obliging the Duke of Albuquerque to abandon his position at Carmona (where he had hoped to cover both Seville and Cadiz), by moving from Ecija upon Utrera (i.e. in rear of the Spanish army), along "a road by Moron, shorter" than that leading to the same place through Carmona. But so far from this road by Moron being "*shorter,*" it is yet more circuitous than the

chaussée; and, moreover, by skirting the foot of the Ronda mountains, it is both bad and hilly.

He furthermore represents the Duke of Albuquerque as falling back from Utrera upon Xeres, with all possible speed, and, nevertheless, taking Lebrija in his way, which town is, at least, eight miles out of the direct road. A French account (*La Pène, Campagne de 1810*) says, the Spanish army fell back from Carmona "par le chemin *le plus direct, Utrera et Arcos sur Xeres,*" — an error equally glaring, for the chaussée is the shortest road from Utrera to Xeres;—in fact, it is as direct as a road can well be, and leaves Arcos some twelve miles on the left! We may suppose, in attempting to reconcile these discrepant accounts, that the main body of the duke's army retreated from Utrera to Xeres by the chaussée; the cavalry by Arcos, to cover its right flank during the march; and that the road by Lebrija was taken by the troops withdrawn from Seville, as being the most direct route from that city to Xeres.

[58] Don Maldonado Saavedra viewed it in this light, imagining that, in the Itinerary of Antoninus from Cadiz to Cordoba, two distinct roads were referred to; one proceeding direct, by way of Seville, whence it was taken up by another road, afterwards described, to Cordoba; the other (starting again from Cadiz) traversing the Serranía de Ronda to Antequera, and proceeding thence to Cordoba by Ulía. Florez, however, disputes this hypothesis, conceiving that but one route is intended, and that from Seville onwards it was given, not as a direct road, but merely as one by which troops might be marched if occasion required. But why, if such were the case, a road should have been made that increased the distance from Seville to Antequera from 85 to 121 miles, he does not explain; and I confess, therefore, it seems to me, that Don Maldonado Saavedra's supposition is the more probable. The distances, however, between the modern places which he has named as corresponding with those mentioned in the Itinerary do not at all agree; and he also, in laying down the road from Cadiz to Antequera, has made it unnecessarily circuitous. The following towns will be found to answer much better with those mentioned in the Roman Itinerary, and the line connecting them is one of the most practicable through the Serranía.

Iter a Gadis Corduba, milia plus minus 295 sic.

	Roman miles.
Ad pontem (Puente Zuazo) m. p. m.	12
Portu Gaditano (Puerto Santa Maria)	14
Hasta (near La Mesa de Asta)	16
Ugia (Las Cabezas de San Juan)	27

Orippo (Dos Hermanos)	24
Hispali (Seville)	9
(returning now to the Puente Zuazo, we have to)	
Basilippo (a rocky mound and ruins between Paterna and Alcalà de los Gazules)	21

[59] Olbera, according to Saavedra.

[60] This disagreement with the heading is in the original.

[61] Cura de los Palacios.

[62] The diminutive of Venta.

[63] Are they English?

[64] Literally—on which foot the business was lame.

[65]

> He who shelters himself under a good tree,
> gets a good shade.

[66] Name and surname.

[67] Beneficed clergyman.

[68] Glance—from ojo, eye.

[69] Good for study.

[70] The lower orders of Spaniards, generally speaking, imagine that Protestantism implies a denial of the Godhead in the person of Our Saviour, and consider that but for our eating pork, like *Christianos Viejos*, we should be little better than Jews. For the whole seed of Israel, they entertain a most preposterous dislike; so deep rooted is it, indeed, that I once knew an instance of a young Spanish woman—far removed from a *low* station in life, however—who was perfectly horrified on being told by an English lady that Our Saviour was a Jew. Her exclamation of "Jesus!" was in a key which seemed to express wonder that such a blasphemous assertion had not met with the summary punishment of Annanias and Sapphira. I have no doubt but that the bad success which has attended the *Cristina* arms is attributed by the lower orders less to the incapacity of Espartero and Co. than to the Jewish blood flowing in the veins of Señor Mendizabel.

[71] Mapping the town.

[72] A Spanish side-saddle; or, more properly, an *arm-chair*, placed sideways on a horse's back, with a board to rest the feet upon.

[73] Female attendant.

[74] Managing person.

[75] Ages ago.

[76] Many Roman Emperors.

[77] As it is said, by an Englishman named Marlborough, and other very distinguished persons.

[78] Palacios, posadas, y todo—i.e., palaces, inns, and *every thing*.

[79] Throughout Spain.

[80] For every thing it has a cure—look you, &c.

[81] Youngster.

[82] The poor old Tio could not have acted under "proper directions," as I am informed that he died the year following my last visit to the *Hedionda*.

[83] I drink no other—never any other—I cook and every thing with it.

[84] Even to its bad smell.

[85] Little walk.

[86] A game that bears some resemblance to Boston.

[87] The Invalid.

[88] The water—nothing but the water—there is nothing in the world more salutary.

[89] They say that he was one of those lords, of whom there are so many in England.

[90] Heaps of gold.

[91] To me it appears.

[92] The Spaniards considered tea a medicine.

[93] A gentleman in whom perfect confidence might be placed.

[94] Yes, sir; that is true.

[95] Pastures.

[96] There are many robbers hereabouts—last year (accursed be these rascally Spaniards!) a good fowling-piece was stolen from me in this confounded narrow pass, &c.

[97] These beggarly Spaniards, &c.

[98] Young lady of the house.

[99] Very well *combed*, literally—her hair well dressed.

[100] Unequalled.

[101] A young girl I am bringing up for (*i. e.* to be) a countess.

[102] Now, gentlemen, it is necessary to load—these cowardly Spaniards always fall suddenly upon one; and, if we are not prepared, we shall be all netted, like so many little birds.—We are all well armed with double-barrelled guns, and, with prudence, we shall have nothing to fear—but ...! prudence is necessary.

[103] In these parts, no evil-disposed persons whatever are to be met with; that sort of *canaille* know too well who Louis de Castro is.

[104] A gazpacho, eaten hot.

[105] Literally, *beds*—spots frequented by the deer.

[106] Wolf.

[107] The position taken up by the sportsmen is called the *cama*, as well as the haunt of the game.

[108] A day of foxes—an expression amongst Spanish sportsmen, signifying an unlucky day.

[109] Literally, light—here used as *"fire!"*

[110] A wild boar! zounds!

[111] Yes, it is a sow.

[112] To escape from the thunder, and encounter the lightning.

[113] The war-cry of the Spaniards.

[114] I precede you with this motive, and in the shortest possible time *all will be ready.*

[115] Very dear friend of mine; aprec'ion, abbreviation of apreciacion; esteem.

[116] Go you with God ... and without a horse.

[117] An ounce; i. e. a doubloon.

[118] Get down directly.

[119] Perhaps a flight of woodcocks will arrive to-night. Is it not true, good father?

[120] "It is infested with banditti at each step. Is it not true, Don Diego, that that rocky path beyond Alcalà is called the road to the infernal regions?" "Yes, yes—as true as holy writ."

[121] Rock of Sancho.

[122] The little stream that empties itself into the sea, near Tarifa, is called *El* Salado, *par excellence*, in consequence of the great victory gained on its banks by Alfonso XI.; but, properly speaking, it is El Salado *de Tarifa*.

[123] Hirtius, Bel. Hisp. cap 7.

[124] Ibid. cap. 8.

[125] Dion—Lib. 48.

[126] Dion and Hirtius.

[127] Cap. 27.

[128] *Singilia Hegua*, corrected by Hardouin to Singili Ategua.—The ruins of Singili are on the banks of the Genil (Singilis) to the north of Antequera.

[129] It is a mere boast, however, for, according to Rocca, the French entered the town and levied a contribution.

[130] Scanty *vecinos*—a *vecino*, used as a *statistical* term, implies a hearth or family, though literally a neighbour. The Spanish computation of population is always made by *vecinos*.

[131] He does not understand.

[132] Have no anxiety.

[133] Mapping the country.

[134] Town.

[135] Fair and softly.

[136] Nonsense.

[137] Should this good woman be yet living, I suspect her opinion on this point will have undergone a material change—like that of most Spaniards.

[138] With polite mien and deportment.

[139] What a rare people are these English!

[140] Mentioned by Hirtius—Bell. Hisp. Cap. XXVII.

[141] The salutary waters of the divine Genil.—Don Quijote.

[142] Dion and Hirtius.

[143] Zurita and Hardouin maintain, that it is not in the old editions of Pliny.

[144] Foreign gentlemen.

[145] The wheel of fortune revolves more rapidly than that of a mill, and those who were elevated yesterday, to-day are on the ground.

[146] These *Salvo conductos* were by no means uncommon in those days. A friend of mine offered to procure me one to ensure me the protection of the celebrated *José Maria.*

[147] Forward, forward, heartless deceiver!

[148] There is no wedding without its morrow's festival.

[149]

> Between the hand and the mouth
> the soup falls

[150] Holy face.

[151] Uninhabited place.

[152] Distant from Cordoba 300 stadia.

[153] Distant fourteen miles from the Guadalquivír.

[154] *Illiturgi quod Forum Julium.*—Pliny.

[155] Titus Livius, lib. 28.

[156] Pliny.

[157] To the parlour! to the parlour!

[158] Be not afraid.

[159] Stew.

[160] Literally, that he could no more.

[161] I, the king.

[162] With us, I am sorry to say, "the honour of knighthood" has, in too many instances, become rather an acknowledgment of so many years' *good salary received*, than of any meritorious service performed.

[163] A very small copper coin.

[164] And this is a teapot!

[165] A pillow!

[166] What voluptuous people!

[167] A stone—a flint.

[168] How! without horses, without mules, without any thing, save steam!

[169] The estate, so called, was bestowed on the Duke of Wellington, as a slight acknowledgment of the distinguished services rendered by him to the Spanish nation.

[170] Santa Fé, built by Ferdinand and Isabella during the siege of Granada, and dignified by them with the title of *city*, is a wretched little walled town, of some twelve or fifteen hundred inhabitants; and, excepting two full-length portraits of the Catholic kings contained in the church, possesses nothing worthy of notice.

[171] Eating; to use the expression of one of the peasants we conversed with.

[172] *Itinerary of Antoninus.*

Malaca to Suel	21	m. p. m.
To Cilniana	24	"
To Barbariana	34	"
To Calpe Carteia	10	"
Total	89	miles.

Pomponius Mela has made sad confusion of the itinerary from Malaca to Gades (of which the above is a part), by introducing Barbesula and Calpe, and mentioning Carteia twice; but, on attentive observation, it is evident he intended to imply that the road bifurked at Cilniana, one branch going straight to Carteia by Barbariana, the other making a detour by Barbesula and Calpe, and rejoining the former at Carteia; the distance from Malaga to Cadiz, by the first route, being 155 miles, by the latter 186.

[173] Pliny.

[174] Published in 1765.

[175] "Two leagues" are his words—meaning Spanish measure, or eight miles English; since he estimates the league at four miles.

[176] Otherwise called Horgarganta.

[177] Florez fixes Salduba where I suppose Cilniana to have stood, i. e. on the eastern bank of the Rio Verde, about two miles to the westward of Marbella. Cilniana he places at the Torre de Bovedas, a site to which the objections above stated apply equally as to the position assigned to that place by Mr. Carter.

[178] Pliny places Salduba between Barbesula and Suel.

[179] Marbella is a fine place, but do not enter it.

[180] This may appear at variance with what I have said in computing the distance from Malaca to Calpe Carteía in Roman miles—viz., only eighty of eighty-three and one third to a degree of the meridian: but, besides that the distance from Malaga to Gibraltar is at least three English miles greater than to Carteía, the measurement I here give is along a winding pathway, that makes the distance considerably more than it would have been by a properly made road, even though it had followed all the irregularities of the coast.

[181] Bell. Hisp. cap. xxix.

[182] Journey from Gibraltar to Malaga.

[183] Traces of the first-named of these Roman roads may yet be seen about Tolox. The latter was one of the great military roads mentioned in the Itinerary of Antoninus, and, doubtless, existed long before that work was compiled.

[184] Hirtius, de Bell. Hisp. xxix. et seq.

[185] Great allowance must be made for exaggeration in enumerating the strength of contending armies in those early times, since even in these days of despatches, bulletins, and Moniteurs, it is so extremely difficult to get at the truth. The battle of Waterloo offers a remarkable instance of this, for no two published accounts agree as to the respective numbers of the belligerents, and one which I have read—a French one, of course—swells the force under the Duke of Wellington, on the 18th June, to 170,000 men!!!

[186] The inscription is given at length in Florez España Sagrada.

[187] The source of the Sigila, now called El Rio Grande, is twenty-five English miles from Cartama, following the course of the river.

[188] Certainly *not* Mr. Carter's, than which I never saw a more complete caricature. Not one of the rivers is marked correctly upon it, and the towns are scattered about where chance directed.

[189] Hirtius Bell. Hisp. xxviii.

[190] Ibid. xli.

[191] An account of which place has already been given in Chapter I. of this volume.

[192] "Don Ferdinand the Seventh, by the grace of God, king of Castile, Leon, Aragon, the Two Sicilies, Jerusalem, Navarre, Granada, Toledo, Valencia, Gallicia, Majorca, Seville, Sardinia, Cordoba, Corsica, Murcia, Jaen, the Algarves, Algeciras, Gibraltar, the Canary Islands, the East and West Indies, islands and terra firma of the Great Ocean; archduke of Austria;

duke of Burgundy, Brabant, and Milan; Count of Hapsburg, Flanders, the Tyrol, and Barcelona; Lord of Biscay and Molina, &c."—The seeming wish to avoid prolixity, implied by this "&c." is admirable.

[193] *Clean* blood.

[194] At any price.

[195] These love affairs are much to my taste.

[196] Attractions—literally, *hooking* qualities.

[197] In fine—as it was captain for captain.

[198] Not a bit.

[199] Would to God!

[200] Eating her life.

[201] A Post league is equal to 3 British statute miles and 807 yards.

[202] To Algeciras, by boat, saves 4 miles.

[203] This is the only stage that is not perfectly practicable for a carriage.